DATE DUE			
Aug 15 '72			
Dec 13 '72			
Jan 4 '73			
Jun 25 '75			
Oct 2 '75			
Feb 19 '76			
Oct 11 '76			
Oct 6 78			
Feb 14 80			
Feb 7 '81			

the

band

director's

guide

THE

BAND   GUIDE

director's

written

and

edited

by

kenneth l. neidig

Prentice-Hall, Inc.
Englewood Cliffs, N. J.

© **1964**
by PRENTICE-HALL, INC.
Englewood Cliffs, N. J.
The Band Director's Guide
by Kenneth L. Neidig

785.07
N31b
79380
Aug. 1972

Library of Congress Catalog Card No. 64-16430

PRINTED IN THE UNITED STATES OF AMERICA

21488—B & P

Sixth Printing.....March, 1970

To

my parents for the ability
my teachers for the background
my friend, Tom Ecker, for the chance
my wife and family for the necessary time

this book is dedicated.

Preface

Music schools throughout the United States generally do an excellent job of preparing the music student for a career in instrumental music; however, the school band director soon discovers that there are a great number of things he must know which were not necessarily a part of his degree training.

He soon discovers that he needs more money for his program than the board has appropriated . . . the townspeople are full of candy . . . he has a problem.

Maybe he should have taken that new degree his school offered and become a "sales engineer."

The hardheaded business manager asks about "net annual reserve for depreciation allowance on capital expenditures for equipment." . . . *What?*—he has a problem.

Maybe he should have done his undergraduate work in business administration.

The majorettes have been doing the side twirl in ten different positions, and are more than ready for something new . . . he has a problem.

Maybe he should have been a physical education major . . . or married a baton twirler.

He finds his band lacks the prestige of other school organizations; he cannot attract the top students. How can he create an atmosphere of acceptance, and how does he sustain this over a period of time? . . . he has a problem.

Maybe he should have enrolled in the psychology department.

He wants to start a stage or dance band, and finds that his legitimate training is an excellent foundation, but that he needs some special help with jazz style, and the organizational problems of this type group . . . he has a problem.

Maybe he should have gone on the road with Stan Kenton (or Ace Brigode) when he had the chance.

But he didn't do any of those things then. What does he do now? Clinics, magazines, trial and error? He still has a problem.

The solution of these problems—and many others like them—is a very important factor in the success (or failure) of today's band director. The list of "things they didn't teach me in college" (or more accurately, "things I didn't learn because I didn't know they were so darn important") is a long one. Such a list could well fill a book; in fact, it has filled this one.

Successful bandmasters *have met, and conquered*, their problems through study, hard work, brilliant insight, and a great deal of experimentation over long periods of time. Through this one volume you will have the opportunity to receive the benefits of the cumulative knowledge and experience of great band directors.

Each has had many years "in the business."

Each is a recognized expert in his field.

Each has produced notable, lasting results.

Realizing that it is probably unrealistic, and perhaps somewhat selfish, to expect to make the job of the school band director any *easier*, it is our hope that through this generous sharing of ideas, techniques, and experiences, the very important work being carried on in school systems throughout the country may be made more meaningful to the student, more satisfying for the director, and more beneficial to the community.

Contents

Building
A Permanent
Successful Program

by **Paul Behm**

Mason City, Iowa

Paul Behm

has been director of the
famous Mason City (Iowa)
High School Band since the
fall of 1950. He holds the
Ph.B. (Bachelor of Philoso-
phy of Education) degree from Creighton University of Omaha, Ne-
braska, and an M.S. in Education and Music from the University of
California at Los Angeles. He has done additional work at the State
University of Iowa and the Vandercook College of Music in Chicago.

The graduate of a very small high school with no band program,
and originally a science and mathematics teacher, Paul Behm just
"drifted" into band directing at Logan, Iowa. After seven years he
moved on to Grinnell, where he stayed 10 years before directing the
City High School Band in Iowa City for two years, just prior to his
move to Mason City.

His musical family is composed of his wife Marjorie, who plays
piano accompaniments for many of the high school students, his sons
Chuck, flutist in the school band, Gary (clarinet) and Dennis (French
horn), both of whom are Iowa band directors.

Mr. Behm is a member of the American Bandmasters, American
School Band Directors, National Band, and the Iowa Bandmasters
Associations. He is a past president of the Iowa Music Educators
Association.

2

The permanent, successful band program must be consistent, serve the school, and stay within the framework of the educational system. Performance level, number of participating students, and expenditures for music and equipment should not show extreme variation from year to year. The instructional staff should remain the same over long periods of time.

EDITOR'S NOTE: The band program in the schools of Mason City, Iowa was started in the fall of 1927 by Gerald R. Prescott, and almost immediately the group was able to earn a Division II rating at contest. Since that time the band has not received any contest rating other than a Division I. From 1931–50 Carleton Stewart was director of the band, during which time it gained national recognition. In 1934 the first separate instrumental music building to be built for public schools in the United States was completed in Mason City, where it still serves the high school bands and orchestras. In 1958 with the opening of *The Music Man* on Broadway, the world knew Mason City, but by the name of "River City"—an alias invented by the show's creator, Mason City-born Meredith Willson. In 1964, under the direction of Paul Behm, there were seven instrumental staff members instructing over 800 band and orchestra students in this midwestern community of 35,000 inhabitants. This is truly a successful, permanent program.

The band directors of a public school educational system should be regular members of the school faculty who direct organizations which are part of the educational system of the community and dedicated to fulfilling the needs of the school and the community.

The successful band program must have the full support and

cooperation of the school administration, which must be kept informed of the plans and actions of the directors at all times. It is the responsibility of the administration to establish the school policies and it is the responsibility of the directors to carry out those policies which pertain to the band program. Should the directors not like or disagree with these policies, then a better solution would be for them to seek another situation.

The support and cooperation of the school patrons must also be secured. This may be done most simply by giving them their money's worth. The "patrons" of a school are the parents of the students, not the "downtown" people who have no children in the schools. The parents of the boys and girls in the school bands want, within reason, an enjoyable experience for their children. They want them to learn something about music and to have a pleasant association in a large group; but they want something beyond this. They are trying to bring up what might be called "decent kids" and to help in training them they expect good wholesome group experiences from the band.

Many students who go through the Mason City program are well prepared for college and eventual professional work, because we insist that they play as well as they possibly can here. But we are not in the business of developing professional musicians. While many of our former students have never played their instruments since graduation from high school, none have ever told us that they were sorry that they played while in school. They build fine record libraries, attend concerts, and will enjoy all forms of music in every way with a sense of appreciation that they could have gained in no other way.

TECHNIC OR BAND CLASSES: BASIS OF OUR PROGRAM

The Mason City band program was started in 1927 when James Rae, the high school principal, worked with Gerald Prescott to set up a number of band instrument classes, using a rotating class schedule which subsequently was adopted by many schools throughout the country. With this system, each week the student attends one band class, averaging five students, instead of his regularly scheduled academic class. Each week he misses a different period; thus he misses only one class per subject each month. A junior's schedule might look something like this:

Period 1—Algebra II   miss the first week
Period 2—History   miss the second week
Period 3—English III   no class scheduled
Period 4—Band   band
Period 5—Chemistry   miss the third week
Period 6—Study and Gym   miss the fourth week

In September 1962, after nearly 35 years of successful operation, it was found desirable and possible by the high school administration and band directors to abandon the rotating schedule in favor of a permanently fixed band class schedule.

The new schedule is as follows: All band students are assigned to the Music Hall for their study halls, and each student is taken out of one study hall per week for his band class.

Period 1—B♭, alto, bass clarinets
Period 2—trombones, baritones, tubas, percussion
Period 3—no class scheduled
Period 4—band
Period 5—cornets, French horns
Period 6—flutes, oboes, bassoons, saxophones

During these four daily periods, Monday through Thursday (16 periods), 32 classes are set up averaging about six students per class, and the classes are grouped according to like instruments and ability.

These small, like ability groups are the basis of our entire teaching procedure. We select material that is appropriate to the ability and development of each particular class and then assign, teach, test, and seat. A typical class lesson follows this pattern:

1. The director chooses four exercises of eight measures or so from the assignment. Each student plays each exercise individually and the director gives numerical grades.

2. When all have played, the grades are totaled. The student with the highest score sits first chair in the class and others follow in order.

3. A new assignment is made and taught.

As we score the students, we cultivate their ability to judge others, and thus themselves, by calling attention to the reasons for our preference of one above the other. The students do not vote. Making these selections is part of our job.

There is a strong competitive spirit among our people, since these results determine the students' position in the band. We feel that competition is an ever-present fact of life and to deny it is unrealistic. There are many girls in our bands. One reason could be that here they find the competition which so many boys enjoy through athletics.

REQUIREMENTS AND STANDARDS

Most of the students who come into the high school band have been through the Rubank Advanced Method. We have no required course of study and no minimum standards or requirements. We find that the students make their own requirements and set their own standards. We only demand that they behave themselves and do the band and themselves some musical good.

GROUPING

The entire high school band is grouped and assigned as follows:

The High School Band includes everyone in the high school band program and performs whenever facilities will permit the seating of a group usually in excess of 150.

The Marching Band includes everyone in the high school band. During the football season varsity football players do not march at games, but they attend rehearsals and do some drilling so that they are able to march at functions other than football games.

The Symphonic Band includes the top 90 to 100 players selected on the basis of ability and the needs of the instrumentation. This band performs at contests and on other occasions when space is limited, or when the music to be performed is best suited to a group of this size.

The Concert Band consists of all players in the high school band who have not been selected for the symphonic band. It rehearses at the same period, and performs as a separate unit several times during the year. (Staff and facilities allow simultaneous rehearsals.)

The Pep Band varies from 40 to 60 players according to the needs of the pep meetings and games. The pep band occasionally takes an out-of-town basketball trip.

The Stage Band consists of 25 of the top players selected from the high school band. This group rehearses twice weekly at 7:30 A.M.

FEEDER SYSTEM

We have no elementary school pre-band instrument training classes, and we do not use a musical aptitude test to select students. Experience has shown us that the best method is to give the student the instrument and teach him how to play it. Our staff consists of two men in the elementary schools, three in the junior highs, and two in the high school. Too many times students have been denied musical training on the basis of a low aptitude score, only to transfer to another school and become good players. During the summer before they enter the third grade, we start those who want to on a regular band instrument—including the trombone. Many people have told us that third graders are "too young" to play the trombone, but they make this comment only *before* they have heard these students play.

EQUIPMENT

Parents must furnish flutes, clarinets, alto saxophones, cornets, and trombones. At one time we owned six flutes and had trouble finding flute players, so we sold the flutes and told the parents they would have to buy their own. Now we normally have over 20 flutists in the high school band, and more than 150 in the system. However, we do want to own oboes, bassoons, alto and bass clarinets, tenor and baritone saxophones, French horns, baritone horns, tubas and all percussion instruments, so that we can select the people who will play these instruments.

The following is a list of the school-owned band instruments in the entire Mason City school system:

14 oboes
11 bassoons
 6 alto clarinets
10 bass clarinets
 9 tenor saxophones
 4 baritone saxophones
 8 bell-front alto horns
12 single horns in B♭
 8 single horns in F

23 double horns
30 baritone horns
 8 E♭ tubas
 6 BB♭ tubas
24 sousaphones
 6 recording basses
 5 full sets of percussion equipment

FINANCING THE PROGRAM

The Board of Education pays salaries and buys and maintains instruments and music. All instrumental music students in the entire school system each school year pay a nine dollar activity fee, which is payable at the Board of Education office. The six-week summer fee is three dollars. These funds, used to provide those materials and services not legally purchasable by the Board of Education, make facilities and equipment available which would be difficult to acquire any other way on such an equitable basis. No student who is unable to pay the fee is denied the opportunity of participating in the program. Work may be provided by either the school principal or the music instructor so that the student may earn the money for his fee.

The money in the Instrumental Music Activities Fund is expended by a purchase order from the director of instrumental music and signed by the high school principal.

A budget for each fiscal year is prepared by the director of instrumental music and presented to the Superintendent of Schools for his consideration. It has been the custom of the Superintendent to present the budget to the Board of Education for its approval.

RELATIONS WITH STUDENTS

Since more time is spent in rehearsing than any other single band activity, obviously the students must enjoy this period or they will soon leave the program. The director must see that something is accomplished musically in these sessions. Students know whether they play well or not, and whether others have genuinely enjoyed their performances. While we give a letter award to the seniors in May when we play for the high school students for the last time, we find that the day to day rehearsal atmosphere is far more important to the success of a program than any number of awards. We do try to glamorize the seniors somewhat, since we feel that these older students should be the controlling influence in the group.

You must be demanding, but very careful, in the application of pressure. The "soft sell" is the best, since if you high-pressure a student you are going to lose him when the going gets tough. You can push students to a certain point; when you get beyond that point you are in trouble. A sort of "teacher's sense" of human nature tells you where this point is.

Personally, I am not a believer in extremely rigid discipline. I feel it drives many good students from the program. The door to my office is always open and the students feel free to discuss anything they wish. When I go into a rehearsal, I want the band members to give me their attention and let me work. I do not wish to be a policeman.

DROP-OUTS

Although we certainly do not encourage our students to drop out of the band, we are aware that some students have become very successful in other areas after leaving the band. We recognize the right of anyone to decide to make a change in his life, and so drop-outs do not disturb us. Students who do not play well constitute 95 percent of our drop-outs.

On entering the tenth grade all students decide on a three-year course of study. After conferences with guidance counselors and administrators their plan is set and it then becomes very difficult for a student to get into or out of the band, since any change will upset the rest of the high school class schedule.

STABLE POPULATION HELPS

Although the superior teacher will probably be able to develop an acceptable program anywhere (and a poor one can wreck an established one very quickly), there is one factor, with its subsequent influences, which makes one community more receptive than another: *stable population.*

If 100 students are started in the elementary school and only 10 of them reach your high school, you are defeated immediately. The fact that the same people continue to live in the same community year after year leads to an atmosphere of stability which is reflected in a consistent Board of Education interpretation of what the patrons wish in a school system. Mason City is in the middle of the agricultural area, where families remain for many years. I think this has a lot to do with our success and with why so many fine bands come from the Midwest.

THE DIRECTOR

The best course of action for a man approaching a new position—whether it be to start a new program, revive one, or continue a fine one—is to keep quiet and go to work. He should not talk about what a fine job he did where he was teaching before, and how "this isn't the way we did it in X-ville." He should never talk about the terrible mess his predecessor left him and how hard he is working to get it straightened out.

Good teaching is the only thing that will last. The impatient director may find some "gimmick" which will bring him to the attention of others more quickly, but if he does a good teaching job day after day, that *later* day will come when people will look at him and realize what fine work has been going on all of the years before. Recognition for his band and himself may be slow in coming this way, but it will endure as a permanent, successful program, because it is built on such a solid foundation.

Organization
And
Business Management

by **John W. Worrel**

Cincinnati, Ohio

John W. Worrel

has been Supervisor of Music for the Cincinnati, Ohio, School System since 1960. For the 10 years immediately preceding this appointment, he pursued a very successful career in teacher training and brass instruction at the University of Kentucky.

His early life centered in Kansas. He was born at Fairview in 1915, was graduated from high school in Atchison in 1933, and went on to Kansas State Teachers College for the Bachelor's degree in 1938. After four years of military service in Army bands, he earned a Master's degree, in 1947, from George Peabody College for Teachers in Nashville, Tennessee. While on a fellowship at the University of Illinois, in 1957, he received the Ed.D. degree. Other college credits have been earned at Lindsborg College, Bethany, Kansas; the Conservatory of Music in Cincinnati, and the University of Kentucky.

Bill Worrel is well known in Kentucky, Tennessee, Indiana, South Carolina, and Kansas as a judge, speaker, and guest conductor. He has been a finalist with Leopold Stokowski's All-American Youth Orchestra, directed church choirs, and taught both vocal and instrumental music in Wilson, Lincoln, Atwood, and Salina, Kansas.

His varied background of experience includes two seasons as first trombonist with the Miami, Florida, Symphony, and time on the road with the Lawrence Welk dance orchestra.

12

The ultimate goal in every area of music education is better instruction for each individual student who comes under the guidance of the school. It is especially important to remember this when considering organization and business management since in this area it is especially easy to become entangled in the minutiae which can divert a teacher from accomplishing the primary aim.

The school is often the largest business establishment in the community. A large and specialized staff must be hired not only to teach students, but to provide physical support as well. In the Cincinnati music department, for instance, we employ a man who does nothing but tune the more than 1,000 pianos in the system. This is big business and it must be conducted as such. Smaller cities and towns have proportionately smaller school systems, but they are quite often still the biggest industry in town.

The band director has a moral and a legal responsibility to the taxpayers to run his portion of the community's largest industry with honesty and efficiency.

Directors seem to fall at various places along an efficiency scale: At the one extreme we have the man who is completely *dis*organized; he is the epitome of the "real artist" type—a superb musician, but he just cannot keep anything organized. At the other end there is the man who is completely organized, but a terrible musician!

The successful band director must be just as good a business manager as he is a musician, because the musical result achieved by the band will be directly influenced by the quality and effectiveness of his business management. The number of people who attend his concerts, the quality of instrument on which his students play, and similar factors, are strictly *business-organizational* items which affect the *musical* result.

The job of the band director is becoming more complicated every year. With so many new products being developed, and with the tremendous expansion of publisher's catalogs, it is impossible to try to remember everything. He must have some system of retaining facts and materials so that he can put his hands on them when he needs to.

The name of a fine alto sax concerto often escapes me, but in my saxophone file not only is the title listed, but the composer, arranger, publisher, and the grade of difficulty as well. There is also a note that Bill Jones played this composition at the 1959 state music festival.

THE FILE OUTLINE

This is the system which I use as a depository for reference materials. There are six sections, and each section is subdivided as much as becomes necessary for the topic and the interest of the director. (Only those sections of particular interest to the band director will be subdivided here.)

The same outline is used to file materials in two different places:

1. *The filing cabinet.* The actual piece of material (score, magazine article, sales literature, instruction booklet, etc.) is placed in the cabinet according to the outline. File dividers separate the sections, and file folders are used to organize the sub-sections.

2. *The 4x6 card file.* Notes on the many facets of music education are placed on cards and filed according to the outline. This file can be used to retain information gleaned from a brass clinic, for example, whereas a comprehensive list of brass solos received at the same clinic would be placed in the *filing cabinet.*

File Outline of Music Education Materials

SECTION 1: ADMINISTRATION AND SUPERVISION

I.   General Library References
II. Philosophy of School Music
III. Objectives of School Music
IV. History of School Music

Headings I–IV should be subdivided into the following "reference series":

A. General Works
B. Books
C. Magazines
D. Pamphlets, Trade Papers
E. Unpublished, and Notes
F. Audio-Visual

V.   Curricula
A. Course Offerings
   1. Credit
   2. Core
   3. Theory-harmony
   4. History-appreciation
   5. General Music
B. Proportion
C. Integration, Correlation
D. Evaluation
   1. Grades
   2. Awards
   3. Tests

VI. Scheduling
A. General
B. Sample Schedules

VII. Housing–Plant–Equipment
A. Goals
   1. Plans
   2. Qualifications
   3. Specifications
B. Building Equipment
   1. Acoustical
   2. Lighting
   3. Ventilation–Heat
C. Maintenance Problems
D. Other Equipment
   1. Uniform–Robes
   2. Audio-Visual
   3. Instruments
   4. Risers
   5. Miscellaneous

VIII. Records–Reports–Forms
  A. Letters to Parents, Students, Others
  B. Personnel File
  C. Marching Band
  D. Library
  E. Uniforms
  F. Instruments

IX. Finance
  A. Securing Funds
    1. Regular Sources
    2. Outside Sources
    3. Parents' Clubs
  B. Budgeting Expenditures (bids, insurance)
  C. Salary (sources, averages)
  D. Records (fines, ledgers)

X. Public Relations
  A. Newspapers
  B. Radio-Television
  C. Posters
  D. Other

XI. Performances
  A. In School
  B. Out of School

XII. Community Activities
  A. Concert Series
  B. Directing Civic Music Organization
  C. Personal Performance of Instructor
  D. Musicians' Union

XIII. Selection of Music
  A. Publishers
  B. Composers-Arrangers
  C. Ordering of Music

XIV. Securing Students
  A. Surveying Potential of School
    1. Tests
    2. Pre-Band Instruments

       3. Personal Interviews
   B. Creating Interest
       1. Publicity
       2. Demonstrations
       3. Speeches
   C. Instrument Rental Plans

XV. Organization of Classes
   A. Extra-Musical Considerations
       1. Selection of Personnel
       2. Guaranteeing Future Instrumentation
       3. Discipline
       4. Seating Plans
       5. Chairing, Part Assignments
       6. Camps
   B. Musical Considerations
       1. Score Preparation and Editing
       2. Interpretation
       3. Adaptation of Scores
       4. Intonation and Temperament

XVI. Supervision
   A. Definition of Duties
   B. Teacher-Training
       1. Conferences (individual)
       2. Teachers' Meetings
       3. Clinics
       4. In-Service Training
   C. Professional Organizations
   D. Critique Teaching
   E. Inspection
   F. Research

SECTION 2: BAND

I.   Concert Band
II. Marching Band
III. Stage Band
IV. Baton Twirling

Subdivide headings I–IV into the following "reference series":

    A. General Works

    B. Books

    C. Magazines

    D. Pamphlets, Trade Papers

    E. Unpublished, and Notes

    F. Audio-Visual

V. Music

    A. Training

        1. Methods

           a. beginning

           b. intermediate

           c. advanced

        2. Technical Studies

           a. beginning

           b. intermediate

           c. advanced

        3. Tunes

           a. beginning

           b. intermediate

           c. advanced

    B. Serious

        1. Overtures and Concerts

           a. collections

           b. by grade (I–VI)

        2. Religious

           a. general

           b. by seasons

         3. Waltzes, Minuets

        4. Marches

           a. collections

           b. concert only

           c. street

    C. Popular

        1. Collections

        2. Current Hit Tunes

        3. Standards

        4. Waltzes

        5. Latin-American

        6. Jazz

    7. Semi-classical
    8. Folk
       a. American
       b. by country
    9. Patriotic
   10. Novelties
   11. Stage Band Instrumentation
  D. Accompaniments
    1. To Solos
      a. vocal (S, A, T, B)
      b. instrumental (score order)
    2. To Ensembles
  E. Massed Music
    1. With Chorus
    2. With Other Groups
  F. Marching Band Only
    1. Precision Marching Shows
    2. Football Field Shows

SECTION 3: ORCHESTRA AND STRING ORCHESTRA

I.   References (subdivide into the "reference series")
II. Orchestra Music (subdivide like Band Music section)
III. String Orchestra Music (subdivide like Band Music section)

SECTION 4: ENSEMBLES

I.   Strings
II. Woodwinds
III. Brasses
IV. Percussion
V. Mixed

Subdivide each, in order by size, as follows:

  A. Duets
  B. Trios, etc. to "Woodwind Choir," "Brass Choir," and "Percussion Ensemble"

SECTION 5: INDIVIDUAL INSTRUMENTS AND ENSEMBLES OF LIKE INSTRUMENTS

I.   Strings

II. Woodwinds

III. Brasses

IV. Percussion

Subdivide each into the individual instruments, in score order, then further subdivide as follows:

1. General
2. Recordings
3. Manufacturers
4. Methods and Studies
5. Solos
6. Ensembles of Like Instruments

The Filing Cabinet

Out of the stacks of material which arrive in the mail every day, you will probably have a real need for some portion of it— eventually. Obviously you cannot start a heap in the corner and next year expect to find "that booklet with the red cover" from last September's mail. There must be some definite place to "put it to bed" until it is needed.

It may be a sample score for a new mambo for band. Looking in the file outline (handy on the desk), you find that the score should be filed under Section 2 (Band), V (Band Music), C (Popular), 5 (Latin American). Write "Sec 2 V C 5" at the upper right hand corner of the score, put it in the file basket, and your student assistant will see that it gets to the proper place in the filing cabinet. The next year when a fine jazz drummer transfers into your school from Latin America, the sample score of just the piece for the annual pop concert will be waiting in the file.

The 4x6 Card File

Perhaps during your Army service you may have had the opportunity to know professional musicians. When Xavier Cugat's drafted drummer tells you an authoritative Latin-American drum method is the one by Isabelo Marrero, published by Marks, you can use this information later when you want to teach all of your drummers to play this exciting style of music (instead of waiting for the transfer student to arrive), if you have noted the name of the book under Sec 5 IV in your 4x6 card file.

BIDS AND SPECIFICATIONS

The band director must have a current, thorough knowledge of the industry that supplies him with all of the raw materials which are so necessary to effective instruction. I have a 35-page file of names, addresses, and specialties which I correct every time there is a move, sale of business, or shift of emphasis in the music industry. The director who maintains such a list will know, for instance, that there is one company which for years has specialized in school electronic equipment. When choosing a stereo unit for the band room, he would probably then consider their set with the kick-proof grill, rather than the beautiful piece of name-brand furniture which looked so nice in his friend's living room.

The director certainly must know quality and be sure that he gets it, but if he tries to prepare minute specifications on everything he buys, it will consume all of his time, and probably require that he earn an engineering degree as well. He must learn to depend on source material. When he does set specifications, he must be careful to prevent some really insignificant point from eliminating an otherwise very acceptable product.

No matter how small the school system or how insignificant a purchase may seem, I am a great believer in the sealed bid system. Since regulations vary, the director should be aware of his own individual state law regarding bid-letting. Many dealers do not like bids since it usually becomes such a "cut-throat" affair, and they may indicate that you will not get much service from them unless you give them all of your business. This is one reason why directors fall into the trap of dealing with just one company. It is better to pay for service, rather than throw all the business one way, regardless of bids.

CHOOSING INSTRUMENTS

The businessman-director should set up some impartial method of choosing instruments. Many school systems call all of the instrumental staff together and ask them to judge the quality of several different brands played by professionals behind a screen. Another method is for each instructor to test the offerings of all companies and choose the models which are acceptable for use. Bids are then requested only from these companies. Experts may be called in by the director in a one-man operation. Perhaps a cooperative agreement among several directors, each specializing in a different instrument, could be worked out.

BUSINESS RELATIONS

One of the most reliable experts is the manufacturer's representative. The man with whom we are dealing today is generally a very reputable person who is quite often at the mercy of his own research department. For example, most bassoon manufacturers know that there is one company which has come up with a superior material, and most representatives will admit it.

Every businessman respects the buyer who is well informed and knows quality merchandise when he sees it, but "chiselers" are not popular—or effective, either. I recall reading of an experiment in which two men were sent out to get bids from five different car dealers who knew nothing of the plan. The first man schemed, chiseled, argued, etc. The second was a meek sort of fellow who agreed with almost everything the dealer said. In every case the final price secured by the "purchaser" was nearly the same, although they had seen identical dealers.

DO NOT TAKE COMMISSIONS

I have known band directors who have been successful for many years, and suddenly they become involved in a scandal. I recall one in particular. He started taking five percent, 10 percent, then a dealer offered him 20 percent of the gross sales in the school in return for an exclusive agreement. Later the whole thing was exposed and the school board had to say: "Now we're sorry . . . you've been doing a good job for us for 20 years, but we're going to have to fire you on this account."

The band director must be honest and completely aboveboard. The bid system protects you in this respect.

THE BUSINESS OFFICE

While there will be great differences in the space available, certain facilities are needed by every director. Figure 1 shows both a "budget model" office plan, and also what is possible with the use of top quality furniture.

Figure 1: Office Plans *

"Plush Model"

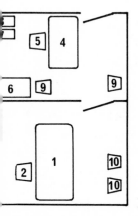

1. Executive desk, with out-of-sight wastebasket (76" x 36")
2. Executive posture chair
3. Bookcase (52")
4. Secretary's desk, with out-of-sight wastebasket (65" x 30")
5. Secretary's chair
6. Combination cabinet (38" x 24")
7. Four-drawer letter file cabinet
8. Letter file with 4 x 6 card file
9. Side chairs (no arm rest)
10. Side chairs (with arm rest)

"Budget Model"

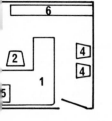

1. Right-hand "L" unit
2. Desk chair
3. Four-drawer letter file cabinet
4. Side chairs
5. Card file box, 4 x 6
6. Wooden shelving (floor to ceiling)

There are many items which are essential to the efficient operation of a business office. The following list includes those items which band directors will find most useful:

Office Equipment and Supplies Check-List

typewriter	cellophane tape dispenser
adding machine	desk nameplate
desk letter trays	memo pad
rotary telephone index	desk organizer
desk spindle	desk set

* Based on material provided by All-Steel Equipment Co., Aurora, Ill.

stationery rack (desk drawer)

sponge moistener

4x6 cards

4x6 file guides

filing folders

letter size file guides

file folder labels (color coded)

ledger

dictionary

calendar

binder covers

clip boards

pencil sharpener

steel cash box

3-hole punch

paper punch

magnifying glass

shears

tubular coin wrappers

currency wrappers

rubber stamps

bond typing paper

bond envelopes

onion skin

carbon paper

address labels

metal clasp envelopes

rubber cement

all-purpose glue

rubber bands

paper clips

staples

thumb tacks

ruler

eraser

gummed reinforcements

duplicator master units—plain

duplicator master units—music lined

BUDGETS

In supervising both the raising and spending of funds, the director must keep absolutely complete and accurate records of all transactions, no matter how insignificant they might appear. He should train student helpers, but he must also condition himself to be accurate and efficient with small sums of money so that he will be capable of controlling larger amounts. Even directors in very small systems quite often are responsible for extremely large fund raising campaigns and the subsequent expenditure of the proceeds.

Ideally, sufficient money for all needs is appropriated by the Board of Education and the director need only be concerned with making intelligent purchases. However, this situation is certainly not widespread, and most men find themselves having to spend much time and effort in the planning and execution of successful fund raising drives.

Not By Bread Alone

Most directors rely on candy as their "bread and butter," but are always on the lookout for new methods. One director arranged for band parents to purchase an ice cream stand in a good location; another sold advertising on slides projected onto a rear-view screen on a roof facing heavy traffic; others sell Christmas trees. The wise director tailors any method to his own particular community, considering the *mores,* economic level, spending habits, saturation point, attitude of the businessman, and the unique talents of the students and himself.

Fringe Benefits

Fortunately there are very important by-products which may be enjoyed through fund raising campaigns by booster clubs. Parents working together generate increased enthusiasm concerning the band —among themselves and in the community. The hard worker who raised the money to purchase an English horn appears at his first concert (bringing with him a row full of guests) and beams with pride when that exotic instrument has a solo.

There is ample opportunity for the application of psychology in budgeting. Since the average group of parents will show more enthusiasm when asked to raise money for uniforms than would be apparent if they were asked to buy a contrabass clarinet, it is best to put the clarinet on the school budget request, and leave the glamorous purchases to the boosters. It is the same patient technique which develops a flashy marching band with glittering uniforms and dazzling football shows while planning the purchase of a contrabass clarinet and the formation of a balanced woodwind choir which will perform Bach fugues.

HAVE A PLAN

The following is a sample five-year plan [1] which can be used to install an instrumental music program in a new school.

This plan will result in the following school-owned instruments and equipment at the end of a five-year period. After that it should be possible to maintain a 55–60 piece band for approximately $2,000 per per year. This figure includes repairs, replacement of instruments and uniforms, and additional music.

---

[1] From *An Administrator's Guide to the Instrumental Music Program in the Public Schools,* G. Leblanc Corp., Kenosha, Wisconsin.

40—Pre-band instruments
2—Piccolos
2—Oboes
2—Bassoons
1—Alto clarinet
2—Bass clarinets
1—Tenor saxophone
1—Baritone saxophone
4—French horns

3—Baritones
4—Sousaphones
1—Set concert drums
1—Set marching drums
1—Set tympani
1—Set bells
2—Pair cymbals
30—Music stands
60—Uniforms

FIRST YEAR . . . . Budget of $4680
20—Music stands $9 ea. . . . . $ 180
40—Pre-band melody instr. $1 ea. 40
 1—Bass drum (34" x 16") 85
 2—Snare drums (8" x 15") $60 ea. 120
 1—Pair of cymbals (16") 50
 1—Sousaphone (BBb) 500
 1—Baritone 290
 2—French horns $270 ea. 540
 1—Baritone saxophone 350
    Music 250
35—Uniforms $65 ea. 2275

SECOND YEAR . . . . Budget of $3115
 1—Oboe . . . . $ 325
 1—Bass clarinet 500
 1—Tenor saxophone 280
 1—Baritone 290
 1—Sousaphone (BBb) 500
 2—Parade drums (12" x 15") $75 ea. 150
 1—Scotch bass drum (10" x 28") 80
 1—Pair of cymbals (14") 45
 5—Additional music stands 45
    Music and marching folios 250
10—Additional uniforms $65 ea. 650

THIRD YEAR . . . . Budget of $2420
 1—French horn . . . . $ 270
 1—Baritone . . . . , . . 290
 1—Bassoon 500
 1—Set of tympani 450
 1—Piccolo (C) 95
 1—Set of bells 90
    Music 250
    Repairs . . . . , . 150
 5—Additional uniforms $65 ea. 325

FOURTH YEAR . . . . Budget of $2420
1—French horn (double) . . . . $ 370
1—Sousaphone (BB♭)   500
1—Oboe   325
1—Bass clarinet   500
    Music   250
    Repairs   250
5—Additional uniforms $65 ea.   325

FIFTH YEAR . . . . Budget of $2415
1—Piccolo (C) . . . . $ 95
1—Sousaphone (BB♭)   500
1—Bassoon   500
1—Alto clarinet   350
5—Additional music stands $9 ea.   45
    Music   300
    Repairs   300
5—Additional uniforms $65 ea.   325

In a more mature band program the director—working toward the objective of full support from the school for all instructional costs, including equipment, and using the money from the efforts of the band boosters club to underwrite trips, social functions, and other so-called "extras"—should work out a definite plan for accumulating and spending the funds which, in his estimation, are necessary for a successful program.

INSURANCE

Most large businesses consider insurance an absolute necessity. The band director will probably find that the Board of Education has insured the building and the music room furniture, but he may have to prepare a complete list of all instruments and other musical equipment so that these too will be covered. Moth damage insurance on uniforms is often overlooked.

On Instruments. Since the school board insures so much equipment, the premium rate they are able to secure is quite low. Those who own their instruments are often able to take advantage of this rate if the director will set up a system for them to do so. If the Board is already dealing with an insurance company, that company should be consulted as to the exact procedure and the rate which would be charged. If the director is expected to handle his own insurance, then the bid technique should be used.

On Trips. Terrible accidents have occurred on band trips. If you do not have insurance on these trips, and the parents want to, they can make it extremely difficult for you. Compared to the trouble you could get into if you do not have it, trip insurance is very inexpensive.

Any company doing interstate business must be bonded, but there are various forms of bonded transportation. Even if a bus driver tells you he has insurance on all passengers, ask to see this bond yourself. He may not really know what he is talking about, or he might even be trying to deceive you in order to get the business. After an accident has occurred and the parents have brought a lawsuit against you for negligence, it is too late to buy trip insurance.

THE COPYRIGHT LAW

Unfortunately, many band directors break this law almost hourly —for football shows, especially. The man who creates the work should have the right to the money which it produces, but the composer is being deprived of the fruits of his labor by what seems to be common practice among band directors. We have a moral obligation to the composer and to the industry which supplies us with the music on which we build our instrumental programs. The "Music Copyright Law Guide" [2] spells out very clearly what you *can* do and what you *can't* do under the United States Copyright Law. (*See* Fig. 2.)

Figure 2

Music Copyright Law Guide

A. Even though music is protected by copyright under the United States Copyright Law there are various things which you can do without securing permission of any type and without fear of infringing.

You may purchase a copyrighted musical composition, orchestration or other form of published music and do the following with it:

---

[2] Copyright © 1960 and 1962 by MUSIC PUBLISHERS' PROTECTIVE ASSOCIATION, INC. and MUSIC PUBLISHERS' ASSOCIATION OF THE UNITED STATES, INC. *This guide may be reprinted in its entirety without permission, provided the above copyright notice and this notice appear in each reprint. Permission to reprint excerpts from this guide must be secured from the copyright owners.*

Music Copyright Law Guide (cont.)

1. You may sell it or give it away.
2. You may perform it in private, or in public for non-profit.
3. You may use it for teaching in a classroom, at home or in a pupil's home. Solely for teaching purposes you may write symbols and indicate instructions upon it.
4. Provided the composition has already been recorded by others, under the authorization of the copyright owner, for the manufacture of phonograph records serving to reproduce the same mechnically, and provided further that you notify the copyright owner by registered mail of your intention to make such use (with a duplicate of such notice to the Copyright Office, Washington 25, D. C.), you may make similar use thereof upon making monthly payments of the statutory royalty to the copyright owner.

B. If you wish to make some other type of use which is not described above, you should write to the copyright owner for specific permission in each instance. The following are some of the things you cannot do without specific permission:

1. Reprinting, duplicating or copying the work or any part of it by any method or means whatsoever.
2. Arranging, adapting, orchestrating, translating or making any new versions of the work or any part of it.
3. Photographing or reproducing the work or any part of it by any method or means, including on film or slides or by opaque projector.
4. Performing the work in public for profit.
5. Recording the work by any method or means or for any use or purpose, other than as provided in "A. 4" above, including in synchronization with motion pictures or for television, and whether on records, film or tape.
6. Writing of parodies upon lyrics.

To avoid infringement, the right to do each or any of these acts must be cleared, and the clearance of one particular right does not clear any of the other rights. All rights are separate, distinct and independent. For instance, the clearance for broadcast does not carry with it the right to copy, or to arrange, or to record; clearance of the right to record does not carry with it the right to perform. The obligation is upon you to make certain that the right involved in the act you intend to do has been cleared.

C. If you have occasion to perform the composition publicly for profit, guide yourself as follows:

Music Copyright Law Guide (cont.)

If the performance is to be in a theatre or over a radio or television station, in all likelihood the theatre, radio or television station will have a license for you to perform the musical composition publicly for profit. However, it is your obligation to make certain of this and to secure a license if there is none.

If the performance is to take place elsewhere, there is less likelihood that the establishment has a license for you to perform publicly for profit and in such event a license must be secured. There are three important performing rights societies which license the great majority of copyrighted works: American Society of Composers, Authors and Publishers (usually referred to as "ASCAP"), 575 Madison Avenue, New York 22, New York; Broadcast Music, Inc. (usually referred to as "BMI"), 589 Fifth Avenue, New York 17, New York, and SESAC, INC., 10 Columbus Circle, New York 19, New York.

If you have occasion to present a musical play or other dramatic work or a musical composition from a musical play, with costumes and/or dialogue on the stage at your school, church or elsewhere, whether for profit or nonprofit, you must secure from the owner of the work or his agent a license or permission.

D. When you see the word "Copyright" or the distinctive © printed on a piece of music, it is the notice that protects the copyright owner of the work and authorizes him to exclusively exercise and enforce all rights secured to him under the United States Copyright Law, and at the same time it is the notice that informs *you* that the exercising by you of any such acts, including those described in B and C above, *unless authorized*, will subject you to liability under such law.

A printed copy of a musical composition published in the United States, bearing no copyright notice, indicates that the composition is in the public domain in the United States and may be used freely. However, if an arrangement, adaptation or other version of such a work has been copyrighted, utmost caution must be exercised in treating the same as you would any other copyrighted work. But notwithstanding such copyrighted arrangement, adaptation or other version, of a work in the public domain, you are still free to treat the basic composition as being in the public domain. A work in the public domain reprinted in a compilation is not protected, even though the compilation itself is copyrighted, unless the reprint is a copyrightable or copyrighted arrangement, adaptation or other version thereof.

This guide is made available free of charge by the following associations:

Music Copyright Law Guide (cont.)

MUSIC PUBLISHERS' PROTECTIVE ASSOCIATION, INC.
460 Park Avenue
New York 22, New York

**MUSIC PUBLISHERS' ASSOCIATION OF THE
UNITED STATES, INC.**
609 Fifth Avenue
Fourth Floor
New York 17, New York

OTHER LEGAL MATTERS

It is helpful if you have a band member who is the offspring of a local attorney. The band boosters club can use the father's guidance, and so can you. There are many situations which at first may seem harmless that actually can lead to real trouble. For instance, there have been times when a newspaper has published a picture which was not too flattering to a child, and the parents have sued the director for releasing it.

We send a release form home with each child who is in a picture (each time he is in a picture) and the parent has to sign it before we will release the photo.

ADMINISTRATIVE FORMS

The director who desires an efficient operation must develop a system of forms. By using these you can do "as a matter of form" many things which you might otherwise forget. If you create the form as you need it, and then file a sample in the proper place you will have it when you need it again. Even though it may prove necessary to revise the form, it will be much easier to make this revision than it would be to make a new one.

Forms which you may want to develop to fit your own school and community situation are the following:

Information to Parents, Students, Others

Questionnaire survey

Follow-up note to parents
Practice records
Problems of child
Announcement of summer classes
Band rules, policies, information handbook
Band parents' club meeting notice, organization
Tryout policies, procedures, ratings

Director's File on Personnel

Permanent record master sheet
Seating chart
Merit award system
Pupil semester schedule
Enrollment chart, by instrumentation and grade
Private instruments for sale
Record of appearances

Marching Band

Rosters—in marching formation (easy to check attendance)
Game routines
Trip bulletins, performance announcements
Rules of conduct, wearing of the uniform

Library

Check-out cards
Folder check-out receipts
Library file cards (composer, title, classification)

Uniforms

Inventory record
Regulations regarding use, care, cleaning

Instruments

Inventory record
Regulations regarding use of, care, cleaning
Long-range purchase plans
Instrument cabinet storage assignments

Suppose the Board of Education has decided to build a new school—certainly not an uncommon decision with our exploding population. You may have the opportunity to advise the architect on the music portion, or to check the plans when presented. If you have sufficient information available you can make sure you have adequate facilities. If you do not know these things, you may be unhappy with the result, since many architects do not know what special things are needed in a music building or room.

A Memory Aid

Most of us, given several days to think about it, might come up with a complete list of the things which are necessary, but without a form it is likely that when checking the plans we would forget or overlook some very important part of the requirements.

There is a prominent state college with a beautiful music building; however, someone failed to include a single electrical outlet in the band room. This is quite embarrassing to the administration, because when you visit them you see an electric cord running across the hall to a classroom, which is the closest source of power.

There is another band room in another school with such a low ceiling that the sousaphone players cannot stand up on the top riser. They also have a terrible time getting out the door.

Somebody just did not have a form to check these things out. We have developed a check-list (*see* Fig. 3) which is used in checking blueprints for a new school. I find that it helps me to check those things which I know, but cannot remember accurately while going over the many pages of a complicated set of prints. Remember that a check-list is not a place to keep information. It is not a file, but merely a series of short phrases or words which alert you to specific items or areas.

Figure 3

Check-List of Specifications for Music

NAME OF SCHOOL: ————————————————

ESTIMATED SIZE: ———————————

Check-List of Specifications for Music (cont.)

A. *Auditorium—Room No.* ——

_____ 1. 1200 seating (school of 1800–2100)
_____ 2. near music wing
_____ 3. gratings at side for future organ
_____ 4. corridor (# _____) to music tall enough

B. *Choral Rooms—Room No.* ——

_____ 1. separate Choral and Band rooms
_____ 2. wider than deep
_____ 3. windows at back
_____ 4. 1800–2400 sq. ft. (120 pupils)
      5. Risers
_____   a. semi-circular
_____   b. 6 risers
_____   c. 6–8″ high
_____   d. 36″ wide
_____   e. space in front: piano, etc.
_____ 6. no support posts
      7. Vestment (Robe) Storage Room (# _____)
_____   a. 120 sq. ft.
_____   b. lockable door (# _____)
_____   c. 48″ wide doors
_____   d. tall doors
_____   e. mirror
      8. Music Library Room (# _____)
_____   a. 70 sq. ft.
_____   b. built-in storage
_____   c. ceiling height
_____ 9. tackboard
_____ 10. chalkboard
      11. light plugs, outlets
_____   a. 3 in front
_____   b. 1 in back
_____ 12. ceiling height: 18 ft.
_____ 13. wall patch acoustical-treatment
_____ 14. ceiling acoustical

C. *Band Rooms—Room No.* ——

_____ 1. wider than deep
_____ 2. windows at back
_____ 3. 2,760 sq. ft. (120 pupils)
      4. Risers

Check-List of Specifications for Music (cont.)

C. *Band Rooms—Room No.* _____ (cont.)

_____   a. semi-circular
_____   b. 4 or more risers
_____   c. 6–8″ high
_____   d. 48″ wide
_____   e. top riser: 72″ wide
_____   f. space in front: piano, etc.
_____   5. no support posts
     6. Instrument Storage Room (# _____)
_____   a. 288 sq. ft.
_____   b. 2 doors for traffic pattern
_____   c. doors high (door # _____)
_____   d. 48″ wide doors
_____   e. no sill under doors
_____   f. doors lockable
_____   g. _____ ceiling
     7. Uniform Storage Room (# _____)
_____   a. 168 sq. ft.
_____   b. lockable doors (# _____)
_____   c. no sill under door
_____   d. tall doors
_____   e. 48″ wide doors
_____   f. mirror
     8. light plugs, outlets
_____   a. 3 in front
_____   b. 1 in back
_____   9. ceiling height: 18 ft.
_____ 10. wall patch acoustical-treatment
_____ 11. ceiling acoustical
    12. 2 doors: exit and entrance
_____   a. tall (# _____)
_____   b. wide: 48″
_____ 13. chalkboard
_____ 14. tackboard
    15. Band Music Library Room (# _____)
_____   a. space elsewhere _____

D. *Practice Rooms/Dressing—No.* _____

_____   1. near music and auditorium
_____   2. 4 rooms _____
_____   3. 150 sq. ft. _____
_____   4. window for supervision

Check-List of Specifications for Music (cont.)

D. *Practice Rooms/Dressing–No.* _____ (cont.)

_____ 5. mirror
_____ 6. ceiling height

E. *Offices–Room(s) No.* _____

_____ 1. one for both _____ separate _____
_____ 2. 168 sq. ft. for two
_____ 3. light plugs, outlets
_____ 4. windows into both rehearsal rooms for supervision
_____ 5. ceiling height
_____ 6. ventilation

F. *Miscellaneous*

_____ 1. brushed paint, no spray
_____ 2. coat hooks–choral
_____ 3. coat hooks–band
_____ 4. band room isolated from choral (sound-wise)
_____ 5. lockable from rest of school
_____ 6. loading area (door # _____)
_____ 7. outside entrance doors (# _____)
_____   tall _____
_____ 8. soundproof air-heat ducts
_____ 9. workspace: water, sink
_____ 10. workbench
_____ 11. clear traffic passage from horn storage room to band rehearsal
         room

ESTABLISH A BASIC INSTRUMENTATION

In purchasing new instruments the director must analyze his school population. If the school is in an economically poor part of town we provide more instruments like the cornet and clarinet. However if the area has a high level of economic support we do not buy any of these "personal size" instruments, because we know that if the parents can afford it, the student will show a lot more interest and take a lot better care of *his own* instrument. In these schools we spend our money on oboes and bassoons and the "unusual" type of instrument. We establish our basic instrumentation for each school dependent on its size and the type of student in attendance.

Once he has established this basic instrumentation, the director must develop a priority list of purchases of new instruments to fill his requirements. He must also plan for funds to repair and eventually replace the instruments he is now using—at the same rate at which they will be wearing out. *The Band Instrument Inventory and Depreciation Record* [3] is an excellent form to use in such planning.

A Business-like Manner

All well-managed businesses have a schedule of depreciation and a routine appropriation of money to replace equipment. Using this method prevents being caught without funds for a necessary replacement and helps to eliminate tremendous differences in appropriations from year to year. Most important, it puts the band director's request for funds on a firm, business-like foundation.

Early in my teaching career I went to a school board with a 10-year plan based on this system of setting aside a net annual reserve for depreciation allowance. They told me, "We hadn't planned to appropriate much money for band instruments this year, but we're so impressed with the business-like manner in which you have approached this whole problem that we are going to give you everything you have asked for."

Believe me, that was plenty! I was able to buy a complete instrumentation, including contrabassoon, contrabass clarinet, and all the rest.

Making Entries. As soon as the instrument is purchased the director should fill in the information at the top of the form, as illustrated in Figure 4. On the first line of the cost record he should enter the acquisition cost, and since this is the total expense to date, enter that same amount in the accumulated cost column. If he does not have the cost information on an old instrument he can estimate both the present value and the life expectancy, and start from there (*see* Fig. 4).

Whenever he receives a repair bill the detailed "repair record" on the reverse side should be filled out, and the date and expense entered on the cost record. The expense should then be added to

---

[3] Blank forms are available from Conn Corporation, Elkhart, Ind.

determine the new accumulated cost. This must be done each time there is any money spent on the instrument.

At the end of the year the director must go through all of his forms (which he should keep in a separate binder) and fill in the year's changes (as listed on page 39).

Figure 4: Band Instrument Inventory and Depreciation Record

Band Instrument Inventory and Depreciation Record

Name of Instrument ____ O B O E ____ Make __D. KAYE__ Model __IWW__ Finish ____ Serial __62862__

From Whom Purchased ____ The Laurel Music Company ____ Date ____ August 30 ____ 19__ 64__

COST RECORD

COST, REPAIRS & REPLACEMENTS	MO.	DAY	YR.	EXPENSE		ACCUMULATED COST	
Acquisition	8	30	49			400	00
Repair #1 (3rd year)	6	9	52	10	00	410	00
Repair #2 (5th year)	4	5	54	10	00	420	00
Repair #3 (7th year)	7	4	57	45	00	465	00
Repair #4 (10th year)	1	10	59	13	00	478	00
Repair #5 (12th year)	8	30	61	3	50	481	50
Repair #6 (14th year)	12	20	63	12	00	493	50

DEPRECIATION RECORD

YR.	DEPRECIATION RATE %	NET ANNUAL RESERVE		ACCUMULATED RESERVE FUND		NET BOOK VALUATION		APPRAISAL	
								VALUE	DATE
1	25%	100	00	100	00	300	00		
2	13%	52	00	152	00	248	00		
3	12%	49	20	201	20	208	80		
4	8%	32	80	234	00	176	00		
5	8%	33	60	267	60	152	40		
6	7%	29	40	297	00	123	00		
7	7%	32	55	329	55	135	45		
8	7%	32	55	362	10	102	90		
9	7%	32	55	394	65	70	35		
10	6% 100%	28	68	423	33	54	67		
11		10	93	434	26	43	74		
12		11	81	446	07	35	43		
13		11	81	457	88	23	62		
14		17	81	475	69	5	81		
15		17	81	493	50	-0-			
16									
17									
18									
19									
20									

Estimated Life Expectancy of Instrument as Result of Repairs ____ 5 ____

COPYRIGHTED
JULY 1942
C. G. CONN LTD.

1909-X

REPAIR RECORD OF	O B O E	D.K A Y E		62862
	INSTRUMENT	MAKE		SERIAL NUMBER

	DESCRIPTION OF REPAIR	REPAIRED BY	DATE	COST
1.	Replace pads as needed Straighten bent rods	E.Curtis	6-9-52	$ 10.00
2.	Clean and adjust	E.Curtis	4-5-54	$ 10.00
3.	Complete overhaul	D.Kaye factory	7-4-57	$ 45.00
4.	Repair bridge keys	E.Curtis	1-10-59	$ 13.00
5.	Pads	"Chu's Fix-it"	8-30-61	$ 3.50
6.	Replace pads as needed. Clean and adjust	Barry Repairs	12-20-63	$ 12.00
7.				
8.				
9.				
10.				
11.				

1. Determine the current dollar amount of depreciation. This is done by multiplying the accumulated cost by the current year's depreciation rate. If the accumulated cost is $400, and the first year depreciation is 25%, then the dollar amount is $400 × .25 or $100. This figure is called the *net annual reserve* and should be entered in that column.

2. The cumulative total of the net annual reserve amounts is shown in the *accumulated reserve fund* columns.

3. The *net book valuation* is the accumulated cost less the net annual reserve.

4. Total the current net annual reserve figures from *each* of the charts. This is the figure which must be appropriated each year to be certain that funds will be available to purchase a new instrument when the present one is totally depreciated. Pass this total figure along to the Board of Education. In this way the musician-businessman does not beg for money each year, but merely informs the administration of its annual obligation to protect the capital investment in musical equipment.

Extra Life. Since the cost of repairs has been added to the acquisition cost and depreciated along with it, at the end of 10 years (although the instrument has been depreciated 100%) there will still be a balance remaining on the net book valuation record. In this example, through repairs, we have increased the life of the oboe. After the tenth year the director must estimate the remaining life expectancy. If he feels that another five years have been added by the repairs, as in this example, then he will put aside one-fifth of the remaining net book valuation each year, adding the cost of any additional repairs to the net annual reserve for that year.

At the time the instrument must be replaced, the accumulated cost and the accumulated reserve fund will be equal. This will allow a school to keep the stock of instruments at a constant level. In an inflationary economy the wise administrator will compensate for the increase in the purchase price of a new instrument. In a deflationary economy the reserve fund will be in excess of the cost.

As in many other areas, the band director can get valuable help from other departments (in this case the commercial) and build good will and friendships in the process. The best friend you have is quite often not the one for whom you have done the most, but the one who has done the most for you.

SPEND TIME TO SAVE TIME

Many schools allow one hour a day for all of the band director's out-of-class activities. This is really not enough. I would estimate that the man who is doing a conscientious job could spend this one hour in school and one hour out of school—as a minimum. About half of this time might be classified as business management. The other half would be choosing music, general planning, etc.

Although the director will spend considerable time "getting organized," and "being businesslike," he will really save time in the long run. For example, if you have your band music numbered and keep it in order, when you pass it out it is going to flow more smoothly onto the students' stands. When you call it in, and there is a piece of music missing, you immediately know what piece of music it is, and to which student it was assigned. You can call the student to your office and say, "I checked out No. 14 to you. It is not here. You owe 50¢."

When you get the same arrangement out later all the solo cornet parts will *not* be missing. The typical band music library too often has 15,000 alto horn parts and not a single solo cornet part in the files. They are all to be found in the instrument cases—of the alumni!

WHY BOTHER?

Many directors do not attempt any organizational system because of the apparent magnitude of the task. They begin to sense the size of the whole music business and get panicky, thinking that it so big and so complicated that they are not even going to bother with it. They say, "I'll just live on a year-to-year basis."

But if you will start with what you are doing *today*, and organize that, you will be starting to build up a backlog of organization which will accumulate more quickly than you realize.

If you are going to hand out a band arrangement tomorrow, then today number the parts, put the data on a 4 x 6 card. Just that much— just that one number you are going to play tomorrow: do this and you will be at least one step more organized than when you started.

This sort of progress is slow. You cannot organize a band library, for instance, in a month, or six months, or even a year. You may not have time to do it in two years. What you need is to *organize yourself*, and work at it a little each day. Organize what you can, when you can, and then do not worry about the rest of it.

The organizational techniques described in this chapter can save you the time which is so precious in your job. If a man has to be a father to his family, a leader in the community, and all of the other things which are demanded of successful band directors, then he must make the absolute maximum use of his time and effort. He cannot do this if he is always slowed down by insignificant details.

Proper organization and business management is not an end in itself, but a means to free the band director's mental and physical powers for the really significant problems of his job.

Public

Relations

by **Al G. Wright**

Purdue University

Al G. Wright

serves as Head of the Department of Bands at Purdue University, Lafayette, Indiana, where he holds the rank of full professor. He was Director of Music and Conductor of the Band and Orchestra at Miami, Florida, Senior High School for 14 years before moving to Purdue in 1954. Born in 1916 in London, England, his early education was received in the public schools of Pontiac, Michigan. His BA and M.Ed. degrees were earned at the University of Miami.

Under his direction Miami High became recognized as having one of the outstanding high school instrumental music programs in the country, and he has brought the Purdue Symphony Band and the "All American" Marching Band to a standard of excellence which ranks it among the finest in the nation.

Mr. Wright has been a leader in the field of music education for many years and has held a number of state and national offices, including the presidency of the National Band Association, and membership on the board of directors of both the Music Educators National Conference and the American Bandmasters Association.

He is a contributing editor of the *Instrumentalist*, the author of the marching band text *The Show Band*, and has been responsible for numerous articles in national professional music magazines.

The many different ways to tell people what you are doing are known collectively as "public relations"—"PR."

Obviously the first requirement of a good PR program is that you *do something*, but it is equally important that you then make sure the people know about it. This means not only must you create a band program which is good for the students, the parents, the school, and the community; but it also means that you must develop the ability to disseminate news and information which, without bragging, makes these same people conscious of what a good program they have.

Public relations is an essential part of your job, not something extra to be passed along to someone else, or to be done only when you have some "spare time."

Sometimes called promotion, publicity, public information, human relations, etc., PR actually involves all of these things, held together by the common element of *communication:* with the students, the parents, your school associates, and the general public.

A knowledge of newspaper procedures and techniques, a command of the spoken as well as the written language, and the ability to use the typewriter are all extremely valuable. Until courses in journalism, public speaking, and typing are added to the music education curriculum, the band director will have to pursue these studies on his own.

Too many times PR responsibilities are looked upon as a great burden, when actually much can be done in conjunction with other duties. Since you have to make up a list of selections for your program, for instance, you can just make an extra copy, write a few explanatory notes at the top, and send it on down to the newspaper. Even when you write a full news release, there is no need to go beyond four good paragraphs, and don't try to tell *all* the details—just who, what, when, where, and why.

As the director of the band you must be certain that the "projected image" (to use the Madison Avenue term) of the band is the one *you* desire, not a student or parent version.

Your PR organization may include students who write for the school paper, provided you see and approve every story (and rewrite almost all of them) before publication. Both students and parents may do the "leg-work" associated with gathering materials, delivering stories, and complaining (but only a little bit) when a story does not get in the paper.

You alone have the responsibility for *everything* connected with the band. Don't duck it. If you choose a student or parent committee to help run your public relations program, make certain that they can handle the job, and that *you can handle them.*

A PR Routine

Every band director knows that he must get up early and go to bed late if he expects to get his job done, but as more and more demands are placed upon his time it becomes even more important for him to set up certain rigid regulations which will make for maximum efficiency and the best of relations between himself and the public. Here are a few suggestions:

Answer Your Mail Every Day. The problems do not go away. Tomorrow the letter will still be there. Even if you just scratch "yes" or "no" on the bottom of the page and send it back, do it right away.

Plan Your Work Schedule in Advance and Stick to It. If you have publicity to write for an approaching concert, say to yourself, "Tomorrow I will write the piece in my one o'clock planning period" (and in the interest of good PR never call it a "free period"—even when you're talking to yourself). Do not accept any visitors; stay away from the bull session in the teacher's lounge; don't even answer your phone, but do get off by yourself and go to work.

Develop a Professional Attitude. Do not allow parents to just "drop in" on you, any more than you would walk up to your doctor on the street and begin to describe symptoms. When the parent of one of your high school students just "comes by to say hello," step outside the band office door and say: "I'm terribly sorry but I just can't see you now . . . I'm all tied up. How about tomorrow at 3?"

After about a year of this, all of the parents will realize that they should call and make an appointment. This procedure will give you a chance to gather your information together so that you can talk intelligently with the parent about the progress of his son or daughter.

This is not being cold or aloof, but just plain professional behavior; as such it is excellent public relations. You have to be careful how you do it.

Don't Be a Slave to the Telephone. Keep one in the office for your convenience in *calling out.* At Miami High School I set up a schedule of student assistants to answer the telephone and to keep a record of incoming calls. I was never called to the phone from a rehearsal, even for long distance. If I wanted to shut myself up and do some work I felt I had just as much of a privilege of withdrawing from the phone as I did of withdrawing from people. Of course the students were alerted that if the principal called, *I was there!*

PLANNING PUBLICITY

The three basic phases of publicity are like the famous sermon analysis:

(preliminary)—"First, you tell them what you're going to tell them.

(last-minute) —"Then you tell them. . . .

(follow-up) —"After that, you tell them what you just told them."

Effective publicity must be carefully planned and then executed according to that plan. Proper timing is especially important. Since many things are often forgotten in the rush and excitement of preparing for a major event in the life of the band, it is best to use a check-list to make sure that the things which you know need to be done are taken care of at the proper time.

The "count-down" should begin at minus three months, but if the band is going to appear at a national event, such as the Cherry Blossom Festival or the Rose Bowl Parade, it should be announced immediately upon selection, even though the event may be nine months away. Once a month "keep it warm" by releasing stories about practice sessions, fund-raising, trip-planning, etc. Note that in the *Major Event Planning Outline* [1] (*see* Fig. 5), the tasks associated with public rela-

---

[1] Developed by Gladys Stone Wright and reprinted with her permission.

tions are an integral part of the entire planning procedure, not something extra.

Figure 5

Major Event Planning Outline

TARGET ————————————————————

DATE OF EVENT ————————————————————

Count-Down	Action	Completed
3 months	Event on calendar	———
	Physical facilities obtained	———
	Students notified of event	———
	Possible program of music considered	———
2 months	Tentative program established	———
	Props and stage scenery construction planned	———
	Needed items and materials obtained	———
	Extra personnel involved (guest soloist, parent committees) contacted	———
1 month	Program firmed up	———
	Posters to Art Dept. or Printer's	———
	Tickets to Art Dept. or Printer's	———
3 weeks	Posters distributed	———
	Tickets distributed for sale	———
	First publicity announcement	———
2 weeks	Check on ticket sales	———
	Set up publicity release to include details	———
	Program to printer's or mimeograph department	———
	Appoint following committees:	
	Ushering	———
	Ticket	———
	Security	———
	Decoration	———
	Transportation	———
1 week	Invite special guests	———
	Prepare publicity release (daily if possible)	———
	Contact local civic clubs to make announcement of event	———

Count-Down	*Action*	*Completed*
	Supply copy to local radio and TV for announcing	
	Are committees working?	___
	Prepare announcements, introductions, etc. that will be made by you at the program	
	Proofread programs and arrange for delivery 2 days before concert	___
	Double-check physical facilities, *i.e.,* stage, stands, etc.	___
	Remind band of uniform requirements	
	Check Director's uniform	___
2 days	Pick up programs	
	Release final publicity material	___
	Double-check committees	___
Following Concert	Thank all persons involved for contributing to successful program by letter or phone.	___
	Complete checking of tickets and money.	
	Return all borrowed items.	___
	Compare critique of event for possible use next year.	
	Prepare post-event publicity.	___

DEALING WITH NEWSPAPERS

Except in the case of an ax murder by your second oboist, newspapers will probably never come knocking on your door in search of information. Their life blood is the *press release*—material about an event generally unknown to the press which is fed to them by those people who *do* know about it.

The easier you can make it for the man who will be using your material, the more he will appreciate your sending it, and the more likely he will be to print it.

Every newspaper has its own saturation point for promotional type releases, but there is no limit for true *news* items. In some large communities, or where the paper is overloaded with school events, no matter what is happening, you may be able to get only three mentions in the paper: two weeks, four days, and one day in advance of the event. In a community with one high school and one local paper they will usually run stories more often than that, however.

Many times an alert director can create items which will pass as "news," even though on close analysis they may be pure promotion.

Stories should be presented well in advance of the time you would like them published. Your release might get into a choice spot if you wait until late to submit it (since newspapers make up their front page last, and most small town editors often use inside pages-type material to fill space), but, for the same reason, it might not get in at all.

It is best for each director to sit down with his local editor and find out how much material the paper wants to handle, the type of item they are most interested in, the deadlines they observe, and the best size for photographs.

Since there are so many places in the necessarily rapid writing, make-up, and printing operations of a newspaper where errors may slip in and cause mistakes in the final edition, you should not be critical of their efforts. Don't let Mrs. Smyth visit the editor to point out that she is *not* one of "those common Smiths" who spell their name with an "i"; and don't you call about that either, or to complain that you didn't get enough space, or that your picture was too close to the girdle ads. Just continue to send accurate, concise, well-written stories in the acceptable form, and realize that the important thing is that your material *is* being published, and that the newspaper is doing the best it can.

Preparing News Copy

Newspaper stories should be like the old saying about majorettes' uniforms: long enough to cover the subject and short enough to be interesting. Be sure to give your readers the answer to the five important questions: Who? What? When? Where? Why?

Read the news stories in today's paper again, this time as a literary critic, and analyze the style so that you can imitate it. You will find the writing to be simple, easily understood, factual, and to the point. If you find any opinions expressed they will be in the form of a quotation from someone connected with the story.

Notice that even if you stop reading after the first few sentences you have still been exposed to the essential facts. This is because a good news story is written using a series of short paragraphs, each telling the story in a little greater detail, so that the editor can print as much or as little as he has space for at any given time. Compare different editions of a large metropolitan daily to see how the same story may be used in different versions.

The mechanical requirements, standard throughout the industry, are:

1. Use only one side of a sheet of 8½ x 11 plain, white paper (no letterhead).
2. Type the copy. Never submit a handwritten release.
3. Use one page whenever possible. If you must go to two pages, be sure to end the first with a complete paragraph and put (MORE) at the bottom.
4. Indicate when you want the story released, by the appropriate phrase: "For release January 1," for example. If you want to give an exclusive ("beat") to one outlet, you can say: "For *your* immediate release; for general release January 10." Be careful when playing favorites.
5. Include the name, address, and phone number of the organization and the person from whom the editor can secure additional information if he needs it.
6. Begin the actual story a third of the way down the page, leave a wide margin on both sides, and double space (triple if possible), so that the editor has plenty of room for corrections, additions, and typesetting instructions.

Proofreader's marks can save time for you when you are rewriting material or checking copy for publication. Your local newspaper or print shop should be able to supply you with a set.

Mechanically duplicated sheets (ditto, mimeo, etc.) are accepted by newspapers if it is a general release of information, but they resent receiving *news* items in this form. When your band goes on a tour, for instance, you can use mimeographed material, since the information will go to so many outlets. "Localize" the story by writing at the bottom: "John Jones, of 150 Elm Street, is the president of the organization sponsoring the concert in your city." This will allow the local editor to give it to his rewrite man who then calls 150 Elm Street to get his lead paragraph for the story.

Carbon copies should be made of any release you prepare. In addition to protecting yourself against loss of the original, and having a model for your release on the same event next year, you will find it interesting to compare the published article with the material you submitted. When a parent whose name was left off the refreshment committee list comes in to complain, you can point to her name on the carbon and show that you had no malice aforethought, but that it was simply an oversight by the newspaper.

Never send a carbon copy to the newspaper; the editor won't know for sure if you made a mistake and kept the original yourself, or whether you sent it to the competing paper. Neither assumption makes for good public relations.

PHOTOGRAPHS

The picture you see reproduced in a newspaper is actually a group of tiny dots made by photographing the original print through a half-tone screen (a glass plate ruled with a grid of opaque lines). The dots seem to disappear when viewed from a normal reading distance. Since the dots increase in diameter as the original varies from white to black, the published photo appears, to the naked eye, almost exactly like the original.

A comparison, using a magnifying glass, of the photographs in this book with those in a newspaper will reveal a difference in the number of dots used. The quality and the cost of the reproduction is determined by the number of lines per linear inch in the screen used to make the cut. The use of both a coarse screen (with fewer dots) and the rough newsprint paper stock greatly reduce the original quality of a sharp print.

These mechanical limitations must be considered with the other technical and aesthetic requirements for a good photograph in developing your over-all concept of publicity pictures.

The picture itself must be newsworthy, properly composed, and in good taste. Prints must be sharp and clear, glossy surfaced, with a little more "punch" (increased contrast) than normal. Box camera type snapshots are rarely acceptable. Backgrounds should be plain so that the figures stand out. Poor backgrounds can be eliminated prior to publication by brushing them out with white opaque.

Vertical pictures are best since the basic form of a newspaper depends on a contrast between horizontal headlines and a series of vertical columns underneath. Photo sizes are identified by the relationship to the width of a column of type (1¾"). Individual portraits are "one column cuts"; an informal group (three is a good number) might be a "two column cut." As the *width* of the photograph you submit increases, your chance of getting in the paper decreases.

Find out the reproduction process which your local papers are using and choose your photographs accordingly. If they use the engraving process, it is best to send them 8x10 prints, because when the plates are made they can reduce the size, and thus (by concentration) increase the clarity. The paper using the Fairchild Plate process, which produces a plate the same size as the original, would first have to reduce your 8x10 print to a new print in a smaller size. The necessity of extra time, effort, and expense, might cause an editor to eliminate the story entirely, whereas if you submitted a smaller print (which costs less anyway) both the photo and the story would probably be run.

A different pose should be sent to each paper in town, and you should try to distribute your "best shots" equally.

The name of the individuals or organization should be typed on a sheet of paper and taped to the back of the print so that it will fold over the top edge and protect the glossy surface. It can be torn off before use. Do not print anything on the back of the photograph itself as the pressure (especially from a ball point pen or a typewriter) will emboss the opposite surface and make it impossible to use the print.

Photographers

A student photographer should be appointed, preferably the youngster whose father owns the local photo shop. Even if most of the boy's pictures are of poor quality, you will find that when something really important comes up, his father will do the job.

When a professional photographer comes to take a picture for the newspaper or the high school annual, the band director should already have the poses in mind. In the case of a large group photo, he should have everything set up and ready to go. Be sure that every face is seen.

Photo Ideas

Personal portraits of guest soloists or conductors, band members or parents who have received special honors, or the director himself, may be used. A personal photo should be updated every five years to make sure that the wrinkle and hair count is at least somewhat consistent with the live version.

Small group photos, such as parents' committees, band officers, or sections of the band can be very effective. A row of trombone players coming downstairs provides an interesting effect in the desired vertical format. In picturing majorettes care must be taken never to use a low camera angle or to show the inside of the thigh.

Large group pictures are usually not run by newspapers because the small faces are lost in the screening process.

"News" photos. You are limited only by the saturation point of the publication and by the extent of your own imagination in the variety of reasons for "news" photos. Here are a few suggestions:

1. New students in the band (beginners, transfers, or those from the feeder system).
2. New officers for the year (marching officers in the fall, concert officers later on).
3. New section leaders, newly promoted people, new drum major and majorettes.
4. Posed "action" pictures, taken at a rehearsal of the current week's football half-time show. Make sure everything is just right, and be careful to eliminate empty seats from the photo so that it does not look quite so posed. Use this type of photo only if the formation is impressive enough to compensate for the loss of faces.
5. Summer program: both musical and recreational activities, concerts and awards.
6. Awards and presentations. Give the newspapers a chance to pose the pictures afterwards so that they do not have to wait through a two-hour concert for one shot, and so that you can eliminate the photograpically difficult problem of catching the decisive moment, in a well composed photo, under actual stage presentation conditions.
7. Unique situations. A posed picture of a grade school band is considered to be only of limited local interest, but a photo of the Round Grove (Indiana) Grade School Band appeared in a national publication, because of the fact that *everyone* from the 5th to the 8th grade in the school plays in the band. Figure 6 shows the article.[2]
8. Sometimes you can create a situation which calls for a news photo. Whenever the Miami (Florida) High School Band played out of town we carried greetings from our mayor, first in the form of a framed letter, and later as a scroll. We notified the other city

---

[2] From *Lyons Band News* and *Kjos Music News*. Reprinted with permission.

Figure 6

LYONS BAND NEWS & KJOS MUSIC NEWS

Everyone Plays in the Round Grove, Ind. Grade School Band—everyone, that is, from the 5th to 8th grades. Gladys Stone Wright, Director.

GRADE SCHOOL HAS 100% ENROLLMENT IN BAND

Few schools in this country can boast of the record of the Round Grove Grade School Band, of Round Grove, Indiana, which proudly points to the fact that every student in grades 5 through 8 is a member of the band, which is comprised of 37 players.

The director of this well organized and fine playing band is Mrs. Gladys Stone Wright, who meets with this band Tuesdays, weekly. Mrs. Wright is not only directing this band, but is studying at Purdue University on her Doctorate as well.

Twenty-five of these students entered the Indiana Solo and Ensemble Contest this past year, where they performed admirably. Their new uniforms were purchased through the Classified ads in the Band News recently, and they are very proud of them.

The achievement of the Round Grove Grade School Band should be an inspiration to other small schools throughout the country, and it should prove to them that good small well-balanced bands can be formed in their own schools, and their children can receive the same advantages musically as do children in the larger school systems.

———————

in advance and invariably their mayor would come to the concert for the presentation, bringing with him his local news photographer.

It is wise for the band to adopt a nickname. This will help people to remember the group. The Miami High School organization was called the "Million Dollar Band," not meaning that it cost a million (although sometimes the principal claimed it almost did), but to suggest the expression "it looks like a million dollars," which was popular in those days. I suppose there is a "Billion Dollar Band" somewhere today; inflation has hit even the nickname business.

If you are promoting a concert, the poster can be tacked up on the wall and used as a background for a small group photo. Banners, flags, or drums all make excellent identifying props.

The bass drum should be painted with the name of the band. Clear letters which can be seen from a distance are best. Do not use a fancy script, or a long series of words, neither of which can be read quickly or accurately. It is almost impossible for anyone to look at Figure 7 and wonder where the band came from. Even in the

Figure 7: One of the largest in existence, Purdue University's drum—eight feet in diameter—being used in formation in Ross-Ade Stadium, West Lafayette, Indiana.

panoramic view of the city square in Bogotá, Columbia (made on a South American tour in 1962), which was taken from a great distance, the "P" on the bass drums is still very clear (*see* Fig. 8).

Figure 8: Purdue University Band on Tour in South America

Students should be in uniform, with instruments, and the photos taken so that the name of the band is visible. Since we feel so strongly that uniforms should have some prominent identification feature, we are the only band in the country which must end up a half-time show with "PU" written on the chests of 240 bandsmen for all the amateur comics in the audience to use as their critical commentary on the performance, but they remember which band did the show!

RADIO

Most small town radio stations are very happy to broadcast tape recordings of the local band. Even if the tapes are not technically first rate, the shows are effective because home town kids are playing. You should check with the station manager to determine:

1. The length of show desired. A "fifteen-minute" program, for instance, must not exceed 14½ minutes, including the opening and closing, which usually means 12½ minutes of music, including announcements.
2. The recording level. You must find out how much volume the station engineer wants in order to keep the hiss and background noise to a minimum.
3. The tape speed. Since the quality increases with speed, most stations prefer 15 ips, but will usually accept 7½ ips. The quality of 3¾ ips and 1⅞ ips is not acceptable for broadcast.

If you use a half-track recorder (one that will record on "both sides" of the tape) you must be certain that there is nothing recorded on the other track. The station's full track equipment will pick up the side you want, but it will also broadcast the other side —backwards! If the tape has been used before, it is possible that your school recorder, erasing as it records, will not completely clean off what is underneath, and the more sensitive equipment will pick it up. Using a fresh reel of tape will solve both problems.

When preparing to do a show, do not attempt to record a full program, but rather rehearse a number, make your announcement and record the music, then stop the tape and rehearse the next number. Make the tape complete within itself so that all the radio station (usually understaffed) has to do is to start and stop it; otherwise they may decide to play an LP record instead of trying to figure out what you want them to do and when.

TELEVISION

It is very difficult to do a live TV show with a full band, and for "in person" appearances a few soloists, a small ensemble, or your stage band will be more appropriate for the small studio and the small screen area. However, this exciting medium offers many other fascinating possibilities. Here are three ideas:

1. If your band takes half-time show movies, the station will probably be glad to run short sections of the film that are particularly good (called "clips").
2. By placing 8x10 glossy prints (sprayed with a special anti-glare

mist which wipes off after use) on a bulletin board, the TV camera can move in close and pan across the print. When seen on the video screen the viewer has the feeling of actually being on the site.

3. The same 2x2 slide used in our home slide shows can be projected directly onto the iconoscope (the "tube") for maximum clarity. It can also be shown on a rear-view projection screen, which allows the director to stand in front, with no interference, and indicate the points of interest. Since the color transparency has no grain it produces a beautifully clear image. You can create a complete "communications composition" by taking your own 35mm slides and projecting them in order, just as the stations sequence their advertising slides.

COMMUNICATION WITH PARENTS

As a band director you are the only teacher in the school who must sell parents on the idea of investing from $150 to $300 to get started, spending sizable sums each year on related expenses, and on not really seeing any results for two to three years. While this takes quite a bit of salesmanship in the beginning (the only legitimate sales technique is to maintain a good program), it results in the greatest strength of the instrumental program: a group of parents who have so much time and money invested will support the band and see to it that their children get the most from the experience. The nice part about it all is that they are such *genuinely happy "captives."*

Communication forms should be used to keep the parents advised. The demerit system is used in many high schools. In our plan demerits were reserved for serious offenses (don't give one at the drop of a mouthpiece cap). The parent was notified every time the student received a demerit, starting with the first offense. When this system is first initiated the only change you notice may be an increase in the number of stamps consumed, but when that second letter goes home you will find that the parents become concerned and start to put pressure on the students. In the third letter you request a conference with the parents. If it is necessary to send the fourth, which means "dissociation" with the band, you have ample justification, and the parent has had sufficient warning.

Merit letters. Too many times only the disciplinary problems attract attention and cause comment from the band director while good behavior goes unnoticed or is labeled "expected-normal." In fact, whenever I would forget the name of a student when meeting his parents, I would always tell them: "I only remember the names of those who get into trouble, so your youngster must be doing a real fine job."

Since we sent out demerit letters, we thought it only fair to send a merit letter whenever there was a reason for one. It would usually read something like this:

> Dear Mr. and Mrs. Jones:
> We would like to take a moment of your time to tell you how much we are enjoying having your son Johnny as a member of the "Million Dollar Band."
> Recently he earned a promotion in the clarinet section, and we wanted you to know how proud we are of his progress.
> Sincerely,

You don't have to mention that he was promoted from last chair clarinet to next-to-last chair. The important thing is that the proud parents will be impressed that you took the time to give their son—and therefore them—a pat on the back, rather than the stronger force in a lower area which is the subject of most teacher-parent communications.

AWARDS

An extensive awards system is a necessary part of every high school public relations program. All awards should not be given at the same time, but broken down into various categories and presented at the appropriate occasion. In this way you can avoid the boredom of an endless series of presentations, make the fact that eventually everybody gets an award of some kind less obvious, and spread the publicity and morale building value over the entire school year.

The athletic type awards, such as marching band and majorette letters, should be presented at a high school assembly.

The musical awards, such as the most improved player, concertmaster, or outstanding beginner, should be presented at a band concert. Limit yourself to one or two awards per concert.

The longevity, or "staying alive" awards, such as service bars for a letter or a sweater, should be presented at the annual band banquet.

The outstanding senior award, such as the John Philip Sousa award, if you restrict it to seniors, should be presented at the commencement exercises.

These awards are extremely important to the students and to

their parents. Every parent should be able to say at some time throughout the year, "My Johnny got an award."

COMMUNICATION WITH
THE SCHOOL

One of the most important, and sometimes most difficult, goals of band public relations is to create a favorable "image" of the band and its director in the eyes of the students and the faculty members.

The conscientious band director simply does not have the time to be "buddy-buddy" with the superintendent, play golf with the principal, or be the darling of the faculty bridge club.

Work instead toward building the concept that the band is the *quality* group in school. This can be done by always publicizing prizes, honors, or elections won by band members. Make regular reports to the faculty on how well the band students are doing in their academic work (see to it that they are!). Purdue Band students make grades which are consistently above the average university index, and by publicizing this fact we can answer the standard objection that "band takes too much time away from academic work."

There is nothing wrong with a good strong band program in which there are many activities, provided the program is musical, is good for the students, the school, and the community. If your band program is very popular and growing, you are almost bound to be criticized eventually by some jealous colleague who wishes he could have a program which gets as much attention as yours, but who does not have the slightest intention of putting as much time and effort into it as you do (you've seen him racing the students to the parking lot as the afternoon bell rings).

If you are really sincere in the belief that your program is doing a good job for the students, you can only be amused, never hurt, and maybe even complimented, by the old statement that "the tail seems to be wagging the dog around here."

Work closely with your principal; send him carbons of your activity plans; check things out ahead of time. Remember that: Only a happy school wags its tail, but . . . the tail can wag only as much as the dog wants it to, and even a dog which is about to be shaken violently as a result of the desires of the tail quite often prefers to relax and enjoy it, if you always ask permission first!

Civic club membership allows the band director (and remember there are always many, many "school teachers" in a small community, but usually only one "band director") the chance to talk informally with the civic leaders and to gain considerable stature as a result. When asked to join, even though it will take some of your valuable time, recognize the invitation as both an honor and an opportunity, and do your best to become a respected member of the group.

Concert programs should not serve merely to list the musical numbers to be performed, but should be a part of the public relations program. Names—every student, the parents, officers and committees, the school officials—are an essential part of every printed program. Always list the superintendent, the principal, and the band director—in that order.

Progress reports to the taxpayers may be prepared and published in the papers. This is most effective during March or April when the people are getting ready for the income tax deadline and are very cost conscious. Because of the large number of pupils involved, the cost of music education per pupil will compare very favorably with the average school cost, and you can usually show that the band has one of the lowest per pupil cost factors in the entire system. It should be worded in such a way that you do not directly offend other departments.

Comparing the cost of a band trip to what that same excursion would have cost a private citizen will show the taxpayers tangible benefits of band membership for their children. Make your presentation even more impressive by pointing out the extremely large percentage of the budget which comes from *non*-tax funds.

Never use lump sums. "The River City Band spent only $14,000 last year" is frightening to a man who is paying off a 30-year loan on his $8,000 home, but he will be favorably impressed when that same fact is broken down to the taxpayer's cost per pupil: "The *tax money* spent on each student enrolled in the River City band program last year was $37.42 compared with the national average educational cost per pupil of $415.00."

Tie-in Promotion can be used in cooperation with radio stations and record shops. They will feature commercial albums containing the same numbers you have scheduled for your concert if you will send your program a month in advance so they have time to set it up.

The personnel file can be a valuable bank of information on students and parents alike. You should have complete entries on the occupation and interests of each parent. When you are setting up fund-raising committees, for example, by checking your files you can be sure that doctors, lawyers, and prominent businesmen—all the people who carry sufficient prestige in the community to locate some real cash—are on that committee. If you need uniforms repaired, your file will indicate those non-working mothers with an interest in sewing who would have the time to do the job.

Stock publicity releases in which specific names, places, dates, etc. are inserted into a prepared skeleton are useful when the band is on tour. You can save time, and be sure that your story contains all the proper elements, by preparing a stock form (for your use in writing; retype for release) for each of the more common items: football shows, concerts, parades, etc. Figure 9 shows a stock concert release form which has been filled in.

Figure 9: Stock Form for Publicity Release

River City High School Band
A. Long Baton, director
RIghtway 6-3853

FOR IMMEDIATE RELEASE

Who — The River City High School Band, under the direction of

What — A. Long Baton, will present a concert on Friday evening,

When — May 24, at 8 P.M. This annual spring concert, a

Why — tradition in River City, will be held in the John J.

Where — Flood Memorial Auditorium.

Ralph Mendoza of Mexico City will be featured as guest soloist ~~conductor.~~ The band will play selections

Detail (#1) — covering a full musical range, including Beethoven's Eroica Symphony and My Hero from The Chocolate Soldier.

The fact that the 425 members of the River City instrumental music department will more than overflow the Flood stage is a

Opinion — tribute to the outstanding direction of Mr. Baton, according to Superintendent Neil B. Wright, a former band director.

The concert band will perform works by Mozart, Walters, Yoder, and Persichetti. The woodwind quintet and the

Detail (#2) — "Hungry 5" will also appear. Mr. Mendoza will play ~~conduct~~ "La Virgen de la Macarena." As a special feature, junior Dawn Chaney will sing a memorable arrangement of "Full Moon and Empty Arms."

Commercial — This is the final concert of the current season. A very limited number of tickets will be available at the door for non-subscribers.

(END)

Many local radio announcers, who are often excellent sports-casters, shy away from any description of the half-time show because they feel they do not know enough about what is going on either to give a running commentary or to fill the inevitable "dead air" with related remarks. As a result, your stirring musical arrangements which are so well coordinated with the clever movements of the band may end up, on the radio, as background music for a reading of the first half statistics.

We prepare a press book for each game, and present it to both radio and TV broadcasters one week before the program. The follow-ing items are included:

1. A synopsis of the pre-game, half-time, and post-game shows complete with field diagram sketches, music cues, an explanation of the band's action, and PA announcements.
2. Music credits—the title, composer-arranger, and publisher for each number in the show, listed in the order performed, plus a similar list of repertoire from which we choose music to be per-formed in the stands.
3. Press releases on special events associated with the band's per-formance that day.
4. Biographical material on special guests who will be a part of the show.
5. Background material—in "fact-sheet" form—on the band, per-sonalities, auxiliary units and the director, so that the announcer has some sparkling ad libs available when he needs them.

THIS IS MY LIFE

Biographical material should be prepared in a form which allows you to send mimeographed sheets rather than having to compose a separate letter in answer to each request for information. All three of the basic forms should be sent so that as much or as little as desired is available.

The outline biography, or *vitae sheet*, is a list of the principal events of your life from birth to date.

The biography is a complete account of the highlights of your life —"the long form."

The biographical sketch is the "short form" of about four paragraphs which covers only the most important events.

Be sure that the information is kept up to date. Spelling and grammar must be correct, because quite often you will receive requests from people who are not professional editors, and not used to handling material of this type. The County Festival chairman, for instance, who has a million other things on his mind, may just put your biographical sketch in the program without first rewriting it, proofreading it, or maybe without reading it at all!

TELL OTHERS—FOR MUTUAL BENEFIT

Even though the primary goal of every public relations effort must always be to produce a better program for the students, parents, school, and community, there are numerous personal dividends for the director.

As the local instrumental program grows in size, strength, and popularity, the reputation of its conductor will spread, because every band program is a direct reflection of the ability of the man in charge. When others learn of the band director's accomplishments he is picked for state and national committees, travels, finds opportunities, broadens his experience, and becomes an even more valuable man in his own community.

As a matter of "job insurance" it is always desirable to have built a reputation in the state, or, better yet, throughout the nation. If the local situation ever "blows up," he can move with advantage.

But even as he is receiving personal benefits, the successful director also has an obligation to his profession to share his experiences so that others, and ultimately, the entire music education field, may benefit from his own particular innovations. The phenomenal growth and success of the band movement is being furthered by people who are not afraid to tell others *what* they are doing, and *how* they are doing it.

No editor of a national publication [3] can possibly write to each band director every month and ask him to send in an article on some phase of his program. Since most magazines depend on *unsolicited*

---

[3] Mr. Wright has served in two editorial posts: as President of the National Band Association, which publishes a quarterly newsletter, and as a contributing editor of the *Instrumentalist.*—*Ed.*

manuscripts, every director should sit down and simply tell what he is doing. The thing which may be commonplace to him could be a fresh new idea and just the right solution to a tough problem for some director in another section of the country. Don't be discouraged if all articles are not accepted: different publications have different interests.

First, work hard to develop a program that is beneficial to all concerned, and then don't ever be ashamed to use every legitimate public relations technique to tell other people what you are doing. The jealous will almost certainly damn you, but the wise will be grateful for the information.

Fund Raising

Band Booster Clubs

Uniforms

by **John E. Crews**

Dallas, Texas

John E. Crews

conceived the idea of selling *Manor Texas Fruit Cake* to organizations as an aid to their fund raising plans and started to contact high school bands in 1953. Since that time he has traveled throughout the United States talking to directors and Band Parents Clubs about their financial problems.

Mr. Crews was born in Paris, Texas, and was graduated from the high school there. His study of law at the University of Texas was never completed due to the extreme financial problems he and his family encountered in the depression years of the early 1930's.

He prepared himself for the business world through the study of bookkeeping, typing, and shorthand at a commercial college. He has sold for the Borden Milk Company, worked as a construction carpenter, been an aircraft inspector, and represented a life insurance company.

In 1945 he took a job with the Manor Baking Company of Dallas, Texas, and worked his way up to the position of Office Manager. He entered the fruit cake department in 1952.

They say that money makes the world go around, and while a physical scientist would surely disagree, it *is* easy to see that money does enter into the operation of nearly everything human that takes place on this planet while it is orbiting the sun.

Each of the parts of this three-way chapter has a very definite connection with the dollar, in that funds are usually raised by band boosters clubs (which often exist for that purpose alone), and a great deal of the resulting cash is used to purchase new uniforms.

If you maintain a purely *business* approach to your fund raising activities, *i.e.*, buying quality items at wholesale and selling them at a reasonable profit, you will avoid being classed as a beggar who asks for a handout. By choosing a unique product which is not available locally, and then really giving the public its money's worth, you can even be accepted as a member of the business community.

EDITOR'S NOTE: None of the statements in this chapter is intended by Mr. Crews to reflect discredit on any individual or on any of his competitors, but rather to set forth those high standards of business ethics advocated by all of the many excellent companies who are associated with school bands in their fund raising efforts.

While it would be impossible to acknowledge each individual contribution, it will be obvious to the reader that Mr. Crews' sensitive appreciation of the problems of both the school band director and the businessman have been developed through his close association with many people in many parts of the United States.

WHY RAISE FUNDS?

There are states which provide adequately for practically all of their school needs, including the full operating costs of an active band program, but there are those which merely furnish a room and the director's salary. Somewhere in between are thousands of variations on a share-the-cost theme performed by the board, the boosters, and the band itself—a sort of financial "3 B's."

Funds are raised to pay all of those expenses essential to an effective program which cannot be purchased either because of legal or policy restriction with the limited number of tax dollars made available by the school. When applying for a position it is advisable to determine the administration's philosophy and practice in this area. You should know how much will be furnished, and how much you will be expected to raise.

Many times we give to our children those things which we ourselves had to work very hard to get, saying, "Let's make it a little easier on them." An extreme example of the results of this "silver platter" technique (which ultimately makes it harder on them) is the band whose director told me: "These youngsters have been given everything—instruments, uniforms, music, even their own cars to drive to school—and as a result they have lost all initiative. They have no desire to learn to play or march, and they have almost driven me to the point that I have no desire to attempt to teach them."

On the other hand, when parents and students work together it helps to stimulate mutual interest and respect. Successful fund raising provides this opportunity, as well a chance for students to gain self-confidence through meeting (and selling) new people. It teaches responsibility and dependability, develops self-discipline and good citizenship within the organization, and (always with your proper guidance) presents to the general public a respectable image of today's youth and the organizations they represent.

DONATIONS

I have found bands and directors to have the most successful community relations when donations are *not* solicited. Regardless of the apparent happiness, there are usually strained feelings hidden under the surface.

Beware of the professional fund raising organizations which will come into your community and solicit donations for you on a percentage basis. A great deal of open resentment has been created by the pressure tactics which many such groups employ.

Accepting donations has sometimes put bands and their directors in extremely embarrassing positions. I recall the band which became obligated to a civic organization through a donation by a generous, understanding, fair administration. Then, with the election of a new and very demanding president, the band found itself out of school playing for a large number of events, many of them strictly commercial in nature. The climax came when it was demanded that the band entertain some visiting dignitaries at the president's own personal barbeque. Concluding the performance at lunch time, the band was told, "Thank you," and when the band director stepped up to ask, "Don't my kids at least get to eat?" he was told that not enough food had been prepared for them. Needless to say, that director has not allowed himself to become obligated to any individual or organization since.

ADVERTISING

The ordinary local businessman is asked repeatedly for donations to many worthy causes, perhaps partly because some non-business people feel he has access to an unusual tax escape. Actually unless there is some direct connection with his commercial operation, he cannot list these contributions as a business expense, and so has no special tax advantage over any other citizen who itemizes his gifts to charities. On the other hand, almost every firm does do some advertising, which *is* a deductible expense. When advertising space in a band program or yearbook is sold, however, it is sometimes difficult to determine where advertising ends and donation begins. It is up to the director to make sure every customer gets as much value as possible for each advertising dollar he spends.

FEES

Some schools charge each student a set fee for band participation, based on local economic conditions. All activities are then financed from this fund.[1] If an instrument or uniform rental fee is charged, the proceeds should go into a separate fund to be used only for the repair and maintenance of those items, not for general operating expenses, trips, or special projects.

---

[1] Refer to the very successful Mason City, Iowa system, Chapter I.

A band share of a general student activity ticket including concerts, or a part of the gate receipts of athletic events at which the band
performs probably have more value as status symbols than as fund
raisers, because of the small percentages usually paid. Since most
families are already spending a great deal of money on the education
of their children, many bands prefer to raise the necessary funds
through a total group effort, rather than to charge the individual.

ENTERTAINMENT

The average annual combined income of the amusement, recreation, motion picture, radio, broadcasting, and television industries is
well over three billion dollars. Obviously there is an available market
for entertainment.

When bringing in any outside talent for which the band must
pay, the director must consider the auditorium seating capacity, estimate the number of customers the attraction will draw, deduct the
anticipated expenses, in order to determine which business he will be
in: raising funds or spending money to spread culture.

A great deal of money has been made, and lost, in concert promotion. Certainly the public relations and inspirational value of a fine
concert by an outstanding band is worth even the possibility of *losing*
money to present it, but when you are planning a budget you must
have a reasonable idea of whether to consider this project a potential
source of income or expense.

Plays, variety and minstrel shows, street fairs, amateur nights,
bingo and card parties, beauty contests, and dances have all been successful fund raisers, depending on the community. Many local movie
operators will allow you to keep the money from the sale of tickets
for a special band benefit showing. If the band pays for the rental of a
good film and sells every seat in the house, the owner operates his
concession stand, and the people see a show which is worth the price
of admission, it can be a profitable experience for everyone.

Since certain individuals and groups sometimes object to some of
these activities, you must grasp the prevailing moral code of the town
(through observation and conversation) in order to know what will
be acceptable.

MEALS

Since everyone must eat somewhere, sometime, you can provide them with a pleasant social experience and some incidental musical entertainment by your students, in addition to good food.

Spaghetti, pancakes, fried fish, barbequed chicken, and ice cream have all been used. In Louisiana they have "gumbos" of all sorts (chicken, crawfish, etc.); Kentuckians eat "burgoo" (a kind of beef stew); on the Atlantic coast sea food is very popular. The possibilities are almost limitless. The accent must always be on a good meal at a reasonable price.

LOCAL SALES AND SERVICE

There are always openings for rummage sales because practically everyone has clothing or other items which they are anxious to get out of the house. Not only can the band make money, but also perform a service to the housecleaners and to the needy people who can use the rummage, by selling out all items at a fair price. Pick the site of the sale and plan your advertising with the poorer people in mind so that you can accomplish your dual purpose rather than allow a generous band booster *donator* to take all of those things off your hands which did not appeal to your prospects in the "high rent district."

There is a considerable profit in collecting and selling waste paper. A regular monthly route can be set up.

Band students themselves can organize a babysitting service with all or part of the fees paid to members going to the band. A "Band Car Wash Saturday" has been successful. Pick a paved lot or a large double driveway with water and plenty of parking space, be sure your fee is in line with local prices, and do the best job available anywhere in town. The service stations will not mind because it will take some of the load off their crowded weekend schedules and you will be picking up a lot of the "do-it-yourself" trade they would not get anyway.

Choosing a Commission Sale Item

Consider quality first. Be sure that your band can be proud to sell the particular product at the particular price. If you give the public at least what they have paid for (and preferably more) you can establish a large group of satisfied customers. Strong repeat business is the proof of a good product.

Pick a standard item of general usefulness. If a food product, it should be something which appeals to most of the people.

Note also that the "sale" of identification items such as membership cards, decals, tags, etc., should be recognized as a request for *donations*, since the actual value of these items is extremely small compared to the price usually charged for them.

A higher priced item (up to a point determined by the degree of local prosperity) will require less effort (fewer sales) to return the same profit as one selling at a lower price.

Choosing a Company

Pick a reliable firm, with a history of satisfactory service to schools.

Buy at true wholesale; sell at true retail. Check the usual retail price for an item of comparable quality in a local store or national catalogue. Do not allow a company to sell you a product at a high *retail* price and and ask you to resell it at an additionally inflated figure.

True protection of territory (no sales to your close neighbors) should be guaranteed by the company. Check their record with other customers.

Service must be prompt and accurate, with fast reorder provisions.

Factory fresh merchandise must be sent, not that which has been returned from consignment to someone else.

Packaging should withstand the strain of students carrying products on selling trips.

Sales aids furnished by the company should include circulars, price lists, order blanks, samples, and news releases.

Bookkeeping forms should be thorough and detailed, but easily understood, and not time consuming to use.

Objections from
Local Merchants

Occasionally band directors encounter those who block fund raising drives saying, "Most of the money is going out of town; let's keep the business at home." By offering a quality product which is *not available* locally, you can avoid legitimate objections from local merchants. Ask those who still object to examine the origin of items they themselves offer for sale, and remind everyone that elimination of trade barriers has contributed not only to the tremendous growth of the United States of America, but more recently to the development of the "Common Market" countries.

While it is true that our fruit cake customers, for instance, *do* send the money to Dallas, we buy the pineapple from Hawaii; the cherries come from Michigan by way of Illinois processing plants; the pecans were sent from New Mexico, Texas, Louisiana, or Georgia; the butter was produced in Wisconsin; the white raisins grew in California; the flour was milled in western Oklahoma or Minnesota; the vanilla flavoring was imported through New York; and the eggs may have come from any one of the many farms in a dozen states.

THE SALES CAMPAIGN

It is generally recognized among sales organizations that there are four basic divisions to successful sales activity: planning, prospecting, selling (approach, interview, close), and record keeping.

If you have decided to use the sale of a product as your fund raising method, and have made your selection of the specific product and the supplier with whom you want to work, your next step is to determine the best dates on which to begin and end the sale. The product itself can have a great deal to do with your choice. The traditional candy sale dates, for example, fall before Christmas, Valentine Day, and Easter, with some activity before Mother's Day. Care should be taken to avoid conflicts with other sales and drives, especially in a small community. In a large city a conflict of dates is apt to be more of a mental block than any real hindrance to sales.

THE SALES ORGANIZATION [2]

The project chairman must instill in the other chairmen and team captains (whom he appoints) enthusiasm, cooperation, and the willingness to work. He should hold a strategy meeting with them and plan every phase of the campaign. He must see that each chairman understands his duties and that every worker knows the product he is selling and the services he can offer.

---

[2] This information has been selected and adapted from the sales kit furnished to fund raisers by the Manor Baking Company.

The publicity chairman enlists the support of local newspapers, radio, TV, and other communications media in the area. He provides ample material for their use, timing his releases to achieve the most effective results. Here are a few promotional suggestions:

1. Ask one of your printer members to run off show cards promoting the sale, to be displayed around town. Play up the *reason* for the sale.
2. Ask merchants to give you "plugs" in their regular newspaper, radio and TV advertising.
3. Take a photograph of the club president making the first sale to the mayor. If proceeds are to be used for band uniforms, have two band members, in old and new uniforms, and a club member photographed with a display of the merchandise for sale. Have a picture made of an especially large sale to a civic leader. As the sale progresses, take pictures of the leading salesmen.
4. Radio and TV news announcements should be made at various key points (before, opening, mid-way, end) of the sale. Use the phrase "public service announcement" when asking for time. Every radio and TV station uses a certain number of these (because of FCC regulation), and they will be happy to use yours (because of local civic pride).

The inventory and distribution chairman maintains ample stock and sees that every member has merchandise on hand by anticipating needs and re-ordering from the company. He receives and checks orders for correctness and damage before signing any freight bill, and keeps records of all transactions. He may need assistants, depending on the size of your organization. The forms he uses are the following (*see* Fig. 10).

Record of items ordered. If you enter the orders placed and note when you receive them, you will always know where you stand with the supplier.

Record of payments to the company. Enter the check or money order number, the amount, date, and the number of the invoice you are paying.

Inventory record. Enter the items you have received in black figures and those sold in red figures. By adding the black and subtracting the red you will know the number of items available for sale on any given day. Continue this from day to day until the end of the sale.

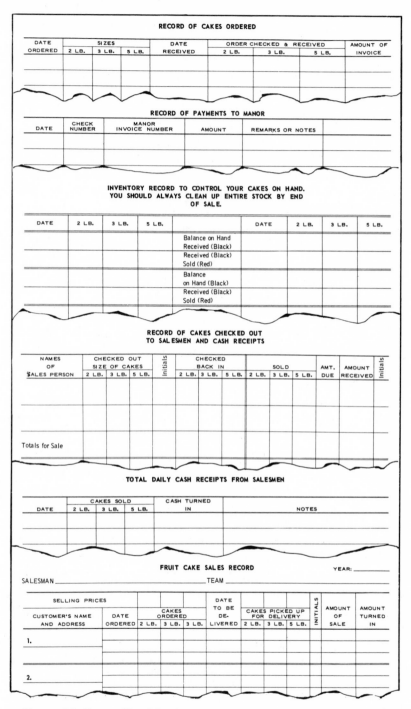

Figure 10: Forms Used by Inventory and Distribution Chairmen

Record of items checked out and cash received from salesmen.
There are three lines for each person selling and a space for totals
provided. You can tell at a glance who is doing the work.

Total daily cash receipts from salesmen. This page gives you a
daily picture of all sales and collections.

Customer sales record. This, the most important record of all for
the group handling an item selling for several dollars or more, should
be used by each salesman to record the customer's name, address, and
details of the sale. Be sure that each salesman turns his sheets in to be
passed on to the next inventory chairman. Each name can mean many
dollars in repeat business over a number of years.

The industrial sales chairman selects team captains who will not
hesitate to call on business and industrial executives. Suggest that they
use your product as a Christmas gift for their employees. This type of
prospect buys early and should be contacted between August and
October.

The house to house chairman selects team captains and meets
with them well ahead of opening day to divide the city and assign
specific territories to each captain. He should determine exact minimum
quotas for each team.

The team captains (both industrial and house-to-house) set individual quotas and make certain that each team member is thoroughly
familiar with the product and the services he is offering. Experience
has shown that the average team captain can supervise about 10
team members.

SALES TECHNIQUES

There are many ideas which professional salesmen in your boosters
club can suggest. Here are a few from personal experience.

The telephone approach can be very effective if you keep accurate records of your sales from year to year.

NANCY (armed with last year's sales list): "Good morning, Mrs.
Smith, this is Nancy Jones of the high school band. We are engaged in
our annual Christmas fruit cake sale, and I see by our records that
last year you bought one 2 pound cake. Now, Mrs. Smith, will one 2
pound cake be enough for you *this* year?"

Competition between teams is very helpful, and many schools
offer prizes to their top salesmen. I feel that cash prizes (in the form

of Government Bonds or gift certificates, if you prefer) are best because it is so difficult to find a prize appropriate for either a boy or a girl which does not duplicate something they already own. If the fund raising project is for a specific trip, the top salesmen can be given spending money as a bonus. Many schools keep an individual record of credit for each student towards band camp, or a special trip.

Each band parent should be encouraged to buy one of the sale items immediately. If they are to sell, they must be completely familiar with the product and have enough confidence in it to become a customer as well as a salesman. Even if they are not actually a part of the sales force, remember that their word of mouth advertising of a quality product, and their recommendations to friends (called "third party influence") is more powerful than all of the drive and push any of your salesmen alone can muster.

BAND BOOSTERS CLUBS [3]

The group organized to promote the welfare of the band must remain under the control and guidance of the band director. Determine what it is you want from your boosters club (financial help, improved public relations, better student-parent-teacher communication, etc.), then set up projects designed to achieve these definite ends, and keep the club busily engaged in the pursuit of progressively more meaningful goals. An agenda must be prepared before every meeting, allowing business to be conducted quickly and efficiently, according to the accepted rules of order. Nothing breeds discontent in a group like this more quickly than either inactivity, or a great deal of activity without permanent achievement. A good motto is "We grow or we go."

Allow the parents to carry on only those activities which *you* feel are in the best interests of the band members, in keeping with school policies, and consistent with community practices. By making sure that all nominees for office have your approval, speaking directly to the membership at meetings (rather than using the president as your spokesman), and making wise decisions based on sound reasoning, you can firmly establish the fact that the club members are the *boosters,* and *you are the director.* The club which feels as though it can overrule a decision by the band director should be disbanded immediately.

---

[3] Based on materials provided by Myron Pearce, Newark High School, Newark, Ohio.

Every boosters club should have some written outline of organization. It may be a formal constitution or merely a statement of policy and regulations, such as that adopted by the Joliet (Ill.) Grade School Band Parents Association.

JOLIET GRADE SCHOOL BAND PARENTS ASSOCIATION
POLICY AND REGULATIONS

1. BAND PARENTS ASSOCIATION: All parents become members of the B.P.A. Meetings are held each second Tuesday of the month at 8 P.M., alternately at Hufford, Gompers, and Washington Jr. High Schools. Your attendance will benefit your child. Dues are $1.00 for the first year and $2.00 each year thereafter. (SCHOOL MUSICIAN magazine is included *after* the first year.)
2. ALL BAND PARENTS shall serve on the Refreshment Committee at Band Parents Association meetings once during the year.
3. BAND MOTHERS: All mothers become members of Band Mothers Club when their child becomes a member of the band.
4. IT IS EACH FAMILY'S RESPONSIBILITY to actively support all fund-raising projects sponsored by this Association.
5. TICKET SALES: To be eligible for any of the B.P.A. sponsored band activities, the minimum number of tickets to be sold by each child for each of the two band concerts is: Jr. High Band—8; 5th–6th Grade Band—6; Beginners' Band—4. In lieu of meeting this minimum quota of concert tickets, the student will pay for the following B.P.A. sponsored activities which he may take part in:

Activity	Est. Cost
All-State, U. of Ill.	24.00
Dist. Solo-Ensemble Contest	5.00
Dist. Band Contest	5.00
Spring Tour	60.00
State Solo-Ensemble Contest	10.00
State Band Contest	10.00
Graduation Pin	3.40
Picnic	2.00
Band Camp	24.00

6. CARE OF INSTRUMENTS AND CASES: It is the responsibility of the parents to see that instruments are kept in the best of playing condition and that the cases are kept neat and clean.
7. CARE OF UNIFORM: It is the responsibility of the parent to see that uniforms are kept clean and covered. It is also the responsibility of the parent to keep the uniform pressed and repaired. Clean collars, shined black shoes, and black socks make the uniform complete.

8. PARADES: It is the responsibility of parents to see that the members of the Marching Bands are available for parades.
9. BUS SPONSORS: Parents who ride the buses as sponsors are to be guided by the following: If there is a parent bus, everyone pays, including sponsors. If there is not a parent bus, sponsors ride free except when it is special long trip.

BAND UNIFORMS

The purchase of band uniforms is often the largest single expense under the director's supervision. Since upwards of $5,000 is usually involved, and uniforms are sometimes used for no more than 10 years, it is obvious that the director must be certain the money is spent wisely.

Style

Most uniforms in use by school bands are a modification of one of the basic styles: *Navy Officer, Lancer, West Point, Military,* or *Eisenhower Jacket.* A shirt and trouser combination is sometimes used. The *Overlay* which will convert a concert uniform into a flashy marching band uniform is very popular. Topcoats are worn by prosperous bands in colder climates. Some bands have taken their school nickname as the springboard to a unique uniform design all their own.

Standard caps and shakos are the Drum Major 14-inch busby, the Drum Majorette 10-inch high shako, the West Point shako, the Austrian or French police shako, the Hussar style shako, the Pershing Cap, the Eight Point Cap, and the soft top Air Force style cap.

Plumes are often added to the shakos and caps. The various types are ostrich, vulture, cocque, upright, wool pompon, and lighted. Citation and breast cords, aiguillettes, knots, and epaulets are used to provide additional color and decoration. These basic designs and accessories are illustrated in Figures 11 and 12.[4]

How to Buy Uniforms

Uniform construction is extremely complicated and it takes a real expert to judge the better qualities, which become apparent to all

---

[4] Illustrations have been selected from the catalogs of just a few of the many excellent uniform manufacturers, to whom we are grateful. The inclusion of any particular company, however, does not necessarily suggest endorsement, any more than the exclusion of the many others would indicate condemnation.—*Ed.*

Figure 11: Basic Uniform Styles (**Group 1**) *

Navy Officer   Lancer   West Point   Military

Figure 11: Basic Uniform Styles (**Group 2**) *

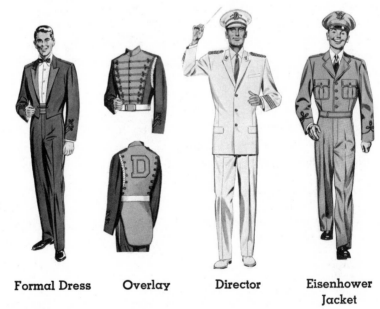

Formal Dress   Overlay   Director   Eisenhower Jacket

* Reproduced by courtesy of E. V. Price Co., Chicago, Ill.

82

THE PLUME

Ostrich   Vulture   Cocque   Upright   Wool   Lighted
Pompon

CAPS AND SHAKOS

West Point   Hussar Style Shako (majorette)   Austrian or French Police Shako

rum Major Busby   Pershing Cap   Eight-Point Cap   Drum Majorette Busby
(14" high)   (10" high)

* From *More Than Meets the Eye,* published by "Uniforms by Ostwald," Staten Island, N.Y.

THE KNOT

Twisted in two and two strands with looped ends.

Twisted in three and three strands.

Two strands, double width, epaulet type.

THE EPAULET

Twisted silk cord edging

Special twirler style

Figure 12: Uniform Accessories **(Group 3)** *

THE AIGUILLETTE

Double strand with ornamental tips at ends.

Two braided cords with ornamental tips with two single strands: one under arm, the other crossed around arm.

One braided cord and two knotted single strands.

THE BREAST CORD

THE CITATION CORD

Two braided cords with ornamental tip at each end.

Three braided cords with three ornamental tips on one end.

One braided cord and two single strands with ornamental tip.

only after considerable use and cleaning. Henry H. Craddock, Sr., has offered some "back of the counter, non-partisan" advice. The following is a digest of his article, *How to Buy School Band Uniforms.*[5]

> *Fabrics.* On uniforms that contain wool, fiber-content labels are required by Federal law. In general, experience points to whipcords as best for band uniforms.
>
> *Shrinkage and colorfastness.* If the fabric is not thoroughly shrunk, a uniform may lose its fit and shape the first time it is cleaned or gets wet. If the fabric is not colorfast its appearance may soon be spoiled by fading. In either event you may have to discard the uniform before getting full value.
>
> *Linings.* Rayon twill linings are most commonly used in uniforms. You can judge the weight and wearing qualities to some extent by the close weave and firm feel of the lining.
>
> *Pockets.* Silesia is the name of the twilled cotton used in coat pockets of good quality uniforms. The best material for pockets in trousers is closely woven cotton twill. Lower grade trousers have coarsely woven pocketing filled with starch to make it look better.
>
> *Coat front.* Materials within a coat, called "coat fronts" in the trade, are *actually the very foundation of a coat.* Though you don't see the materials, you need to find out about them to know how the appearance of the uniform will hold up. Manufacturers of high grade uniforms use high grade canvas made of goat hair spun with rayon. Lowest grades of uniforms have fronts made of

---

[5] Available in full from Craddock Uniforms Co., Kansas City 6, Mo., or the *National Association of Uniform Manufacturers,* 112 E. 19th St., New York 3, N. Y. (reprinted from *The School Musician*).

all-cotton materials or ordinary burlap. Grasp the coat front of a uniform which you know is high-grade and pull your closed hand down over it. It will feel lightweight and soft, not stiff. The front will spring back into shape without a wrinkle when you let go. While you still remember the feel of this high-grade uniform examine one known to be low-grade. The front will feel thick, bulky, and crisp. When you let go you feel the wrinkles left in the inside material. When you get the feel of these two extremes, practice judging in-between qualities.

Collar interlinings. Roll a corner of the collar up and forward. If the interlining is good material, the corner will flip back into place; if it is sized cotton, it will turn back slowly.

Shoulder padding. The best padding (fine cotton) is soft, lightweight, free from lumpiness; cheap padding (coarse, lumpy cotton or paper) feels thick, heavy, uneven.

Workmanship. The way a uniform is cut and sewed is even more important to its real worth than the materials. This is oftentimes the largest item omitted to get down to a price.

Shaping uniform coats. After every important inside sewing operation in a high-grade uniform, experts skillfully press and shape the coat. In this way shaping can't come out—it is sewed in by operations that follow and is there for the life of the garment. Low-priced lines of uniforms rush production. There is some flat table pressing, but no shaping. When this grade of uniform is completed, it is put on form presses that actually stamp the shape into the garment so that to many buyers they look as good as the high-grade uniforms. However, this last-minute shaping comes out with wear and cleaning.

Coat linings. In good quality uniforms the lining is smoothly fitted and finely stitched. The lower edge of the coat is bound— "piped," the trade calls it—and fastened over the lining. A small pleat for give is left along the lower edge of the lining. The way armholes are stitched is a pretty good indicator of the quality of handwork throughout a suit.

Buttonholes. Look for neat, strong buttonholes worked on both sides, with close, even stitching and a strong bar opposite the eyelet end.

Selecting your manufacturer. No uniform manufacturer has any edge upon costs of good skilled labor or good materials; but some may be more efficient, with better equipment and management so that pleasing, new, distinctive styling and generous fullness of garments will be the competitive factor.

Summary. "YOU GET ONLY WHAT YOU PAY FOR" and the high pressure salesman with lower price offers, as well as a free uniform for the Drum Major or the Director, or a share of his commission, is a trap for the gullible. Your own detailed specifications and request for a performance bond are the best business procedure. There is no substitute for quality as the best investment.

Consider All Factors

When you have your next opportunity to purchase new uniforms, keep these thoughts in mind:

1. Style can be duplicated, but quality cannot.
2. There is no substitute for superior workmanship.
3. Students grow and membership changes, so:

   Choose a style that will be flattering to either sex.
   Have uniforms identified by *number* rather than *name*.
   Insist on a full cut—for easy alteration.

4. Investigate the financial rating of the firm.
5. Check other customers for quality of service (measuring, re-order, etc.).
6. Arrange payment terms to fit your financial condition.
7. Avoid seasonal rush when ordering.
8. Require a sample uniform for approval. Check it (and some from the regular delivery) against your specifications.

Protect Your Investment

It is not enough merely to purchase the uniforms, you must also secure adequate storage facilities, and instruct your students in proper care habits.

Any corporation which spends thousands of dollars for a new piece of equipment immediately sets up a reserve for depreciation, so that when the equipment has worn out, funds will have been accumulated for prompt replacement. I find many band parents, however, who work extremely hard for a year to raise money (say $8,000) for new uniforms, and then the organization coasts along for the next 10 years enjoying the fruits of that particular group's effort. A 10-year planned program which sets aside money (say $800) each year spreads both the effort and the responsibility to more of the people who will benefit from it. Wise investment of the annual reserve can reduce the burden even more.

VALUE MUST EQUAL
EXPENSE

When you are raising funds, you must offer your potential customers a fair return for the money you are asking them to spend.

When you are operating a band boosters club, you must offer your prospective members a fair return for the effort you are asking them to make.

When you are purchasing band uniforms, you must be certain that you are receiving a quality product which is worth the money you are being asked to pay.

The Director:
His Personal Welfare

by **Traugott Rohner**

Evanston, Illinois

Traugott Rohner

is editor, publisher, and founder of *The Instrumentalist* (1946), and *Clavier* (1962). He spent 27 years as a very effective and influential teacher in the School of Music, Northwestern University, and has been a guest lecturer at the University of Michigan and the University of Wisconsin. His long teaching career has included positions in Marshall, Minnesota (1928–29), where he taught band, orchestra, and science; Asheville, North Carolina (1929–31) in the public schools; Evanston, Illinois (1931–58); and one year teaching mathematics at Northwestern University in the World War II Navy V-12 program.

He holds the BA degree from Central Wesleyan College, the MS from Northwestern University, and has completed all work except a portion of the dissertation towards a Ph.D. in Educational Psychology. Other credits have been earned at the University of Missouri, the Cincinnati Conservatory of Music, and the University of Cincinnati.

Mr. Rohner's sometimes controversial but always thought-provoking editorials appear regularly in *The Instrumentalist*. In addition he has contributed over 50 articles to four different national music magazines, as well as producing numerous books, methods, sound music films, and orchestral arrangements.

The welfare of the band director is an extremely important factor in the success of any school instrumental music program. Quite obviously, if the leader is not healthy, happy, and making some sort of personal progress, his effectiveness will be limited and the overall program will suffer.

Important as these subjects are, however, none of them has come up in the more than 250 semester hours of college credits I have earned. Perhaps this illustrates the typical commencement speaker's announcement that "your education is only just now *beginning* with graduation." The volume of mail I receive either blessing or damning the inclusion of pieces on these personal problems in a *music* magazine indicates that a great number of other college graduates sense the importance of these issues, and feel a need to discuss them.

Earn, spend, but also accumulate

Most band directors spend a great deal of time and effort devising methods to raise large sums of money to pay their band's current operating expenses and to purchase equipment which will help to assure a bright future for the program, yet they often do very little about their own personal monetary needs.

Most musicians have had little financial education and many make serious mistakes in respect to buying insurance, paying taxes, executing wills, making loans, setting up trusts, purchasing a house or other real estate, and financing a car. Those who can least afford to waste a single dollar, unfortunately are the ones most frequently ignorant of sound principles of earning, spending, and accumulating money wisely.

Earning *some* money is usually no problem for the band director, since the supply of instructors has not yet caught up with the demand, and the population is still exploding. The problem, in most cases, concerns the *amount* of money he receives.

In the teaching world, salary schedules attest to the importance of earning at least a Master's degree. Since this work can be taken in summer school, it is often more economical to spend three or four periods of unemployment (laymen call it "summer vacation") than to take off an entire school year.

More and more high schools are paying $7,000 a year and some have increased annual pay schedules to more than $10,000. There is nothing wrong with asking for more pay, but teachers as a whole tend to be too timid when dealing with school boards. Too often they entrust leadership in salary negotiations entirely to their superintendent. They fail to realize that he must be interested in staying in the good graces of the school board, who in turn may be a group of penny-pinching individuals who own considerable property in town, and thus have as their first interest the lowest possible property tax rate. The superintendent needs a strong teacher organization to back up his demands for salary increases. Timidity and meekness may have their place in heaven, but here on earth they are not very productive.

Spending is often determined by social or emotional pressure, rather than any sensible plan based on income. In an attempt to gain prestige some directors will buy a new car almost every year, build an elaborate home, wear overly expensive clothes, join a country club, or entertain often and lavishly.

Just as the private teacher must set his own fee between that of the teacher who charges too little and is not respected and the price of one who charges too much and has no students, the band director must seek his own level in the living standard of the community. The man who drives a 10-year-old jalopy (when he could just as well afford a two- or three-year-old car) may be looked down upon by his students, but generally they will not evaluate him by the car he drives, the house in which he lives, or the clothes he wears—provided that all are of reasonable quality and in good taste.

INVESTMENTS

There are basically two types of investments, *fixed* and *fluctuating*.

Fixed dollar investments include savings accounts, bonds, and

life insurance. Since the principal amount does not change, and the
return is a fixed percentage (often guaranteed), this type will provide
strength in a depressed economy.

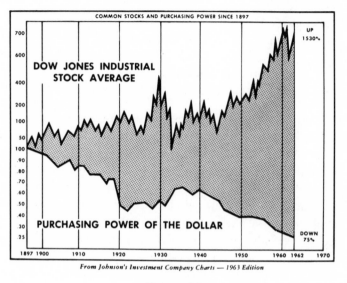

Figure 13

Fluctuating investments include common stocks, real estate, or
anything whose value will fluctuate with the condition of the economy.
They are an excellent hedge against inflation (*see* Fig. 13).

Most wise investors strive for a balance of the two types so that
no matter which way the economy goes they will be successful. A
majority of financial experts, however, predict a gradual continuation of
the inflationary trends we have been experiencing for many years,
and they point out these signs for the future:

Congress and the people are spending-minded.
Labor wants higher wages.
Businessmen and investors are not putting on the brakes.

Let inflation work for you in these ways:

1. Purchase term insurance for *protection*. Avoid other forms of life
   insurance because that portion of the premium not actually used
   for insurance is an investment which brings you only about three
   percent interest.

2. Do not put your savings into fixed dollar type investments.

3. Although one might think it wise to pay off the home mortgage as fast as possible to avoid interest, the opposite is recommended: get as large a mortgage as possible and make future payments in cheaper dollars.

4. Put your money into a fluctuating type of investment. On property investment, be sure to figure all costs, including insurance, taxes, upkeep, interest on mortgage, etc., and then determine the *net* income on the actual cash you will need to invest.

5. *Changing Times* magazine [1] has advised readers to buy stocks if:

   a. Most important, you believe in the future of the United States.

   b. You stick to long-term investing and avoid the temptation to speculate.

   c. You use care in selecting good-quality companies that show promise of above-average growth through the years.

   d. You space out your purchases over several years and avoid plunking down all your money at once.

   e. You use only spare cash—that is, money you are pretty certain you won't need for some time.

   f. You already have a financial margin of safety in the form of savings and life insurance.

6. Many investors are willing to pay the sales charge and management fee of a mutual investment fund in order to secure their advertised benefits:

   a. Proper selection of securities for income or growth, depending on the objective of the fund.

   b. Broad diversification over a number of securities instead of concentrating the risk in a few.

   c. Constant supervision based on the fact that securities cannot take care of themselves.

In any event, each person must consider investments with the same careful study, selection of competent advice, sensible balance and disciplined regularity with which he has approached his work as band director. Bernard Baruch has said: "We can't cross a bridge until we come to it, but I always like to lay down a pontoon ahead of time."

---

[1] Published by the Kiplinger Washington Editors, Inc., Editors Park, Md.

Continued study offers some tax benefits for the band director. Acceptability of deductions may be tested by asking the following questions:

1. Do you meet the minimum requirements of your profession?
2. Are there courses required of you by your employer for you to retain your position?
3. Is it customary for others in your profession to take the courses?

If the answer is "yes" then you may include them on the tax form. School boards can actually be helpful by making additional schooling a "requirement." *Other deductions* include that for a student (enrolled in school full time for at least five months a year) who may be claimed as a dependent even though he is over 19 years of age, provided the parent pays at least half of his support. A student (or child) must file an income tax return if he makes over $600 per year, but he still qualifies as a deduction for the parent. These items are also deductible:

a. Expenses incurred while taking school-owned instruments to the repair shop.
b. Professional dues and the cost of attending conventions such as MENC, NBA, and state meetings.
c. Expenses you incur in the purchase of your uniform, batons, metronomes, scores, and other items directly related to your position.
d. The portion of light, heat, and depreciation assumed by a room in your home used as an office or studio.
e. Travel expenses *between schools*, but not *from* home *to* school.
f. Social security deductions in excess of $150.
g. Contributions to college scholarship funds. Check your alumni dues: many stipulate that a certain percentage of the dues is reserved for scholarships.
h. Your professional library, including the cost of this book. Since the tax law is constantly changing, seek expert, current information before you "pay unto Caesar. . . ."

SOCIAL SECURITY

Unfortunately, many school teachers are not covered by social security, but every band director should be able to qualify for at least the minimum payments. Income from private lessons, for instance, makes you a "self-employed person." By earning money in this category (private lessons, church choir, dance band, almost *any* summer job) you can raise the amount of your retirement income benefits.

The law makes it possible for men as well as women to retire and receive benefits at age 62. Although few people can live in the manner they prefer on social security payments alone, this money may be used to supplement your other retirement plans. Check with your local social security office for details.

MENTAL AND PHYSICAL HEALTH

Unlike the office or factory employee who leaves all thoughts of the job behind, the band director continues his work long after school hours. He has extra rehearsals, concerts, contests, scores to be studied, and a host of problems requiring his attention while away from the school building. All of these things (plus the elements of conflict present in even the best school systems) lead to wear and tear on his physical and mental stamina.

When a serious problem faces you, it is often better to walk away from it and forget it for a while. This permits the subconscious mind to take over and prevents you from "beating your brains" trying to find an answer. A survey of leading scientists found that 75 percent of them felt their best ideas came to them while away from their laboratories. This "creative pausing" can be achieved by listening to good music, meditating in silence, fishing, gardening, walking, or simply by sitting alone. The band director who values his mental health will plan a daily schedule which permits this relief.

Relaxation is a habit requiring practice and planning, and each individual should determine the form which fits him best. A good book is all that some need. Perhaps getting extra sleep, or spending a weekend doing something entirely unrelated to the daily routine is the answer for you. A hobby can be relaxing, fun, and even productive.

Learn to pace yourself (especially in the final months of a strenuous school year), schedule regular physical checkups, don't take yourself too seriously, above all, laugh a little . . . and remember to relax.

ALCOHOLISM

Five million Americans, one in every 15 drinkers, is an alcoholic whose life span will be shortened by an average of 12 years.[2]

It is not easy to spot a budding alcoholic. In general, according to the National Council on Alcoholism, Inc., he "gulps drinks and complains about the slowness of fellow drinkers. He sneaks drinks before going to a function at which drinks will be served, insists on drinks before lunch and after work, at sports events, etc. He must have drinks for nerves or depression because 'nothing else helps.' He will lie to avoid detection."

The body of the alcoholic becomes addicted to the chemical ethyl alcohol. This condition is an *illness*, not a moral defect, and is so serious that only cancer, heart disease, and mental illness are greater national problems, according to the American Medical Association.

Over 400,000 men and women belong to *Alcoholics Anonymous* which has no dues or fees, is non-demominational, supports no particular medical or religious point of view, and will not attempt to "reform" those who do not seek their help. Doctors, clergymen, psychiatrists, and law enforcement groups all have endorsed AA. Literature is available from the local AA group (most cities have one or more) or by writing to the national headquarters, P. O. Box 459, Grand Central Station, New York 17.

SMOKING

The smoking issue has nothing to do with morals, religion, or credo, but it has much to do with health. The list of studies pointing an accusing finger at tobacco is so large that only those who prefer to deceive themselves can claim no correlation between lung cancer and smoking.

Tobacco, having gotten a physiological hold on a person very similar to that of narcotics, is a rough antagonist. The best way to stop smoking is to resolve to quit altogether, since the gradual tapering off procedure is agonizing and usually unsuccessful.

According to the American Public Health Association, one million persons, now school children, will eventually die of lung cancer

---

[2] Statistics from the American Medical Association and the National Council on Alcoholism, Inc.

if the present trend continues. Our youth have a right to know the facts. We, their teachers, have an obligation to tell them.

RELIGION

It has been said that there are two things one should never discuss: politics and religion; however . . .

The similar fundamental precepts of the various religions are infinitely more significant to the betterment of human beings than the dogma which seem to separate them. Those who are dedicated to their faith are certainly better people than those who are not, regardless of their particular affiliation. A good Jew is better than a poor Catholic and a good Mormon is better than a poor Baptist, for example.

It is extremely unfortunate that emphasis has been placed on the *differences* between religions rather than on the many important principles which are common to all; however, since outstanding and sincere people of every faith usually believe that theirs is the only true religion, we should consider their feelings and apply the "Golden Rule" in our relationships with them.

We should openly discuss the various aspects of different religions as we discuss other important considerations in life, and should oppose fanaticism and bigotry in religion just as strongly as we oppose it anywhere else.

It is indeed gratifying to know that we do not have to close our ears to the music of Mendelssohn because the composer was a Jew, to the works of Bach because he was a Protestant, or to the compositions of Palestrina because he was a Roman Catholic.

COMMISSIONS FROM DEALERS

The mere acceptance of a commission does not necessarily mean the teacher is dishonest, since in some cases a sincere teacher has gone to considerable trouble to select the best buy for the student and has actually earned some kind of compensation. The practice of giving a commission on an instrument sale does *invite* a teacher to be dishonest, as the prospect of monetary gain often crowds out any consideration of the true welfare of a student or his parents.

Whenever the temptation, with a minimum chance of being

caught, becomes sufficiently strong, a "sell-out" can take place. Practically everybody (probably even you) has a sell-out point . . . it may be lower than you think. The "under-the-table" commission-bribe in the instrumental world is equally the fault of the teachers and the dealers. Either group can stop the practice.

Good grooming, proper dress

A survey of thousands of businessmen indicated that it is not necessary to dress expensively, but rather to be well groomed and conservatively dressed, with trousers creased and shoes shined. Businessmen may be more conscious of these items than music teachers, but have you ever overheard students talking about their teachers? Band directors insist on good grooming and proper dress of all students when the band is performing in uniform, but how about the director himself when *he* is "performing" each day under the critical evaluation of these same students?

Part-time jobs

Although salaries have shown significant increases in recent years, superior band directors still do not receive what they should, and many do various other things to make money "on the side."

Under no circumstances should this "moonlighting" undermine the quality of the director's work at school, endanger the welfare of his family, or adversely affect his health. However, there are many capable, young, and healthy men who are not working as hard as they could to build up a financial reserve for that time when they will be able to earn neither extra nor even regular income.

Private instruction can be an excellent adjunct to band directing since it is a pleasant contrast to the rehearsals and full classes most men hold throughout the day. Fields entirely separated from music offer possibilities for extra money, but sometimes do not pay as well since the director is usually not the recognized expert he is considered to be as a teacher of music. A part-time job (instrument repair, insurance sales, camp counseling), wisely chosen, can often lead to a very pleasant occupation when the physical requirements of band directing become too demanding.

Students insist that the director be absolutely fair in all his dealings with them. He should have no prejudices concerning race, creed, sex, or appearance. Tryouts must be conducted impartially, discipline administered with no favoritism, and both criticism and praise offered honestly.

Students do not like a conductor who is too easy on them, who has poor discipline, and who wastes their time (and his) by coming to a rehearsal poorly prepared. Each director should try to eliminate objectionable idiosyncrasies, such as talking too much, thinking that his old jokes are still funny, or displaying any number of peculiarities of dress, behavior, or speech.

Since students like to have their *playing* corrected, but object to being criticized on a *personal* basis in front of the group, the director should develop an attitude which loses the individual during a band rehearsal, and finds him after school in the music office—whenever personal criticism seems necessary.[3]

Teen-age girls are attracted to men almost as strongly as men are attracted to women. The careful band director will always keep a certain distance, placing a "fence" between female students and himself. Actually he should fabricate this same sort of professional curtain for use with *all* students. This is not to imply that the teacher should not take a personal interest in every student and his individual problems, but it does mean that he should maintain the same professional attitude he expects a clergyman or doctor to exhibit.

ATHLETICS AND THE BAND;
RELATIONS WITH COACHES

The relationship between athletic coaches and the band director is pretty much a matter of give-and-take in making demands on their students' time. The following extract material by Otto Graham, Sr., long-time band director in Waukegan, Ill., is a case in point.

By Otto Graham, Sr.

I have had many students play in the band and on one of the athletic teams at the same time. All four of my own boys

---

[3] Mr. Rohner made a survey of the feelings of students toward their directors. His Master's thesis is based on the compilation of the likes and dislikes of every student in 13 Chicago area instrumental programs.—*Ed.*

played in the band. Eugene and Vic played oboe, and Otts [Otto Graham, Jr.] and Dick played French horn. Although all of them went out for sports and tried hard, Otts was the only one who was really successful with it.

I always felt that the activity which was the most important at that time should get the player. The band director should not attempt to dominate everything, but rather to weigh the problem fairly. I've given way many times when it was a rehearsal versus a basketball game, but I would fight very hard to get them for an important concert. The band member who is a regular member of the athletic team should certainly go with the team at all times, but the bench-warmer might as well be utilizing his talents in

Figure 14: Otto Graham, Sr., who retired in 1960 after 40 successful years as Band Director in Waukegan, Ill., has had considerable experience with coaches because of his own interest in athletics and his famous son Otto Graham, Jr., one of the greatest football quarterbacks of all time.

the band. If the coach and I couldn't agree, we'd let the superintendent decide. I never lost a decision from a superintendent—not because of any favoritism; I just never let it go that far unless I had a very strong case.

Otto, Jr. used to play some basketball, too. When he was only a sophomore he wasn't very tall, but he was already gaining a reputation with the opposing coaches. I remember one time when we played Barrington (Ill.) and our coach took one of our real tall boys out of the game. The Barrington coach called across the floor: "Take that little squirt out . . . he's the one we want out of there!"

Figure 15: Otto Graham, Jr., often described as the "world's finest quarterback," as first chair French horn player.

On one occasion Otts was supposed to play basketball the night we were scheduled for a trip to a very important state music festival. The opposing team was mediocre and no real importance was attached to the game. The superintendent backed me up, Otts made plans to play with the band, but the coach said that if he didn't stay and play with the team he would have to turn in his uniform the next day.

I said, "Okay, he'll turn it in right now, no need for it to go to waste . . . he'll bring it in right after school."

Well, did that coach's face change . . . and, of course, Otto never did have to turn in his uniform.

"Music Remains a Part of Me"

Eugene played first oboe with the U.S. Marine Band in Washington, D.C. for 20 years, and is now the owner of a music store and an oboist with the Tulsa (Okla.) Symphony. We discovered his perfect pitch one morning when he, his mother, and I were eating breakfast, and Otto, Jr. was practicing his violin in the living room. Suddenly, Eugene (he was 10, Otto was 8) called out: "Otts! You play the wrong pitch!" I thought to myself, "I wonder what he knows about that?" His mother went in to check it on the piano, and sure enough, it *was* wrong.

In 1938 when Otto was an all-state football and basketball player he was also the first chair horn player in the band and orchestra and a member of the Waukegan High School Brass Sextet, which placed first in national competition. He was a music major at Northwestern University at the time sportswriters were calling him "the world's finest quarterback." When he stopped playing professional football, he began taking piano lessons again.

Quarterbacking is 100 percent timing. Otto feels that music gave him that, so he's a strong believer in musical training for athletes. Otto has said:

> Both sports and music have taught me a spirit of cooperation, competition, poise, and confidence that I hope will remain with me forever. I feel that my early training in music figured heavily in developing that coordination that was so necessary to me as a football player. I am truly grateful, now that my active gridiron days are over, that music remains a part of me that will carry on the rest of my life.

PROFESSIONAL RELATIONS

A superior administrator gives a superior band director a great deal of freedom but still likes to be kept informed. Carbon copies, ditto sheets, inter-office memos are adequate and less time-consuming than personal conferences for most items.

It is always advisable for you to reach your principal or superintendent with the full set of facts before a parent arrives with an incomplete version of the same problem.

You should remember that most administrators have considerable ego (many seek the position because of this motivation), and you should play up to this quality. Ask them to make a short talk at a concert. Always include the names of all your superiors on the concert program, even though they may have contributed absolutely nothing to its production. The next time you begin to dig for money for the band you will note a certain fertility present in soil which has been prepared in this manner.

The Guidance Counselor influences the membership of your band more than any other individual in the entire school system. Since you must have all the best players from the feeder schools, it is impossible to build a superior band if the school guidance department is not "sold" on instrumental music. Talk to the counselors individually, take them to lunch if practical, make friends, and be sure they understand the values of the instrumental music program.

Academic teachers should not be counted "on our side" just because they do not speak out against you at a teachers' meeting. Just one uninformed English or Math teacher can turn students against the band program by casually hinting at the "waste of time of these *non-essentials.*"

If there is a bowling league, golf club, or some other faculty activity, it is very important that you take an active part. You need to be on a first name basis with the entire staff. Although this is extremely time consuming, the rewards in permanent, loyal support are worth it.

School janitors (custodians) and maintenance men are much more likely to cooperate at work time if you *ask*, rather than *tell*, them to set up risers, move chairs, clean the auditorium or band room, etc. These men—as well as all your colleagues—should be treated as equals. Surprisingly enough, this is about all most anyone really expects of another person.

ORGANIZATIONS

Although as a whole teachers have more organizations than any other group of workers (but less organization?), every band director should certainly be a member of the Music Educators National Conference (MENC) for the broad perspective, and the National Band Association (NBA) for more specialized help and prestige.

Through these groups the director has an opportunity to share experiences and ideas with others. Often the personal relationships developed at area meetings or conventions are worth more than the actual facts and figures which come from the official part of the program.

COMMUNITY ACTIVITIES

Every band director is, and should be, an integral part of the entire community. His participation in civic activities is highly desirable, provided that he does not overdo it, and finds that as a result he can no longer carry on his school work properly.

It is not necessary for a director to join the country club or to do other "social climbing" in order to gain the support of this segment of the community. If his work is outstanding, the elite, as well as everyone else, will respect him.

PRIVATE TEACHERS

Since the band director does not have time to give proper individual attention to all students in a system, private lessons should be encouraged whenever competent teachers are available. When a student is receiving private instruction you do not need to worry about his systematic development, and—in a sense—can "forget" about him.

Studio teachers who understand the public school music program invariably support that program. The director must make every effort to establish good relations with the music teachers of the community and to help them realize that they are an important part of the whole instrumental music team.

PERSONAL CONVICTIONS

Many directors lack the conviction and the moral fortitude to stand up for what they know is best, especially if they represent a minority viewpoint. If the crowd is for it, they are for it, but if the crowd is opposed, they will join them.

Although the fundamental goal underlying all of our teaching is the improvement and elevation of human beings, we ourselves have grown apathetic and apparently cannot rise in defense of our beliefs.

Music, and culture in general, are losing time and emphasis in the school curriculum. Tragically, they are not being defeated by the enormous shadows of materialism, but by our own fear of taking a stand against what seems to have been only a normal reaction to Sputnik, which we have let develop into an abnormal trend. *Apathy is the unforgivable sin and the irredeemable error.*

Solutions to the problems discussed in this chapter all have as their underlying objective one of the most elusive of goals: happiness. If it is true that "the busiest are the happiest" then the band director has no worries. If he considers his demanding schedule significant and faces every problem as a challenge, he will rate high on the happiness scale, since what is more exciting, stimulating, and rewarding than to work with human nature itself? If he ever loses his enthusiasm and bogs down in his work, in all fairness to himself and to his students, he should either change jobs or leave teaching altogether.

Research studies reported by John E. Gibson in *Today's Health* have concluded that we are most likely to find happiness by:

1. keeping busy doing our jobs as well as we can.
2. being grateful for what we have instead of regretful for what we do not have.
3. realizing that we cannot bring happiness to others without having it rub off on ourselves.
4. heeding that small voice called conscience, and
5. not being so preoccupied with material things that we fail to realize the vital need to cultivate peace of mind through developing spiritual resources.

Most people place too much emphasis on material acquisitions. They no sooner get a better car, a better house, or a better bank balance, than they immediately set another goal which may be untenable. Happiness does not depend on material wealth. There are as many unhappy people among the rich as among the poor, although if you feel as though you are destined to be miserable anyway, I suppose it's less unpleasant to suffer with money than without it.

It is extremely unfortunate that we human beings often do not fully appreciate our many non-material blessings until we are deprived of them:

—our health and vigor before it is impaired by years of hard work.
—our hearty meals, free of medical diet considerations or calorie counting.
—our deep breaths of fresh air, uncontaminated by the smoker in the airline reserved seat next to us.

—our good parents who solved the problems with their children which are puzzling us now.

HARD WORK

Directing a school band is one of the most enjoyable and stimulating kinds of work, but there seems to be no *easy* way to accomplish superior results. The director who is looking for an easier job—the chap who can't wait to go fishing, golfing, bowling, drinking, or to almost anything but work—wants to escape. Avoiding the unpleasantness of reality may be desirable at times, but rarely does it help solve one's basic problems. Invariably the best solution is to face the facts squarely and tackle the problems directly.

In the pursuit of physical and mental health (and in the long run, maximum happiness) one should never avoid the therapeutic value and the long-lasting personal satisfaction of plain, old-fashioned, honest, *work*, but even so, working *too* hard and *too* long can be a disease. Like any other extreme, this too should be avoided.

OLD AGE

Many men who are comparatively young feel quite old at times; others who have actually grown older sometimes begin to coast or to feel sorry for themselves, and their work suffers as a result.

The way to stay young is to remain youthful *inside:* continue to grow, maintain a cheerful attitude, and stay mentally alive and alert.

One's mental abilities do not have to deteriorate with age. Handel conducted a performance of his *Messiah* at 75; Franklin helped frame the American Constitution at 80; Edison was inventing at 84; and, Titian painted masterpieces at 98.

CHAPTER

Choosing Music

For Performance

Solos and Ensembles
by **13** *outstanding instrumentalists*

Band Music
by **50** *high school directors,*
selected by NBA

The Band Director as Composer
by **Nelson Keyes**
Ford Foundation composer

Frederick Wilkins

Daniel A. McAninch

David J. Gowans

Daniel Bonade

Robert Lowry

Fred Hemke

Himie Voxman

Robert W. Getchell

Phillip Farkas

Harold T. Brasch

Matty Shiner

William J. Bell

Jack McKenzie

Nelson W. Keyes

Anyone who has ever attempted to select "the best" of anything knows that this is a difficult if not impossible task. Still, over a period of time filled with study, performance, teaching, and listening, coupled with regular and diligent searches through stacks of publications, both old and new, outstanding performers, conductors, and private teachers *do find* certain pieces that have become their favorites for a variety of reasons, most important of which is that these have "worked best" *for them.*

While each expert who has contributed to this chapter would be the first to insist that his selections should not be considered the last and only word on the subject, each would also hope that the lists, by specialists with many years of experience, will provide some help for the director in his difficult task of selecting the "right" music for his own particular students.

SOLO AND ENSEMBLE MUSIC

In order to achieve selectivity, each contributor was asked to choose only three solos or ensembles at five levels of difficulty. Obviously, with the wealth of fine material available for most media, the omission of any particular piece does not *necessarily* label it as unworthy of further consideration.

In some cases the experts were specifically encouraged to list their own compositions or arrangements, since it is obvious to all that the pieces themselves have earned the right of inclusion. The omission of such material, while certainly unfair to the contributor, would be even more unfair to the reader who is seeking help in the selection of the best music.

The levels of difficulty referred to are (the roman numeral designations are followed in the subsequent text):

I. For beginners who are probably the fourth, fifth, or sixth grade students in your feeder program.

II. For those students at least in their second year, including those up to junior high school age.

III. For those students who have the instrument under control but lack maturity. These are probably good junior high or young high school players.

IV. For mature students who are still lacking in experience. These are probably 10th, 11th, and 12th grade students.

V. Only for the advanced, very capable player.

FREDERICK WILKINS, *flute soloist and conductor, author of* The Flutist's Guide, *is currently Vice President in charge of development and quality control with Artley, Inc. He makes clinic and concert appearances throughout the United States. His brilliant professional performance and teaching career has included positions with the Radio City Music Hall, Chautauqua, New York City Opera, New York City Ballet, and the "Voice of Firestone" Orchestras, and the Juilliard, Manhattan, Chautauqua, and New York Schools of Music.*

FLUTE SOLOS

I.	Concert Album	Varied	Edition Musicus
	L. Moyse 40 Little Pieces	L. Moyse	Fischer Classical Album
	Two Minuets	Purcell	Rudall Carte
II.	Pearls of the Masters	Various	Cundy–Bettoney
	Classical Album	Various	Rudall Carte
	Adagio	Mozart	Belwin
III.	Minuet	Bizet	Fischer
	Romance	Brun	Rubank
	Sonata No. 7	Loeillet	Southern
IV.	Suite in B minor	Bach	Cundy–Bettoney
	Pleasures of Pan	Various	Cundy–Bettoney
	Fantasie	Faure	Belwin
V.	Sonatas	Bach	Southern
	Carnival of Venice	Briscialdi–Wilkins	Ludwig
	Concertino	Chaminade	Fischer

FLUTE TRIOS

I. Chamber Music for Three Flutes	Voxman	Rubank
II. Flute Sessions	Wilkins–Gerhardt	Shawnee
The Cuckoo	Arensky–Wood	Concord
Fughetta	Bach	Mills
III. Sonata	DeBoismortsen	Boosey–Hawkes
Allegro Giocoso	Haydn	Mills
Trio in G Major, Op. 3, No. 1	Locatelle–Reisman	International
IV. Flute Trio	Tcherepnine	Presto
Dance of the Reed Flutes	Tchaikovsky	Fischer
Classic Fantasy	Warn	Kjos
V. Flight of the Bumblebee	Rimsky-Korsakov	Rubank
Grand Trio in C Major	Walckiers	Zimmerman
Grand Trio in E♭ Major	Walckiers	Edition Musicus

FLUTE QUARTETS

I. Minuet	Bach	Belwin
First Ensemble Book	Buchtel–Paschslag	Kjos
II. Minuet	Bach	Mills
French Clock	Bornschein	Presser
Flute Symphony	Holmes	Rubank
III. Quartet Album	Eck	Belwin
Christmas Morning Suite	McKay	Southern
Tambourin	Guillemain	Mills
IV. First Quartet	Furstenau	Southern
First Grand Quartet in F	Furstenau	Southern
Second Grand Quartet in F	Schneider	Presto

V. Sinfonico Quartet	Reicha	Cundy–Bettoney
Grand Quartet in E Minor	Kuhlau	Southern
Concerto for Four Flutes	Schickhardt	Presto

DANIEL A. McANINCH *is Associate Professor of Music at the University of Louisville, and oboist with the Louisville Orchestra. A native of Little Rock, Arkansas, he received the Bachelor of Music, Master of Music, and Doctor of Musical Arts degrees from the Eastman School of Music. He has served on the faculties of Texas Christian University, University of Kentucky, State University College (Fredonia, New York), and the University of Wisconsin summer music clinic.*

OBOE SOLOS

I. Piece V	Franck	Leduc
Chant sans Paroles	Tchaikovsky	Boosey–Hawkes
Largo (from New World Symphony	Dvorak	Cundy–Bettoney

II. Elegy	Bakaleinikoff	Belwin
Piece in G minor	Pierne	Leduc
Nocturne	Bassi	Rubank

III. Three Short Pieces	Bach–Gillet	Costallat
Concerto in F minor	Telemann	Leduc
Three Romances	Schumann	G. Schirmer

IV. Concerto	Cimarosa	Boosey–Hawkes
Sonata in G minor	Handel	Southern
Concerto in C minor	Marcello	Forberg

V. Prelude and Allegro	M. Theopane	Interlochen
Concerto	E. Goosens	Curwen
Concertino	Mozart	Southern

DAVID J. GOWANS, *Associate Professor of Woodwinds and Theory at Murray (Kentucky) State College, has studied with bassoonists Leonard Sharrow, Angel del Busto, and Gerald Schon. His University studies have been pursued at Wayne and the University of Miami; professional experience includes the position of principal bassoonist with the Havana (Cuba) Philharmonic Orchestra.*

BASSOON SOLOS

I. Cielito Lindo	Buchtel	Kjos
Hermes	Buchtel	Kjos
Sonatine	Weinberger	Fischer
II. Largo, from "The New World"	Dvorak	Cundy–Bettoney
Traumerie and Romance	Schumann	Cundy–Bettoney
Three Pieces	Bakaleinkoff	Belwin
III. Celebre Largo	Handel	Baron
Clown Festival	Kesnar	Cundy–Bettoney
Arioso	Weissenborn	Cundy–Bettoney
IV. Six Sonatas	Galliard	McGinnis–Marx
Ballad and Humoresque	Bakaleinkoff	Belwin
Concertino	David	Cundy–Bettoney
V. Concerto in F	Weber	Cundy–Bettoney
Concerto in B♭ (Op 96)	Mozart	Cundy–Bettoney
Sonata	Hindemith	Associated

DANIEL BONADE, *the "Dean of American clarinet teachers" (many of those on his long list of students hold important positions in orchestras throughout the United States), is now retired in Cannes, France, after an extremely successful career as both performer and teacher. He has played professionally with the Philadelphia, C.B.S., Cleveland, and N.B.C. Orchestras, and served on the faculty of the Cleveland Institute of Music and the Juilliard School of Music.*

CLARINET SOLOS

I. Any solos in beginners' books.

II. My idea in teaching is to wait until a student is able to master his instrument sufficiently before giving him any solos to play because beginners contract bad habits with solos and sometimes cannot get rid of them later. This is just a private opinion, of course.

III. Concertino	Weber	Kjos,
		Cundy–Bettoney
Fantasie	Marty	Cundy–Bettoney
Concerto	Mozart	Fischer, International
		Cundy–Bettoney
IV. Solo de Concours	Messager	Edition Musicales
Solo de Concours	Rabaud	Southern
Second Concerto	Weber	Cundy–Bettoney,
		Fischer
V. Rapsodie	Debussy	Elkan–Vogel
Introduction et Rondo	Widor	Wahn
Fantasie	Ravel	

ROBERT LOWRY, *after 13 years as head of the instrumental music department of Morningside College, Sioux City, Iowa, is now engaged full time as a soloist, guest conductor, and clinician. Both his early* lack *of formal training (he developed many bad playing habits which had to be overcome), and his later* abundance *of experience as a music educator have provided him with a very deep understanding of the problems faced by school clarinetists and band directors. Many contemporary composers have written clarinet compositions for him, some of which are included in the Golden Crest Records, "Bob Lowry and His Clarinet."*

ALTO CLARINET SOLOS

I. A Rendezvous in the Forest	Harris	Barnhouse

	Choral Varie	D'Indy	Elkan–Vogel
	Marche Slav	Tchaikovsky	Belwin
II.	Evening Fantasy	Miller	Belwin
	Melancholy	Whitney	Spratt
	Petite Suite	White	Fox
III.	A Waltz Dream	Strauss	Ludwig
	Adagio (from B♭ clarinet concerto)	Mozart	Cundy–Bettoney
	Serenade	Titl	Fischer
IV.	Leonora	Leoni	Pro Art
	Praeludium	Schmutz	Fischer
	Scene and Air	Bergson	Cundy–Bettoney
V.	Concertino	von Weber	Fischer
	Czardas	Monti	Fischer
	Darkwood	Bennett	Fischer

BASS CLARINET SOLOS

I.	A Rendezvous in the Forest	Harris	Barnhouse
	Aria (from "The Magic Flute")	Mozart	Belwin
	Hercules	Buchtel	Kjos
II.	Marche Comique	Ostransky	Rubank
	Panda Dance	Barnard	Belwin
	Petite Suite	White	Fox
III.	Alborada	Hoffman	Boosey–Hawkes
	Andante and Bourrée	Handel	Barnhouse
	Largo and Allegro	Boni	Rubank
IV.	A Clown Festival	Kesnar	Cundy–Bettoney
	Deepwood	Bennett	Fischer
	Pastorale and Bourrée	German	Rubank
V.	Andante and Allegro	Desportes	Southern

| Ballade | Bozza | Southern |
| Night Wind | Kay | Pro Art |

CLARINET QUARTETS (FOUR B♭ CLARINETS)

I. Let's Play Quartets	Burgstahler	Pro Art
Serenade in F	Sears	Pro Art
Theme	Schubert	Fischer

II. Sarabande	Handel	Fischer
Seven Miniatures	Schumann	Boosey–Hawkes
Twenty-four Clari- net Quartets	Hudadoff	Pro Art

III. Seascapes	Karel	Summy
Six Excerpts	Willaman	Schirmer
Three Bagatelles	Beethoven	Belwin

IV. Pastorale and Dance	Donato	Schirmer
Prelude and Scherzo	Bennett	Fischer
Scherzoso	Schmutz	FitzSimons

V. Prelude and Scherzo	Miller	Belwin
Quartet	Barab	Boosey–Hawkes
Scherzetto	Skinner	Belwin

CLARINET QUARTETS (2 B♭'S, ALTO, AND BASS CLARINETS)

I. Ave Verum Corpus	Mozart	Leonard
Andante	Bonne	Rubank
Temp di Minuetto	Guilmant	Mills

II. Menuet	Schubert	Belwin
Preludial Fantasia	Schmutz	FitzSimons
Woodland Sketches	MacDowell	Ludwig

III. Pastoral	McKay	Barnhouse
Prelude to Autumn	Miller	Belwin
Two Tone Poems	MacDowell	Barnhouse

IV. Finale (from Schu- bert's Quartet)	Willaman	Schirmer
Repartee	Ready	Music Pub. Holding
Rondo alla Turca	Mozart	Southern

| V. Clarinet Rhapsody | Bennett | Fischer |

| Quartet No. 1 | Endresen | Belwin |
| Rondo Capriccioso | Mendelssohn | Schmitt |

FRED HEMKE, *the first and only American ever to win the coveted First Prize in Saxophone at the Paris National Conservatory of Music, is a pupil of the celebrated saxophone virtuoso, Marcel Mule. A member of the faculty of Northwestern University, he also makes numerous solo concert and educational clinic-demonstration appearances.*

ALTO SAXOPHONE SOLOS

I. En Partant	Cui–Mule	Leduc
Deux Miniatures	A. Gretchaninoff	Leduc
Le Bourgeois Gentilhomme	Lully–Mule	Leduc
II. Cantilena	Warren Benson	Boosey–Hawkes
Lament and Tarantella	H. Voxman	Chart Music Pub.
Variations sur un Theme de Claude LeJeune	F. Tournier	Leduc
III. Chanson et Passepied	J. Rueff	Leduc
Sicilienne	P. Lantier	Leduc
Tambourin	Mondonville–Mule	Leduc
IV. An Abstract	David Ward	Southern
Concerto in E flat	Alexandre Glazanow	Leduc
Sonatine Sportive	A. Tcherepnine	Leduc
V. Sonata	B. Heiden	Schott (Associated)
Concertino da Camera	Jacques Ibert	Leduc
Petite Suite	Walter Hartley	Interlochen
Sonatine	Claude Pascal	Leduc

TENOR SAXOPHONE SOLOS

| I. Elegie | Massenet–Grooms | Century |

Angel's Serenade	Braga	Century
On Wings of Song	Mendelssohn–Weber	Belwin
II. Gigue	Aubert–Maganini	Edition Musicus
Suite in C Bourrée	Bach–Mule	Leduc
Arioso	Bach–Kent	Fischer
III. Cypress Song	Karel L.	Boosey–Hawkes
Musette	Leclair–Mule	Leduc
Chant d'Eglise	Philidor–Mule	Leduc
IV. Prelude et Divertissement	Robert Clerisse	Andrieu Freres
Suite for Tenor Saxophone	R. Brancour	Evette Schaeffer, Inc.
Concerto No. 1	Singelee–Voxman	Alfred
V. Ballade	Frank Martin	Universal (Associated)
Sonata IV	Galliard–Rascher	McGinnis and Marx
Introduction and Czardas	Cohen	Witmark (MPH)

BARITONE SAXOPHONE SOLOS

I. Elegy	Massenet	Belwin
Adagio	Corelli–Mule	Leduc
Deux Miniatures	A. Gretchaninoff	Leduc
II. Largo	Handel–Mule	Leduc
Romance	Klughardt–Muller	Jack Sprat
Waltz	Tchaikovsky Harris	Ludwig
III. Andante	Bach–Johnson	Belwin
Canzonetta	d'Ambrosio–Hummel	Rubank
Adagio	Beethoven–Bettoney	Cundy–Bettoney
IV. Chanson à Bercer	Robert Clerisse	Leduc
Interlude Melodie	Fontaine	Pro Art
Sonate	Daniel Lazarus	Durand
Concerto	Singelee–Voxman	Alfred
V. Improvisation et Caprice	Eugene Bozza	Leduc

Serenade Basque	Hoffman	Belwin
Caprice en Forme du Valse	Paul Bonneau	Leduc
Cello Suites	Bach	Peters

SAXOPHONE QUARTETS (2 ALTOS, 1 TENOR, 1 BARITONE)

I. Elegie	Grieg–Taylor	Mills
Hymn	Beethoven	GHM
Saxophone Symphony Album	Holmes	Rubank
Arioso	Bach–Kent	Fischer
II. Quartet for Saxophones	Lucien Cailliet	Belwin
Guardian Angel	Pierne–Nelson	Ludwig
The Cricket	Vecchi–Maganini	Edition Musicus
III. Two Modern Saxophone Quartets	Jack End	Kendor
Sailor's Hornpipe	Henry Cowell	Peer International
Novelette	Sol Cohen	Belwin
IV. Quartet No. 2, Op. 16	Miller	Pro Art
Introd., Recitative and Chorale	A. D. Schmutz	Associated
Prelude and Beguine	V. Williams	Fischer
V. Prelude and Finale	A. D. Schmutz	Associated
Scherzo	Mielenz–Voxman	Rubank
Choral Fantasy	Johnson	FitzSimons

SAXOPHONE QUARTETS (SOPRANO, ALTO, TENOR, BARITONE)

I. None.		
II. None.		
III. Introduction et Scherzo	Robert Clerisse	Buffet Crampton
Marche des Petits Soldats de Plumb	Pierne–Mule	Leduc
Chanson d'Autrefois	Pierne–Mule	Leduc

IV.	Trois Conversations	Paul Pierne	Editions Costallat
	Goldrush Suite	Jack Marshall	Shawnee
	Andante et Scherzo	Eugene Bozza	Leduc
V.	Saxophone–Quartet	A. Glazanow	Boosey–Hawkes
	Quartet No. 1	Russell Howland	Ybra Press
	Introduction et Variations sur Ronde Populaire	Gabriel Pierne	Leduc

HIMIE VOXMAN, *Head of the Department of Music, State University of Iowa, is a well known editor and arranger of woodwind materials. His publications (Rubank), for both woodwinds and brass, include advanced methods, selected studies, solo collections, selected duets, chamber music collections, and the Ensemble Classics Series.*

WOODWIND QUINTET (FLUTE, OBOE, CLARINET, FRENCH HORN, BASSOON)

I.	Masterpieces for Woodwind	Various–Ulrich	Boston
	Six Little Fugues	Handel–Bauer	Boston
	Little Dance Suite	Ward	Mills
II.	Andante and Contradanse in "Ensemble Repertoire"	Mozart–Voxman	Rubank
	Sarabande in D minor	Bach–Henschel	Boosey–Hawkes
	Bainbridge Island Sketches	McKay	Barnhouse
III.	Passacaille	Barthe	Rubank
	Prelude from 2nd Suite, Op. 122	Lefebvre–Waln	Kjos
	Allegro Molto (from K270) in "Ensemble Repertoire"	Mozart–Voxman	Rubank

IV. Petite Suite Miniature in "Ensemble Repertoire"	Balay	Rubank
Divertimento	Haydn–Perry	Boosey–Hawkes
Suite Miniature	Poldowski–Barrere	Galaxy
V. Kleine Kammermusik, Op. 24, No. 2	Hindemith	Associated
Trois Pièces Brèves	Ibert	Leduc
La Cheminée du Roi René	Milhaud	Southern

MISCELLANEOUS WOODWIND ENSEMBLES

I. Seven Pieces for Three Woodwinds (flute, oboe, clarinet)	Various–Hovey	Boosey–Hawkes
Seventy-eight Duets (flute, clarinet)	Various–Voxman	Rubank
Canon et Marziale (flute, oboe, clarinet, bassoon)	Salome–Taylor	Mills
II. Six Easy Transcriptions (flute, oboe, clarinet, bassoon)	Chopin–Gray	Omega
Chamber Music for Three Woodwinds (flute, oboe, clarinet)	Various–Voxman	Rubank
Minuet (flute, oboe, clarinet, bassoon)	Cox	Boosey–Hawkes
III. Chamber Music for Three Woodwinds (flute, clarinet, bassoon)	Various–Voxman	Rubank

Scenes from Childhood (flute, oboe, clarinet, bassoon)	Schumann–Gillette	Witmark
Scherzetto (flute, oboe, clarinet)	Olivadoti	MPH

IV.

Five Divertimenti (2 clarinets, bassoon)	Mozart	Witmark
Aubade (flute, oboe, clarinet)	Wailly	Rubank
For the Gentlemen (flute, oboe, clarinet, bassoon)	Shaw	Mercury

V.

Serenade in C minor, K388 (2 oboes, 2 clarinets, 2 horns, 2 bassoons)	Mozart	Broude
Octuor (flute, clarinet, 2 bassoons, 2 trumpets, 2 trombones)	Stravinsky	Boosey–Hawkes
Suite (flute, oboe, clarinet)	Goeb	Peer

ROBERT W. GETCHELL *is Associate Professor of Brass Instruments at Luther College in Decorah, Iowa. He has taught students of all ages in the public schools of Iowa and at both Bowling Green (Ohio) State University and the Jordan College of Music of Butler University in Indianapolis. He is the author of two volumes each of* Practical Studies for Cornet, Horn, *and* Tuba, *and* Section Studies for Cornets, *published by Belwin, and the* Teacher's Guide to the Brass Instruments *published by Selmer.*

CORNET/TRUMPET SOLOS

I.

Concertino No. 1	Porret	Baron
Country Dance	Harris	Ludwig

The Young Prince	Pelz	Belwin
II. Concertino No. 2	Porret	Baron
The Valiant	Pelz	Belwin
Melody and Scherzo	Ward	
III. Concertino	Louthe	Chester
Impromptu	Buchtel	Mills
Orientale	Barat	Baron
IV. Suite in F	Purcell–Maganini	Edition Musicus
Aria and Allegro	Tenaglia–Krieger	Presser
Suite for Trumpet	Gibons–Cruft	Mills
V. Lento et Scherzo	Barat	Baron
Sarabande et Rigaudon	Clergue	Elkan–Vogel
Concert Etude	Goedicke	Leeds

CORNET/TRUMPET TRIOS

I. Trumpet Threesome	Sartorius	Century
The Three Cubs	Harris	Ludwig
Trio Album	Various–Ostling	Belwin
II. Three of a Kind	Buchtel	Barnhouse
Polka Dots	Buchtel	Barnhouse
Holiday Polka	Meretta	Mills
III. Just for Fun	Herbert	Fischer
Trio for Trumpets	Darcy	Bourne
March and Fanfare	Bach	Marks
IV. Divertissement	Ostransky	Rubank
Suite for Three Trumpets	Busch	Witmark
Air and Variations in B♭	Handel–Goldman	Fischer
V. Sonatina	Donato	Schirmer
Trio	Phillips	King
Three Trumpeters	Agostini–Bainum	Belwin

MISCELLANEOUS BRASS ENSEMBLES

I. Quartets for Brass (Folio)	Quartet	Various– Mesang	Schmitt
Ensemble Classics, Vol. I	Quartet	Various– Voxman	Rubank
Music for Queen Mary	Quintet	Purcell	King
II. Three Short Classics	Sextet	arr. Boyd	Witmark
In Modo Religioso	Quartet	Glazounov	Rubank
March and Gavotte	Quintet	Handel	King
III. Legend and Canon	Quartet	Bright	Associated
Suite Miniature	Sextet	Miller	Belwin
Quartet No. I	Quartet	Whitney	Fischer
IV. Scherzo and Lied	Quintet	Maurer	Mentor
Dance and March	Quartet	Piket	Associated
Quartet No. IV	Quartet	Ramsoe	King
V. Sonata (trumpet, horn, trombone)	Trio	Poulenc	Baron
Divertimento	Quartet	Addison	Williams, Ltd.
Symphony for Brass	Quintet	Ewald	King

PHILLIP FARKAS, *regarded by many as the foremost hornist in America today, serves as Professor of Music at Indiana University. He has held the solo horn position with the Kansas City, Cleveland, Boston, and Chicago Symphony Orchestra. During the summer months he serves on the faculty of the Aspen (Colorado) School of Music and performs with the Aspen Festival Orchestra. Mr. Farkas is the author of two definitive treatises—"The Art of French Horn Playing" published by Summy–Birchard, and "The Art of Brass Playing" (available from Brass Publications, Box 66, Bloomington, Indiana).*

FRENCH HORN SOLOS

I. Our Favorite (from First Division)	Leonard B. Smith	Belwin

Huntsman (from First Division)	Leonard B. Smith	Belwin
Janus: Waltz	Forrest Buchtel	Kjos
II. Andante (from First Division)	Schubert	Belwin
Telestar (from First Division)	Leonard B. Smith	Belwin
Lullaby	Ilyinsky	Kjos
III. Reverie	Glazounow	Leeds
Marching Canon	M. Bradford Anderson	Boosey–Hawkes
Romance, Op. 36	St.-Saëns	Durand
IV. Air de Chasse	Louis Piantoni	Leduc
Intermezzo	Gliere	Leeds
First Movement, Sonata, Op. 17	Beethoven	Fischer
V. En Forêt	Eugene Bozza	Leduc
Concerto No. 2	Mozart	International
Concerto No. 1	Richard Strauss	International

FRENCH HORN QUARTETS

I. Russian Hymn	Pottag Quartet Album	Belwin
My Country 'Tis of Thee	Pottag Quartet Album	Belwin
God of Our Fathers (from "Two Dozen Horn Quartets")	Marvin Howe	Morris
II. Good King Wenceslaus	Marvin Howe Quartets	Morris
Who Is Sylvia?	Marvin Howe Quartets	Morris
Der Freischutz	Pottag Quartet Album	Belwin

III.	Vive L'Amour	Marvin Howe Quartets	Morris
	The Ash Grove	Marvin Howe Quartets	Morris
	In the Church (from "Country Pictures")	Vassily Brandt	International
IV.	Under a Lime Tree (from "Country Pictures")	Vassily Brandt	International
	No. IV from "Five Interludes"	Daniel Lesur	International
	No. III from "Five Interludes"	Daniel Lesur	International
V.	Quartet for Horns on Wagner Themes	Pottag	Belwin
	Six Pieces for Four French Horns	N. Tcherepnine	Edition Musicus
	Fughetta of the Little Bells	Handel	Remick

HAROLD T. BRASCH *was admitted to the U.S. Navy Band in Washington, D.C. in 1936 on the strength of a letter from Dr. Herbert L. Clarke. During the next 20 years, his technical mastery of the instrument, the beauty of his tone and superb musical craftsmanship placed him indisputably among the greatest euphonium soloists of all time. Now retired from the Navy, in Arlington, Va., he devotes his time to clinic and concert appearances.*

BARITONE/EUPHONIUM SOLOS

I.	None.		
II.	Am Meer	Schubert	Fischer
	Because	D'Hardelot	
III.	Atlantic Zephyrs	Simons	Fischer

	The Holy City	Adams	Boosey–Hawkes
IV.	Willow Echoes	Simons	Fischer
	Neptune's Court	Herbert L. Clarke	Fischer
	Stars In a Velvety Sky	Herbert L. Clarke	Fischer
V.	Hungarian Melodies	V. Bach	V. Bach
	La Mandolinata	H. Bellstedt	Southern
	Endearing Young Charms	S. Mantia	

MATTY SHINER, *head of the Brass Department at Duquesne University, has over 25 years of experience as a trombone instructor. He has held the position of first trombonist with NBC's Station KDKA, the Warner Brothers' Stanley Theatre, and the Pittsburgh Light Civic Opera. His students hold important positions in musical organizations throughout the United States.*

TROMBONE SOLOS

I.	Chanson Triste, Op. 40, No. 2	Tchaikovsky	Century
	By the Sea (Am Meer)	Schubert	Fischer
	Autumn (Miniature Concert Series)	Pinard	Fischer
	Evening Shadows	E. Clark	Fischer
II.	Recitative and Prayer–IV	Berlioz	McGinnis and Marx
	Spring's Awakening	C. E. Bach	Cundy–Bettoney
	Berceuse (from "Jocelyn")	Godard	Fischer
III.	Adagio from Concerto for 'Cello	Haydn–Schumann	Witmark
	Little Chief (Polka Caprice)	Arthur Pryor	Fischer
	Annie Laurie Air Varie	Arthur Pryor	Ludwig

IV. Six Sonatas, Vols.   Galliard–E. Clark   McGinnis and Marx
      I and II
    Andante and   J. E. Barat   Southern
      Allegro
    Blue Bells of   Arthur Pryor   Fischer
      Scotland
    Air Varie   Pryor–Cimera   Chart Music

V. Capriccio   Bonneau   Southern
    Sonata for Trom-   Hindemith   Associated
      bone and Piano
    Suite   Bach   Baron
    Concerto en Fa   Handel   Southern
      Mineur

TROMBONE QUARTETS

  I. Chorale Collection   Bach   Rubank
     In Thee Is Gladness   Gastoldi   King
     O Dearest Jesus   Cruger   King

 II. First Suite   Orlander   Schirmer
     Concert Suite No. 1   Clapp   Boosey–Hawkes
     The Lost Chord   Sullivan   Belwin

III. Three Equali   Beethoven   Editions Musicales
     Andante Symphony   Brahms   Rubank
       No. 4
     Festival March   McKay   Barnhouse
     Excerpts from   Berlioz   Edition Musicus
       Damnation
       of Faust

IV. Rakoczy March   Berlioz   Belwin
     Recessional   Haubiel   Fischer
     Three Equali   Beethoven   King

 V. Quartet No. 2   Maas   Cundy–Bettoney
     Concert Suite No. 2   Clapp   Boosey–Hawkes
     Two Fugues   Bach   King (Music for
                                                      Brass)

WILLIAM J. BELL, *"the Dean of American tuba players," is now a member of the faculty of Indiana University. His professional career began with W. W. Norton's Chautauqua Band. Later he was principal tuba and soloist with Harold Bachman's "Million Dollar Band," the John Philip Sousa Band, the Arthur Pryor Band, Pat Conway's Band, the Edwin Franko Goldman Band, Merle Evan's "Barnum and Bailey Circus Band," the Henry Fillmore Band, and "Band of America." His orchestra experience has included the solo tuba position with the Cincinnati, NBC, and New York Philharmonic Orchestras. His students are prominent in the brass ensembles of at least nine major symphonic orchestras. Called by Maestro Arturo Toscanini, "the finest tuba player I have ever heard," Mr. Bell's great virtuosity and outstanding teaching ability have virtually erased the old "oom-pah" conception of tuba playing from the ear of every serious composer and performer.*

TUBA SOLOS

I. Low Down Bass	Bell	Fischer
Massa's in the Cold, Cold Ground	Foster	Belwin
Gavotte	Poppers–Bell	Belwin
II. Jolly Jumbo	Bell	Belwin
Teddy Bear's Picnic	Bratton–McLean	Witmark
Mummer's Parade	Merle	Fischer
III. Billy Blowhard	Kottaun	Fischer
Tarentella	Walters	Ludwig
Barbarossa	Barnhouse	Barnhouse
IV. Concerto No. 2 for Tuba	Ernest Williams	Colin
Recitative and Air ("Messiah")	Handel–C. O'Neill	Waterloo (Ontario)
Air and Bourrée	J. S. Bach–Bell	Fischer
V. Sonata for Tuba and Piano	Hindemith	Schott (Associated)
Sonata for Tuba and Piano	Beversdorf	Interlochen
Sonata for Tuba and Piano	Lebedjew	Edition Musicus

JACK McKENZIE *is Assistant Professor of Music and Bands at the University of Illinois, and conductor of the University of Illinois Percussion Ensemble. He is also teacher of Percussion and Percussion Ensembles at the National Music Camp, and serves as visiting Instructor in Percussion for the Interlochen Arts Academy.*

SNARE DRUM SOLOS

I. American Patrol	Buchtel	Kjos
Den Chief	Ostling	Gamble
Recruits' March	Buchtel	Kjos
II. Scholastic Six-Eight	Stone	Stone
The 400	Harr	Cole
Little Suite for Snare Drum	Goldenberg	Shapiro–Bernstein
III. The Phantom Drummer	Weinberger	Associated
Contest Capers	Mitchell	Kjos
Texas Challenge	Hoey	Southern
IV. General Washington	Heney	Fillmore
Solo for Snare Drum	Hartwig	Music for Percussion
Exhibition Snare Drum Solo	Price	Music for Percussion
V. Six Unaccompanied Solos for Snare Drum	Colgrass	Lawson–Gould
20–40's Sortie	Ables	Ludwig
Brook III	Scholle	Brook

TYMPANI SOLOS

I. Classical March	Noak	Music for Percussion
Andante	Noak	Music for Percussion
Solo Piece	Britton	Morris
II. New Port	Harr	Cole
Dance Primitive	Noak	Music for Percussion

	Sonatina	Tcherepnine	Boosey–Hawkes
III.	6 Graded Tympani Solos	McKenzie	Music for Percussion
	Timpaniana	Bigot	Leduc
	Scherzo	Vito	Frank Drum Shop
IV.	Tympendium	Schinstein	Southern
	Tympolero	Schinstein	Southern
	Fantasy–Scherzo	Noak	Music for Percussion
V.	Sonata for 3 Unaccompanied Kettledrums	Jones	Peters
	Recitative and Improvisation for 4 Kettledrums	Carter	Associated
	Concerto for Tympani	Thrashen	Associated

PERCUSSION ENSEMBLES

I.	First Quartet	4 players	Britton	Music for Percussion
	March for Percussion	6 players	Raab	Music for Percussion
	Quartet	4 players	Ward	Arlington Academy
II.	One Over Three	4 players	Britton	Music for Percussion
	Three Dances	3 players	McKenzie	Music for Percussion
	Theme and Variations	4 players	Goodman	Mills
III.	Sextet	6 players	Siwe	Music for Percussion
	Three Brothers	9 players	Colgrass	Music for Percussion
	Nonet	9 players	McKenzie	Music for Percussion
IV.	Fugetta alla Siciliana	4 players	Benson	Schirmer
	October Mountain	6 players	Hovhaness	Peters
	Introduction and Allegro	4 players	McKenzie	Music for Percussion
V.	Toccata for Percussion	6 players	Chavez	Mills
	Cantile No. 3	6 players	Harrison	Music for Percussion
	4 Holidays	3 players	Bartlett	Music for Percussion

In *The High School Band Director's Handbook*,[1] W. Clyde Duvall writes that the director who is choosing music for performance:

> . . . should pick a type of music that best suits his own band; he should definitely avoid selection of any type that he does not understand or conduct well.
>
> He should take his group's weaknesses and strong points into consideration, avoiding music that contains difficult parts for his weak sections, and selecting numbers that feature instruments or sections that happen to be strong in his organization at that particular time. All of this can be done while he selects numbers from a grade of music that will serve as a *reasonable* challenge to his people. All of us know directors who program the same grade of music year in and year out; not because their band is incapable of further improvement, but simply because it is easier to remain static. Certainly, the members of such a band cannot continue to be enthusiastic about their organization and its progress, and, certainly, the most is not being made of this teaching situation. On the other extreme, there is the teacher (usually the beginner) who selects music that his students simply are not capable of learning or understanding—even if they do a good year's work on it. This director, too, is being unfair to his boys and girls. He is subjecting them to a harmful kind of competition—the kind in which the game is lost before the first ball is pitched.

Through the cooperation of the National Band Association, outstanding band directors throughout the United States were given the opportunity to select the "three very best band compositions ever used—in march, contest, and program categories—on three levels of difficulty."

The following phrases, selected from the many notes accompanying those selection forms which were returned, have been arranged to express the difficulties, as well as the values, of such a selection:

> Trying to pick out the "very best" is a difficult assignment . . . there are hundreds of excellent things I have used over the past 40 years . . . it is sometimes difficult to categorize music . . . the classifications can be a bit off . . . technic is one thing and musicianship or style is another . . . we have tried to think through this list carefully . . . to do it according to our set-up . . . these are the ones with which I have had success . . . hope the enclosed meets your needs.

---

[1] Prentice-Hall, Inc., Englewood Cliffs, N. J., 1960.

We wish to thank the National Band Association, President Al G. Wright, and the following state chairmen and high school band directors, for their cooperation:

Director or Chairman	*City*
Mary C. Askov	Fairbanks, Alaska
Paul V. Backlund	Duluth, Minnesota
Donald Barnes	Kingston, Rhode Island
Wes Barry	Orem, Utah
John M. Bealmear	Portales, New Mexico
Elwyn D. Brown	Columbus, Indiana
David D. Casto	Wilmington, Delaware
William C. Chaloner	Aberdeen, South Dakota
George A. Christopher	Port Washington, New York
Lloyd Conley	Clare, Michigan
Jack Connell	Maryville, Tennessee
Carroll H. Copeland	Lafayette, Indiana
H. Bruce Cullings	Las Vegas, Nevada
William C. Curnow, III	Wilmington, Delaware
Frank H. Diener	Choteau, Montana
Dean Dowdy	Madisonville, Kentucky
William Dwyer	New Hyde Park, New York
William L. Ellett	Ely, Nevada
E. Orville Evenson	Aberdeen, South Dakota
James Ferguson	Vicksburg, Mississippi
Glen A. Fifield	Price, Utah
Ralph I. Finn	Pembroke, North Carolina
Kenneth Forbes	Brattleboro, Vermont
Guy F. Foreman	Laporte, Indiana
Kenneth Geoffroy	Shawnee Mission, Kansas
Clinton W. Graffman	Portland, Maine
John R. Graham	Lexington, Kentucky
Harold V. Halvorsen	Powell, Wyoming
Lawrence E. Hanson	Cheyenne, Wyoming
Herbert Hazelman	Greensboro, North Carolina
Richard A. Hazelton	Browning, Montana
Roger C. Heath	Great Falls, Montana

Director or Chairman	*City*
William Higgins	Key West, Florida
Arthur C. Hills	Holland, Michigan
Eugene Holdsworth	Horton, Kansas
H. Vernon Hooker	San Antonio, Texas
Harold Ikola	Grand Marais, Minnesota
William S. Johns	Fort Knox, Kentucky
Dale Kimpton	Quincy, Illinois
Otis Kitchen	Roanoke, Virginia
Robert W. Krueger	Northport, New York
Michael B. Lamade	Bridgeton, New Jersey
Arne B. Larson	Brookings, South Dakota
Aldie D. Long	Big Rapids, Michigan
John M. Long	Montgomery, Alabama
Kelly Love	Starkville, Mississippi
George H. Low	Warwick, Rhode Island
Clifton L. Mix	Montpelier, Vermont
Donald A. Mattran	Durham, New Hampshire
Stuart A. Morash	Lebanon, New Hampshire
Richard Mylin	Lemmon, South Dakota
David C. McCormick	Cicero, Illinois
Mrs. Ileane McElwee	Phoenix, Arizona
Jack McGuin	Anchorage, Alaska
Dean B. Owen	Dighton, Kansas
Andrew Pappas	Cloquet, Minnesota
Hal M. Polk	Forest, Mississippi
E. Richard Prenshaw	Clinton, Mississippi
Robert P. Rabassa	Lewiston, Maine
Charles Rutherford	Greybull, Wyoming
Jerry V. Schreuder	Fort Benton, Montana
Ralph E. Shank	Martinsville, Virginia
Carl V. Smolik	Crown Point, Indiana
Roger C. Snow	Waterville, Maine
Charles L. Steele	Tucson, Arizona
Logan O. Turrentine	Hialeah, Florida
Franklin H. Unger	Lakewood, New Jersey
Edward W. Volz	Mount Prospect, Illinois
Robert B. Vezzetti	Brownsville, Texas

Director or Chairman	City
Robert J. Werner	Evanston, Illinois
Frank B. Wickes	Wilmington, Delaware
O'Dell Willis	Knoxville, Tennessee
Darrell S. Winters	Sparks, Nevada

March: Easy

Title	Composer–Arranger	Publisher
A Santa Cecelia	Radaelli–Brittain	Kjos
Americans We	Fillmore	Fischer
Billboard *†††	Klohr	Church
Brighton Beach	Latham	Summy
Bristol	Yoder	Kjos
Charter Oak	Osterling	Bourne
Chimes of Victory	Bergeim	Boosey–Hawkes
Conroe	Cannan	Kjos
Crimson and Gray	Keller	Keller
DeMolay Commandery	Hall	Jacobs
Dynamarch	Cacavas	Marks
El Gaucho	Mesang	Southern
Emblem of Unity ††††	Richards	Barnhouse
Empire State Salute	Peterson	Kendor
Flashing Brass	Nyquist	Summy
Frat	Barth–Heine	Fox
Gallito †	Lope–Walters	Rubank
Glory of the Sea	Osterling	Associated
Hey, Look Me Over	Leigh–Warrington	Morley
His Honor *†††††	Fillmore	Fischer
Host of Freedom *	King	Barnhouse
Independentia	Hall–Walters	Rubank
La Banda Nacente	Sbraccia	Kjos
Manhattan Beach	Sousa	Presser
Manhattan Beach	Sousa–Buchtel	Kjos
Marching Song, A	Ployhar	Byron–Douglas
March for King's Reg't.*	Lully–Gardner	Staff
March of the Herald	Nicholls–Leist	Mills
March Onward ††	Luthold	Ludwig
Military Escort ***	Bennett	Fillmore
Night Flight	King	Barnhouse
Officer of the Day	Hall	Lyon & Healy

*   indicates one additional director's recommendation.
†   indicates one additional director's recommendation in another category.

Title	Composer–Arranger	Publisher
Pride of the Pacific	Kleffman	Leonard
Salutation	Seitz	Kjos
Sceptre of Liberty	Olivadoti	Rubank
Shamrock †	Conley	Kendor
Sounding Brass	Maxwell	Southern
Storm King **	Finlayson	Boosey–Hawkes
Symbol of Honor	Mesang	Fillmore
Thunder West	Farrell	Leonard
Totem Pole	Osterling	Bourne
Rocket	Thomas	Kjos

March: Medium

Title	Composer–Arranger	Publisher
Amparito Roca **	Texidor–Winter	Boosey–Hawkes
Army of the Nile	Alford	Boosey–Hawkes
Beaded Belts	Erickson	Bourne
Block M	Bilik	Mills
Brighton Beach **††	Latham	Summy
Burst of Flame *†	Bowles	FitzSimons
Black Horse Troop	Sousa	Fox
Citacion	Smith	Wingart–Jones
Coat of Arms *††	Kenney	Summy
Colonel Bogey	Alford	Boosey–Hawkes
Courier-Journal	Griffith	Midwest
Drums and Bells	Yoder	Kjos
El Capitan	Sousa	Church
Emblem of Unity	Richards	Barnhouse
Fairest of the Fair	Sousa	Church
Footlifter, The	Fillmore	Fillmore
Foundation March, The	Goldman	Mercury
Gallito †	Walter	Rubank
G. Washington BiCent.†	Sousa	Church
Golden Gate	Goldman	Belwin
Grandioso †	Seitz	Seitz
Hall of Fame	Olivadoti	Rubank
His Honor ****†	Fillmore	Fillmore
Inglesina †	Delle Cose	Pagani
Invincible Eagle	Sousa	Church
Jubilee ††	Kenney	Summy
Land of Liberty *	Lee	Leonard
Little Giant	Moon	Fischer

Title	Composer–Arranger	Publisher
Manhattan Beach †	Sousa	Presser
March Electric	Creatore–Falcone	Summy
March of Spanish Soldiery	Smetsky–Lake	Ludwig
Moorside	Holst–Jacob	Boosey–Hawkes
Nutmeggers, The	Osterling	Bourne
Onward (Aufwaerts) ††	Luthold	Ludwig
Parading the Brasses †	Ostling	Bourne
Proud Heritage †	Latham	Summy
Shamrock †	Conley	Kendor
Stars & Stripes Forever	Sousa	Presser
Valdres-Marsj †	Hanssen	Norsk Musikforlag
Vanished Army	Alford	Boosey–Hawkes
With Sword and Lance	Starke–Winter	Boosey–Hawkes

March: Difficult

Title	Composer–Arranger	Publisher
American Salute	Gould	Mills
Barnum & Bailey's Favorite **	King	King
Burlesque March	McKay	Associated
Burst of Flame ††	Bowles	FitzSimons
By Joe, The Tuba	Lavalle	Fox
Chicago Tribune *	Chambers–Roberts	Fischer
Closley March	Fillmore	Fischer
Coat of Arms *††	Kenny	Summy
Commando March *	Barber	Schirmer
Crown Imperial **	Walton–Duthoit	Boosey–Hawkes
Dam Busters' March, The	Coates	Chappell
Earl of Oxford, The	Jacob (Wm. Byrd Suite)	Boosey–Hawkes
Emblem of Unity *†††	Richards	Barnhouse
Fanfare and Allegro ††	Williams	Summy
Febrero	Roncal	Boosey–Hawkes
G. Wash. Bicentennial †	Sousa	Fox
Grandioso †	Seitz	Seitz
Heat Lightning	Bowles	FitzSimons
Inglesina †	Delle Cose	Pagani
January-February March	Gillis	Boosey–Hawkes
Jubilee *†	Kenny	Summy

---

    *   indicates one additional director's recommendation.
    †   indicates one additional director's recommendation in another category.

Title	Composer–Arranger	Publisher
Law and Order *	Alford	Alford
March from Suite in Eb †††††††††	Holst	Boosey–Hawkes
March of the Steelmen	Belsterling	Fischer
March with Trumpets	Bergsma	Mercury
Montartre	Wood–Hawkins	Robbins
Onward (Aufwaerts) ††	Luthold	Ludwig
Parading the Brasses †	Ostling	Bourne
Procession of Nobles †††	Rimsky–Korsakov	Fischer
Proud Heritage †	Latham	Summy
Purple Carnival	Alford	Schirmer
Sons of the Brave	Bidgood	Boosey–Hawkes
Stars & Stripes Forever *****†	Sousa	Church
Valdres †	Hanssen	Norsk Musikvorlag
Washington Grays *	Graffula	Fischer
Wings of Victory	Ventre	Fox
Veterans' March	Pares–Cailliet	Fox

Contest: Easy

Title	Composer–Arranger	Publisher
Air for Band	Erickson	Bourne
Air from Peasant Cantata	Bach–Gordon	Kendor
American Scene	Grundman	Boosey–Hawkes
Balladair	Erickson	Bourne
Belmont Overture	Hermann	Educational Movie Service
Berceuse	Loboda	Brodt
Berkshire Hills	Akers	Bourne
Carnival of Roses	Olivadoti	Mills
Cathedral Canyon	E. Hanson	Ludwig
Colonial Rhapsody, A	Madden	Marks
Concert Overture in G Minor	Lillya–Isaac	Fischer
Crusaders, The	Buchtel	Kjos
Eroica Overture †	Beethoven–Skornika	Belwin
First Swedish Rhapsody ††*	Leidzen	Mills
Folk Song Suite †	Williams	Boosey–Hawkes
Fontainbleau Overture	Bennett	Fischer
Gaillard and Courante	Frescobaldi–Johnson	Rubank
Gavotte (3rd Eng. Suite)	Bach–Willhoite	Shawnee
Golden Gate Overture	Erickson	Bourne
Grand Festival Overture	Zamecnik	Fox

Title	Composer–Arranger	Publisher
Green Domino, The	Grundman	Boosey–Hawkes
Green Meadows Overture	Hanson	Ludwig
King John	Moehlmann	Fischer
King Stephen Overture	Beethoven–Cailliet	Fox
Little Classic Suite	Akers	Fischer
Meditation (Thais)	Massenet	Kjos
Military Symphony in F *	Gossec–Goldman	Mercury
Miniature Chorale and Fugue	Carter	Hansen
Overture for Winds **††	Carter	Bourne
Passacaglia and Fugue	Johnson	Fischer
Prelude Act V–King Manfred *†	Reinecke–Osterling	Ludwig
Prelude and Fugue in B♭ Minor	Bach–Moehlmann	FitzSimons
Prelude and Fugue in G Minor	Bach	Remick
Royal Fireworks Music	Handel–Gordon	Shapire–Bernstein
Second Suite for Band †	McBeth	Southern
Slavonic Folk Suite †	Reed	Hansen
Surprise Symphony	Haydn–Kiser	Leonard
Symphony No. 6 Themes †	Tchaikovsky–Johnson	Belwin
Themes from French Ballet	Johnson	Belwin
Three Gates of Gold	Frangkiser	Belwin
Three Modern Chorales	Gordon	Bourne
Toccata for Band **††	Erickson	Bourne
Trauermusch	Mozart	Ludwig
Two Woodland Sketches	MacDowell	Rubank
Waltzes from Symphony No. 5	Dvorak	Rubank

Contest: Medium

Title	Composer–Arranger	Publisher
Afternoon of a Faun	Debussy–Walters	Rubank
Ballad for Band	Gould	Chappell
Ballet Parisien *	Offenbach–Isaac	Fischer
Ceremony for Winds	Cacavas	Bourne
Chorale and Alleluia †	Hansen	Fischer
Court Festival	Latham	Summy
Dance for Three	Rossini–Hazelman	Mills
English Folk Song Suite	Williams	Boosey–Hawkes

---

     *   indicates one additional director's recommendation.
     †   indicates one additional director's recommendation in another category.

Title	Composer–Arranger	Publisher
Eroica Overture †	Beethoven–Skornika	Belwin
Elsa's Procession (Lohengrin) *†††	Wagner–Cailliet	Remick
Fantasy on Amer. Sailing †††	Grundman	Boosey–Hawkes
First Swedish Rhapsody *††	Leidzen	Mills
Good Friday Spell	Wagner	Ludwig
Great Gate of Kiev	Moussorgsky–Eymann	Belwin
Irish Tune from Country Derry †	Grainger	Fischer
Jederman Overture	Whear	Ludwig
Jesu, Joy of Man's Desiring	Bach–Cailliet	Elkan–Vogel
Jesu, Joy of Man's Desiring	Bach–Leidzen	Fischer
Mannen Veen	Wood	Boosey–Hawkes
Meistersinger, Die, excerpts †	Wagner–Osterling	Ludwig
Moses–Portraits from Bible	Work	Shawnee
Mozart Festival	Johnson	Rubank
Original Suite, An	Jacob	Boosey–Hawkes
Pageant ††††	Persichetti	Fischer
Prelude Act V–King Manfred ††	Reinecke–Osterling	Ludwig
Psyche and Eros	Franck–Harding	Kjos
Sequoia	LeGassey	Kjos
Slavonic Dances, Op. 46	Dvorak–Johnson	Rubank
Suite, First, in E♭ ******††††	Holst	Boosey–Hawkes
Suite, Second, in F *†	Holst	Boosey–Hawkes
Symphonic Suite ††	Williams	Summy
Symphony No. 1 (Finale) †	Kalinnikov–Bainum	EdMus Svc.
Symphony No. 2 (Finale)	Erickson	Bourne
Symphony No. 6 Themes †	Tchaikovsky–Johnson	Belwin
Symphony in E♭ (Finale)	Saint-Saëns	Witmark
Toccata †	Frescobaldi	Mills
Toccata for Band ††††	Erickson	Bourne
Universal Judgement ††	DeNardis	Fischer
Variation Overture	Williams	Ludwig
Winter Scenes	Johnson	Belwin

Contest: Difficult

Title	Composer–Arranger	Publisher
Au Pays Lorrain	Balay–Chidester	Fox
American Overture for Band ††	Jenkins	Schmitt

Title	Composer-Arranger	Publisher
Barber of Seville	Rossini–Lake	Fischer
Benvenuto Cellini Overture	Berlioz–Henning	Schirmer
Canzona	Mennin	Fischer
Celebration Overture	Creston	Templeton
Chester Overture **	Schuman	Presser
Chorale and Alleluia †	Hanson	Fischer
Divertimento for Band	Persichetti	Ditson, Presser
Cumberland Gap	Jenkins	Schmitt
Fanfare and Allegro ††	Williams	Summy
Fingal's Cave	Mendelssohn	Fischer
Flying Dutchman Overture	Wagner–Overgard	Schirmer
Four Way Suite	Coates	Chappell
Good Friday Spell	Wagner–Slocum	Mills
Il Guarany Overture †	Gomez–Clark	Fischer
Lincolnshire Posey	Grainger	Schirmer
Meistersinger, Die, excerpts †	Wagner–Osterling	Ludwig
Night on Bald Mountain	Moussorgsky–Paynter	manuscript
North Sea Overture ††	Hermann	EdMus Svc.
Overture 1812 †	Tchaikovsky–Lake	Fischer
Overture for Band	Mendelssohn	Schirmer
Pageant **††	Persichetti	Fischer
Pines of the Appian Way	Respighi	Ricordi
Polka and Fugue (Schwanda) ††	Weinberger–Bainum	Associated
Prairie Overture	Ward	Galaxy
Prelude and Dance †	Creston	Ricordi
Procession of Nobles *††	Korsakov–Leidzen	Fischer
Richard III	Germon–St. Clair	Fox
Sea Portraits †††	LeGassey	Kjos
Suite, First, in E♭ *††††††††	Holst	Boosey–Hawkes
Symphonic Suite ††	Williams	Summy
Symphony No. 1 (Finale) †	Kalinnakov–Bainum	EdMus Svc.
Symphony No. 3	Giannini	Ricordi
Symphony No. 4 (Finale) †	Tchaikovsky–Safranek	Fischer
Symphony No. 5 (Finale)	Shostakovitch–Righter	Boosey–Hawkes
Symphony No. 8 (Unfinished) †	Schubert–Cailliet	Fischer
Symphony in B♭	Hindemith	Schott (Associated)
Symphony, New World (Finale) †	Dvorak–Leidzen	Fischer

---

     *   indicates one additional director's recommendation.
     †   indicates one additional director's recommendation in another category.

Title	Composer-Arranger	Publisher
Toccata †	Frescobaldi–Slocum	Mills
Toccata and Fugue in D minor	Bach–Leidzen	Fischer
Toccata and Fugue in D minor	Bach–Wright	Chappell
Universal Judgement ††	DeNardis	Fischer
William Byrd Suite	Jacobs	Boosey–Hawkes

Program: Easy

Title	Composer-Arranger	Publisher
Alda Overture	McCaughey	Fischer
Allegro, Adagio, Alleluia	Akers	Fischer
American Folk Rhapsody	Grundman	Boosey–Hawkes
Bolero Non	Kurtz	Mills
Café Rio	Cacavas–Gould	Chappell
Calif of Baghdad	Boldieldieu	Fox
Caribeguine	Schaefer	Fischer
Elegy for Moderns	Howard	Kendor
Fantasy–Amer. Sailing Songs **†	Grundman	Boosey–Hawkes
Fantasy for Band †	Erickson	Bourne
Fantasy for Flute	Leader	Leonard
Festival Day Overture	Thomas	Robbins
Folk Song Suite †	Williams	Boosey–Hawkes
Fughetta	Stainer–Righter	Schmitt
Golden Glow Overture	Johnson	Boosey–Hawkes
Gyp. Baron March Paraphrase	Strauss–Walters	Rubank
Hymn of Freedom	Brahms–Tolmadge	Staff
Impressions of Scottish Air	Ployhar	Byron–Douglas
Interval Town	Grundman	Boosey–Hawkes
Joshua	Yoder	Kjos
Kentucky 1800	Grundman	Boosey–Hawkes
Little English Suite	Jackson	Witmark
My Fair Lady †	Lowe–Herfurth	Chappell
Nobody Knows Trouble I've Seen	Ployhar	Byron–Douglas
Oasis *	Kepner	Ludwig
Overture for Billy	Erickson	Bourne
Overture for Winds ††††	Carter	Bourne

Title	Composer-Arranger	Publisher
Panis Angelicus	Franck	Fischer
Parade of the Icicles	Dedrick	Pro–Art
Pastels	McRae	Summy
Pavane	Ravel–Johnson	Rubank
Second Amer. Folk Rhapsody	Grundman	Boosey–Hawkes
Scenes from the Sierras †	Bennett	Fischer
Si Trocadero	Walters	Rubank
Six Little Songs (Nursery)	Myers	Leonard
Slavonic Folk Suite †	Reed	Hansen
Sleeping Beauty	Yoder	Hansen
Street Scene	Newman–Bennett	Robbins
Studio One	Osser	Leeds
Suite Italienne	Bilik	Southern
Summer Evening Serenade	Isaac–Lillya	Fox
Three Sketches for Band	Morrissey	Marks
Toccata for Band *††††	Erickson	Bourne
Toy Symphony	Haydn–Gardner	Staff
Two Hymns (Faith Looks Up)	Mason–Griffith	Midwest
Three Chorale Preludes †	Latham	Summy
Vista Carribean	Ployhar	Summy
Welsh Folk Suite	Davis	Ludwig
Aueignung (Dedication)	Strauss–Davis	Ludwig

Program: Medium

Title	Composer–Arranger	Publisher
Anacapri	Yoder	Elkan–Vogel
Ballet Music from Pr. Igor †	Borodin–Bennett	Mills
Bluebells of Scotland	Anderson	Mills
Blue and Gray, The (Civil War)	Grundman	Boosey–Hawkes
Bolero Espagnol	Lecuona	Marks
Burlesk for Band	Washburn	Boosey–Hawkes
Colorama (Fantasy in Color)	DeRose–Yoder	Big Three
Cuban Fantasy	Kepner	Summy
Driftwood Patterns	Work	Shawnee

---

    *   indicates one additional director's recommendation.
    †   indicates one additional director's recommendation in another category.

Title	Composer–Arranger	Publisher
Elsa's Procession (Lohengrin) ††††	Wagner–Cailliet	Remick
English Folk Song Suite	Williams	Boosey–Hawkes
Fandango	Perkins–Werle	Mills
Fantasia on Alleluia Hymn	Jacob–Duthoit	Chappell
Fantasy for Band †	Erickson	Bourne
Fantasy on Lady of Spain	Evans–Hunsberger	Fox
God and Country Overture	Wingard	Leonard
Grand Symph for Band (Finale)	Berlioz–Goldman	Mercury
Holiday for Winds	Osser	EdMus Svc.
Irish Tune–County Derry †	Grainger	Fischer
Lil' Abner Overture	DePaul–Reed	Commander
Malaguena	Lecuona–Cacavas	Marks
Matador	Cacavas	Bourne
My Fair Lady †	Lowe–Herfurth	Chappell
Ode	Herman	EdMus Svc.
Overture for Winds ††††	Carter	Bourne
Pageant ††††	Persichetti	Fischer
Pensionat, Das	von Suppe–Lake	Ludwig
Peter Schmoll	von Weber–Smith	Pro–Art
Procession of Nobles †††	Korsakov–Leidzen	Fischer
Relax *	Yoder	Kjos
River Jordan	Whitney	Schirmer
Rush Street Tarantella	Yoder	Kjos
Scenes from the Sierras †	Bennett	Fischer
Sea Portrait **†	LeGassey	Kjos
Serenade for Band	Persichetti	Elkan–Vogel
Sound of Music, The *	Rodgers–Bennett	Williamson
St. Lawrence Suite	Gould	Chappell
Suite Francaise	Milhaud	Leeds
Suite, First in E♭ ††††††††††	Holst	Boosey–Hawkes
Suite, Second in F ††	Holst	Boosey–Hawkes
Symphony in C minor	Williams	Morris
Three Chorale Preludes †	Latham	Summy
Trauersinfonie	Wagner–Leidzen	Associated
Variations on a Folksong	Schuman–Erickson	Bourne
Victor Herbert's Favorites	Herbert–Lake	Witmark
Viva Mexico Suite	Morrissey	Marks
Voice of Freedom	Rubinstein–Cailliet	Boosey–Hawkes
Water Music Suite	Handel–Kay	Presser
Windjammer	Gould–Yoder	Chappell
Yellowstone Suite *	Klein	Boosey–Hawkes

Program: Difficult

Title	Composer–Arranger	Publisher
American Overture for Band *†	Jenkins	Schmitt
Ballet Music–Faust	Gounod–Laurendeau	Fischer
Ballet Music–Prince Igor †	Borodin–Bennett	Mills
Candide Overture	Bernstein–Beeler	Schirmer
Carousel Waltz	Rodgers	Chappell
Dixie Fantasy	Cailliet	Boosey–Hawkes
Elsa's Procession (Lohengrin) *†††	Wagner–Cailliet	Remick
Euryanthe	von Weber	Fischer
Fanfare and Allegro ††	Williams	Summy
Fledermaus, Die	Strauss–Cailliet	Boosey–Hawkes
Gay Nineties Ov. for Band	Lang	Mills
Geo. Washington Bridge	Schuman	Schirmer
Gypsy's Five Side Dream	Fultz	Mills
Hurricane	Yoder	Kjos
Il Guarany †	Gomez–Clark	Fischer
Incantation and Dance	Chance	Boosey–Hawkes
Italian In Algiers	Rossini–Cailliet	Fox
Jericho Rhapsody	Gould	Mills
Kiddie Ballet	Hermann	EdMus Svc.
La Fiesta Mexicana	Reed	Mills
Mademoiselle Angot (Ballet)	Lecoca–Mohanpt	AMP
Music for a Festival	Jacob	Boosey–Hawkes
Nordic Symphony	Hanson	Summy
North Sea Overture *†	Hermann	EdMus Svc.
Overture 1812 †	Tchaikovsky–Lake	Fischer
Parade of the Charioteers	Rozsa	Big Three
Polka and Fugue (Schwanda) *†	Weinberger–Bainum	Associated
Porgy and Bess	Gershwin–Bennett	Gershwin
Prelude and Dance †	Creston	Ricordi
Second Suite for Band †	McBeth	Southern
Serenato	Anderson	Mills
Siegfried's Rhine Journey	Wagner–Cailliet	Remick
Solemn Fugue	Williams	Summy
Suite of Old Amer. Dances ***	Bennett	Chappell

---

*   indicates one additional director's recommendation.
†   indicates one additional director's recommendation in another category.

Title	Composer–Arranger	Publisher
Symphony for Band, First	Erickson	Bourne
Symphony No. 4 (Finale) †	Tchaikovsky–Safranek	Fischer
Symphony No. 8 (Unfinished) †	Schubert	Fischer
Symphonic Suite ††	Williams	Summy
Tap Roots	Skinner	Skinner
Tristan and Isolde–Liebestod *	Wagner–Godfrey	Boosey–Hawkes
Tulsa **	Gillis	Mills
Universal Judgement ††	DeNardis	Fischer
Waltzes from Rosenkavalier	Strauss–Cailliet	Boosey–Hawkes
West Side Story–Prologue	Bernstein–Gilmore	Schirmer
West Side Story–Selections *	Bernstein–Duthoit	Schirmer, Chappell

NELSON KEYES *is currently Composer-in-Residence for the city of Louisville, Kentucky. Under a grant from the Ford Foundation he devotes a third of his time to the public schools, a third to the University of Louisville, and a third to individual organizations. He has studied composition with Kent Kennan, Wilbur Ogdon, Arnold Schoenberg, Halsey Stevens, and Ingolf Dahl. His teaching positions have been with the Los Angeles City Schools, Long Beach (Cal.) City College, University of Southern California. He spent two years (1961–63) as a Ford Foundation Composer for the Louisville Public Schools where he had an opportunity to practice what he suggests in the piece which follows.*

THE BAND DIRECTOR AS COMPOSER

The perplexing problem of repertoire, especially new repertoire, is a permanent and often unwelcome companion of the conscientious band conductor. The search for interesting, fresh, appropriate material usually involves examination of many works, which are not suitable, in order to find one which comes close to serving a given purpose. Too often the searcher falls back on familiar material, performs the same few pieces again and again, and fails to broaden his own horizons or those of his students.

A potentially rich and, for the most part untapped, source of music for band is the director himself, writing arrangements and original pieces for his own particular group. Even a director who has little writing experience possesses the great advantage of intimate knowledge of his players' abilities, and he can compose or arrange for the exact instrumentation of his group. And as the training offered by American music departments grows in breadth and quality, more and more music education graduates will have the necessary skills and background for efforts in this direction.

The principal reason for specially written material is the wide variation among bands in size, instrumentation, and ability. Published pieces must be playable by a number of different instrumentations, which results in cross-cueing of solos, overloading of other parts, and a waste of the great variety of color available in the wind ensemble. All of these difficulties disappear in music intended for one particular group; solos can be given to the strongest players, easy parts to the weakest, and doubling for the unmusical reasons of security and optional instrumentation can be done away with.

Appropriate training for the director-composer is already available and in some cases required in music education curricula. Such training should include studies in counterpoint, instrumentation, orchestration, and band arranging as well as composition and music structure. A broad knowledge of twentieth century music would be necessary to keep the director-composer's works from being a pale imitation of older styles. Of course, even the best education will not make every director a respectable composer, and it is not suggested that all directors write for publication—in fact, just the opposite—but it is a reasonable supposition that an energetic and talented director can create valuable material for his own players and frequently improve on the typical commercial product of the publishers.

The conductor who is dubious of his creative abilities can begin writing with arrangements of simple tunes, composition of warm-up exercises, or other uncomplicated pieces that his band has need of. From these he can proceed to transcriptions of larger pieces—the Baroque organ repertoire is a large and excellent source—or to original works of modest size. Whatever he writes will be tailor-made for the group and therefore worth his time and effort.

CHAPTER

The
Feeder
System

by **Charles S. Peters**

Joliet, Illinois

Charles S. Peters

is Supervisor of Instrumental Music for the Joliet, Illinois Public Schools (Grades 1–8). Born in Joliet in 1913 (the year the Joliet Boy's Band was organized), he played in both the grade school and high school bands, and was appointed director of the Championship Joliet Grade School Band on October 14, 1942. He was elected to the American Bandmasters Association in 1957, the only grade school director to be so honored.

Mr. Peters began the study of the cornet, at the age of nine, with Mrs. Jessie Fields (a pupil of H. A. Vandercook who founded the Vandercook School of Music which Peters later attended). He also studied at the Chicago Symphony and Roosevelt College Schools of Music, Joliet Junior College, and Western State Teachers College of Kalamazoo, Michigan. He played trumpet professionally for radio station WLS (NBC) in Chicago.

"Chuck" Peters, the author of the *Master Method for Band* series, has appeared as speaker, soloist, adjudicator, and guest conductor in nearly every state of the Union.

When the Joliet Grade School Concert Band won so many first place awards that it was given an Honorary Division I Superior Rating and asked to present a concert rather than compete, Director Peters secured permission for the training band to enter instead. This second band then proceeded to win first division ratings each year. Joliet students have won over 6,000 first place medals during Mr. Peters' tenure as director.

152

"They say that in Joliet babies teethe on oboe reeds," narrator Jimmy Stewart quips in the film *Holiday for Bands*, for which our band provided the background music. Although we wish that were true, we find that we have to sell our program just as hard as any other band in the United States.

No organization can continue to be effective without a strong recruiting and training program. Since the relatively short time a student spends in high school does not allow sufficient time for effective training *and* performance at an acceptable level, high school directors must build their programs on the basic training the students receive in a junior high band. Obviously the level of eventual attainment possible in the most experienced performing organization is determined in large measure by the musical level at which the students enter that group.

A junior high band, however, at the same time it serves as a feeder for the high school band also demands a feeder system of its own. For the ultimate goal we have set for our students in Joliet, beginning in the fourth grade is a must. We progress slowly but solidly, in the beginning, start a little acceleration in the fifth and sixth grades, and give them a big push in the seventh and eighth.[1]

The successful high school instrumental music program must include a triple level of feeders—beginner to elementary, elementary to junior high, and junior high to high school—with an over-all plan and smooth transitions between phases.

---

[1] This has resulted in a band of symphonic proportions, consistently superior ratings at contests, and polished performances of university and professional level literature.—*Ed.*

The children in Joliet are not "special," although they are good kids and we like them very much.

The school board does not spend unusual sums on the band, and, although we receive considerable support, they actually spend less per capita than most schools.[2]

We do not take students out of class unreasonably. One of our administrators told me: "Chuck, before I came here everybody told me that you even taught arithmetic with band instruments in Joliet, and I thought I would really have some problems . . . well, I've found that you take the students out of class *less* than the other three schools with which I have been associated."

We do work hard. Our students, parents, and instructional staff have found that there is no substitute for hard work. You must work hard to build, and even harder to maintain, a good program.

We do have the full cooperation of the parents. I spend a great deal of time and effort in personal interviews and phone calls making certain that the parents understand our program. I feel that our drop-out rate of approximately five percent is a direct result of this effort, since of those students who do drop, we have found that about 90 percent have parents who are not interested.

Most students do study privately. The system is an outgrowth of a "buddy system" begun many years ago which utilizes advanced players and alumni as the majority of the teachers.

THE PARENTS

It is very easy for each of us to become so involved in what we are doing that we assume everyone in town knows about it. Recently we opened up a new music department in a school which had been in Joliet for over 50 years. Many people who came to our band parents meeting there had never been in the school before, although they had spent their entire lives in Joliet. They had seen the band on parade and read about it in the paper occasionally, but had never *really noticed* until their child reached the age when he had an opportunity to start playing an instrument. We must sell each new group of parents.

---

[2] About $5,000 annually for 650 students enrolled.

Every detail of the students' life in the band from beginners' classes to graduation is explained at the very first meeting with the parents who are interested in enrolling their children in the program. We leave no stone unturned, and they realize that their children are embarking on a worthwhile endeavor.

These parents, just as others in communities all over the world, feel that their children gain many things in addition to music training from band membership. One of our parents, Dorothy N. Fletcher, has expressed this feeling in a poem:

To MR. CHARLES PETERS

by *Dorothy N. Fletcher*

I guess he hypnotizes them
Yes, I'm sure it's true
Otherwise, how would he get them,
To do the things they do.
Skip hardly ever washed his face,
And never combed his hair.
But now he always does them both,
I simply stand and stare—
He's perfectly willing to wash his hands,
And always wants a clean shirt.
Of course, I really am quite pleased
But, just a little hurt.
To think for years I have tried
To influence him this way;
To help improve these habits
I've done everything, I say.
All at once it is important,
To always be on time.
I can't help it, I simply wonder
If it is that "Boy of Mine."
It's—Mr. Peters will and Mr. Peters won't—
It's—Mr. Peters says and Mr. Peters don't.
I know there are other mothers
Who feel just as I do,
But might not remember
To say these things to you.
So—little by little
I'm beginning to understand;
That my son learns more than music
In Mr. Peters' band.

Rehearsals and Meetings

We invite the parents to our beginners' and elementary rehearsals on Saturday mornings and to our City Band practice on Monday evenings. Each week we have 50 to 60 parents observing each session. We rehearse just exactly as if we were behind locked doors. If a student gets into trouble, he receives the same treatment as he would if the parents were not there. The parents like it that way.

Parents sign in at each of the nine meetings of the Band Parents Association and the students get credit for their attendance. At the end of every meeting we announce the number present and the percentage of the people from each school who have come out. One of our performing groups plays at each of the meetings, and their parents always turn out 100 percent.

Many years ago I noticed that the children of the parents who were interested enough to come and talk with me about the program and who understood what I was trying to do, became the top-notch players. On the other hand, the students who didn't produce too much —even though they had talent—were the ones whose parents seemed to be unconcerned. Ever since, I have spent almost as much time explaining the band program to the parents as I have spent teaching the students.

PRIVATE LESSONS

Our version of individual instruction started out many years ago with a "buddy system" in which the older, more experienced, players were teamed with the beginners. This personal attention not only helped the "students" a great deal, but the "teachers," who were extremely proud of their positions, learned a lot themselves—just as every band director learns *so* much when he actually gets out of school and begins to apply what he has gathered from books.

As the "older buddies" entered high school they began to charge the younger ones 25 cents for a lesson, and, as junior college students, increased their fee to one dollar. In 1926–27 when I was a student in the Joliet Grade School Band, the price had reached $1.50, and most of our teachers have held that line ever since!

Of the approximately 50 people who teach these private lessons, less than five are full-time professionals. The others are band and orchestra alumni who do it to assist and perpetuate the program which helped them in the same way.

This system is a tradition in Joliet, and almost every band student takes one lesson per week. A similar plan can be initiated in any community by asking the older players to help the younger ones. After all, a traditional practice has not existed forever, but has had a *beginning* at some definite point in the past.

SCHOOL STAFF AND
SCHEDULE

In addition to my position as supervisor, the school board has provided for two band and two orchestra instructors. Each two-man team has charge of a junior high (7–8 grade), and the elementary schools which feed it.

For the first 44 years of the band's life all rehearsals were held outside of school time (noon, before and after school, evenings, and Saturdays). Since 1956 some school time has been used.

Grades 1–3. Public School Music Classes. These concern singing and the enjoyment and appreciation of music. Some of the classroom teachers—on their own—teach pre-band instruments, but we have no concentrated program. If I had the time and the staff, I would schedule pre-band instrument classes in every elementary school. Every student would also study drums (on the pad) for one semester: counting time is that important.

Grade 4. Beginner Band. Classes are held once a week on school time (40–60 minutes) during their general music class time, and on Saturday morning (90 minutes). Most students take one private lesson per week.

Grades 5–6. Intermediate (Training) Bands. Classes and lessons continue as in the fourth grade. Bands are formed.

Grades 7–8. Junior High Band. Full band rehearsals are held five times per week during the school day. Section rehearsals are held before school. The top players are selected for the All-City Band.

RECRUITING

During the spring we introduce the instruments in each third grade room, using large pictures, recordings, and playing demonstrations by advanced students and instructors. We create a lot of interest by passing the instruments around and letting the students actually hold them.

After the summer vacation we go back to see these children who are now in the fourth grade and give them our own aptitude test, which includes part of the McCreary and Pan American tests, as well as some of our own devices. Although we feel that there is no completely valid aptitude test for instrumental music, the excitement of taking the test builds interest and the test itself does help us to find some of the better students.

We list the top 50 percent (usually about 500 students), and ask each teacher to recommend those who are the most promising, who would benefit from the program, and who are academically capable. Since there is also some expense involved, we ask the teachers about the family's financial condition. After these conferences, we send out about 300 letters of invitation to the parents.

Those who come to the meeting announced in the letter hear a very thorough explanation of the entire program. They are told very explicitly what we expect from them and what they can expect from us. In a general information sheet for beginners we express our idea of this fair exchange of effort:

> The Joliet Grade School Band is known throughout the U.S. and Canada as the finest. We consider it an honor for any of the boys [3] to be a part of this renowned group. We expect to keep our good name. This is done with the finest staff money can buy plus the most interested boys and parents we can find.

We discuss absolutely everything at the meeting and the parents can sense that it is a big program and a good program. We are so thorough that they go away feeling that we are really going to give them something worthwhile.

We ask those who are still interested to send their children the following Saturday morning. Since we are a public school, we do not exclude anyone who wants to start.

CLASS ORGANIZATION

On Saturday mornings we conduct a class in music fundamentals for all the beginners. There is a lot of blackboard work, with the em-

---

[3] Joliet has been a "Boy's Band" since its organization in 1913.

phasis on counting time. During the four to five weeks spent on this instruction, the directors are contacting parents and allowing students to try the instruments.

We keep an eye on balance, but in most cases the students start on the instrument of their choice. Instruments are furnished by the school for a six-month period. After that time the parents buy an instrument from the dealer of their choice. A letter is sent to indicate when they should make this decision. Trial-rental plans can be used in communities which do not have enough instruments to provide this service.

Using a Method Book

The use of supplementary material is necessary no matter what book you are using. My *Master Method for Band Series, First, Second, and Third Performance* books, and the *Master Drills* book [4] are mostly a compilation of the mimeographed material I have written and used over a long period of time to supplement all of the many fine method books we have had through the years. Even though our students go through the *Master Method* series, I still use additional mimeographed material to supplement them.

Progress

Learning fundamentals thoroughly pays off later. We do not feel that the students have to go home the first day and "play a tune for mother"; and, since we have explained the program so thoroughly to the parents, "mother" does not expect it.

During the first two weeks we spend a lot of time with the mouthpieces alone, playing the whole notes and the whole rests on the first page of the book. We stress a hard, correct embouchure in the very beginning, because we know that no matter how long an advanced band works on intonation, they will never be able to play in tune if the embouchures are basically incorrect.

The further along we go in the book, the slower we go because we are always going back to review. If the students are not taught a system of counting time you will always have to teach them each new piece by rote. As soon as we reach quarter notes we go back and play the whole notes in the first lesson as four quarters; when we hit eighth notes we return to the beginning and "trade in" all notes for eighths.

---

[4] Published by Neil A. Kjos Music Co., Park Ridge, Illinois.

Sometimes we have the lower instruments play as written, the middle range play as quarter notes, and the high ones divide into eighth notes. All combinations are used and the student soon begins to understand the 2:1 relationship between eighth, quarter, half, and whole notes.

This same review technique is used when we teach various articulations, three volumes (loud, medium, soft), and three speeds (fast, medium, slow). When we return to the early pages the student can concentrate on that one new item we have just introduced, without the added problems of range, fingering, etc. found on the later pages.

All beginners have their instruments before November 1, and by the following summer (when the beginners enter the 5th–6th grade training bands) we are ready to start on Book II, but continue to review Book I. Whenever a student runs into difficulties, we inform his parents by checking appropriate items on a form letter.

MAKING THE TRANSITIONS

It is important that the same basic procedure be used in both the training and the advanced bands. Instrumentation must be balanced, and younger students must be brought along at the proper time to take over the responsibilities of members who graduate. The turnover should be controlled so that a solid nucleus of outstanding players remains from one year to the next, avoiding "good" and "bad" years as much as possible.

There should be a logical progression in difficulty of music from one group to the other. We have a number of filing cabinets reserved exclusively for our training band library, and the directors try to take the students through a good portion of it during the two years they spend in this organization.

The Fifth and Sixth Grade Band serves as the direct feeder for the advanced junior high bands. As supervisor of the grade school instrumental music program I am in a position to maintain these important controls, as can the many directors who handle the entire program from beginning through high school band all by themselves. In larger systems it is important for the elementary, junior high, and high school directors to meet periodically to plan a unified approach to their individual programs.

An eight-week summer schedule is financed by the Joliet Band

Parents Association. There is no charge to the students, but attendance is required of all who are in town. Vacation excuses must be sent, with dates, in advance.

During this time we form our bands for the coming year: the beginners move up to the Fifth and Sixth Grade Bands; sixth graders move to the new Seventh and Eighth Grade Bands; the eighth graders go on to high school. In this way we have the membership of each group set for the opening of school in September, and avoid the uncertainty of organization, and lack of controlled movement from one phase to the next which leads to disinterest and eventual dropping out.

HOME PRACTICE

We feel that each student should spend five hours a week in practice on his own at home; however, the program is so interesting and challenging that many do much more than that. Each student plays in a recital twice a year, and is a member of an ensemble; some play in the stage band; the concert bands play numerous programs from a difficult repertoire. They do not have any trouble filling their five hours.

"The Musical Partnership" which we distribute to the parents, explains in no uncertain terms what is expected of them in respect to the home practice of their children.

THE MUSICAL PARTNERSHIP

Parents and Home Practice
Are an Integral Part of
Success

There is scarcely a more neglected area in the field of instrumental music than that of parent-teacher relationships. The successful and superior student is invariably backed up by an enlightened and progressive parent.

Music study is a three-way partnership composed of teacher, student, and parents. Each member of the partnership has a responsibility. Most parents are eager to be active members of the musical partnership, but need guidance and definition.

Parents' Responsibilities

What are the parents' responsibilities in the musical partnership?

THE MUSICAL PARTNERSHIP (*cont.*)

1. PATIENCE, in repeatedly reminding the student to do his daily stint at his instrument, and in doing this kindly but firmly.
2. ENCOURAGEMENT, when the going is rough. Some things in music are learned easily; others require intensive and repeated application. Parental sympathy and understanding are important.
3. IMAGINATION, in creating a musical atmosphere in the home by tuning in interesting musical programs on radio and TV; inviting into the home friends who also play, and making playing for one another a part of the occasion; adding an attractive recording to the record collection at frequent intervals.
4. COMMON SENSE, in avoiding undue stress on musical work. All healthy children want and need a considerable daily portion of vigorous physical activity. Trying for a balanced schedule of interests into which music practice fits as a natural and compensating element will pay big musical dividends.

Favorable Practice Conditions

As a young person advances in his music study and is presented with increasingly difficult problems in thinking and playing music, the regularity and quality of his preparation become more and more important. Regularity and quality can be promoted if parents will assume the responsibility for seeing that favorable practice conditions are assured. Here are some suggestions as to how this can be achieved:

1. Schedule a regular time for practice. Mornings are best, when minds and bodies are fresh and receptive.
2. See that proper physical conditions prevail: a quiet room, adequate lighting on the music stand, sufficient ventilation, comfortable temperature.
3. Keep instruments well-tuned and in first-rate mechanical condition. Nothing is more discouraging than an out-of-tune piano, a clarinet key that sticks, or a saxophone reed that is defective.
4. Praise work well-done. A congratulatory remark may be interjected during a practice session, or a complimentary comment made later during mealtime.
5. *Never* use practice as punishment. It is advisable occasionally to reschedule a practice period to allow for important conflicting school events, but avoid giving preference to any and all conflicting activities over the practice schedule.

THE MUSICAL PARTNERSHIP (*cont.*)

Parental Help

1. Remind him to practice *new* work *first.*
2. When wrong notes and hesitations keep recurring, suggest:

   a. Practicing in short sections, a few measures at a time.
   b. Practicing more slowly.
   c. Checking carefully the written notes to make sure they have been accurately read.

Parents *can* and *must* have the firmness to insist on what they know is best in the long view, regardless of the frequency, length and volume of resistance. Sustaining interest is a real and difficult problem, and it is perhaps in this aspect of music study where parental action is most important.

THE BUDGET

The school pays instructors' salaries, purchases the percussion equipment, all music, and pays for the repair of the instruments. The Band Parents Association buys all of the instruments used in the beginner program, and the larger instruments in the concert bands, all of which they turn over to the school.

The Parents Association produces a souvenir yearbook. The sale of advertisements alone usually results in an income of about $8,000. The following is a typical proposed budget of the B.P.A., with conservative estimates of income.

Income

Balance Brought Forward	528.70
Band Parent Dues	550.00
Souvenir Yearbook	6500.00
Christmas Concert	1300.00
Spring Concert	1300.00
Rummage Sale	200.00
Ice Cream Social	450.00
Special Project	1600.00
Miscellaneous	400.00
	$12,828.70

Expenditures

Band Camp	700.00
Contest Expenses	1900.00
Graduation Pins	200.00
Instrument Replacement	3191.00
Band Picnic	155.00
School Musician Magazine	147.00
Secretary & Office Expense	735.00
Special Trips	3000.00
Uniforms	1000.00
Summer Band—2 Recitals—Band Camp	1000.00
Convention Expenses	300.00
Miscellaneous	500.70

$12,828.70

TRIPS

Although trips help to make a program popular with the students, they rank way below good parent relationships as a "secret of success." We have a quota system, worked out with the parents, which sets the number of tickets each student sells for the Pre-Christmas and Spring Band Concerts:

Beginners	4
5th–6th Grade	6
Junior High	8

It is a wonderful feeling for the students who have worked so hard preparing for a concert to see a full house when the curtain opens. If they do not care to sell the tickets, they can pay their own way on the trips, but it always costs a great deal, so they sell the tickets.

Periodically we have a "double the quota" trip for the students who have sold twice as many tickets as the minimum required. These trips are strictly for pleasure, often to nearby Chicago for Cinerama, the Symphony, baseball games, Museum of Science and Industry, Kungsholm Restaurant, the puppet show, etc.

The City Band takes a three- to five-day trip every year, spending between five and ten thousand dollars. We have been to New York, California, Mexico, usually taking a long trip about every third year.

BAND . . . AND ORCHESTRA?

I have always believed that a complete school music education program should offer band, orchestra, and choral music. I appeared before the school board twice a year for 12 years, until they finally gave me permission to hire an orchestra director.

Joliet has been a *Boy's Band* from the beginning. Since we have always had a waiting list of boys, putting girls in would only result in putting boys out, and we have never felt that was any improvement.

For this reason, girls make up about 90 percent of the orchestra, but each year more boys are entering. The program is gradually growing in size and strength. It was started in 1953, whereas the band was organized in 1913.

The two organizations are run side by side: every class, every concert, every picnic, every trip for the band is matched with a similar experience for the orchestra. We hope that someday girls will have a choice between band and orchestra, but we do not want to take a chance on losing the orchestra by allowing that choice too soon.

WHERE IS THE END?

In over 25 years of teaching instrumental music I have never found the upper achievement limit of grade school youngsters, no matter how I have challenged them. Even the year we performed my transcription of the Tchaikovsky *Pathetique Symphony* they had not reached their limit, although that was as hard as I have ever pushed a group (or myself!).[5]

You must create a program which is a constant challenge to all the students, regardless of their age, ability, or how much additional effort they want to put into it. The wonderful thing about music is that no matter what the present level of achievement may be, there is always something *more* to look forward to. There is not a parent or child in our program who has any thought that there is an *end* anywhere . . . they feel that the whole process is just a constant cycle of achieving success, and then setting new goals.

---

[5] The spontaneous eight-minute standing ovation given by the 5,000 band directors at the 1955 Midwest National Band Clinic—which, incontinently, just seemed to explode at the end of the *Pathetique's* third movement—stands out as the highlight of the entire history of Joliet Grade School Bands.—*Ed.*

CHAPTER

Physical Facilities

And

Equipment

by **Mark H. Hindsley**

University of Illinois

Mark H. Hindsley

is Director of Bands, University of Illinois. Under his guidance the Football Band ("Marching Illini") gained tremendous prestige and set extremely high standards which have not yet been surpassed. As Director of Instrumental Music in Cleveland Heights, Ohio, he brought the band from an enrollment of 18 to a first division rating in the national contest in less than four years. This was the only band ever to receive top ratings in concert playing, sight reading, and marching—all in a single year.

Mr. Hindsley was born in Randolph County, Indiana, in 1905, attended Indiana University where he was solo cornetist in the band, and was graduated (*Phi Beta Kappa*) with the highest scholastic honors—in Chemistry! He served as musical director of the Concert Band and of the famous "Marching Hundred" for the four years following his graduation.

In 1934 he became assistant director under A. A. Harding, "Father of the School Band," at the University of Illinois. During World War II he received a direct commission in the Air Force and rose to the rank of lieutenant colonel.

He has written numerous authoritative books and articles, including a still standard reference work among music educators, *School Band and Orchestra Administration*, which Boosey & Hawkes published in 1940.

An authority on wind instrument intonation, his research and inventions have influenced manufacturers in both Europe and America.

168

Physical facilities and equipment do not make the band. Outstanding organizations have grown up in the very poorest of surroundings, but an efficient rehearsal area, adequate storage space, convenient auxiliary rooms, and quality equipment can help a good band to be better.

PRODUCE FIRST

Proper facilities [1] are usually not provided until the program, often working under extreme handicaps, has proven itself. This, paradoxical as it may seem, is a fact of life which band directors have had to face.

The University of Illinois Band was taken over by A. A. Harding (when he was a senior in the college of engineering in 1905) and carried to a position of great fame. In 1928 the band was assigned a barracks type building—a hold-over from World War I. Money was appropriated in 1941 for a new plant, but World War II caused cancellation of construction, and it took until 1955 to get the appropriation back again. Since the present structure is located on the site of the old building, the year of razing and construction was a hectic one for us.

---

[1] Although the thrill of planning a new building of the magnitude of the magnificent University of Illinois Band Building has come only once in the lifetime of only one man (the author of this chapter), the *principles of planning and procedure* employed by Mr. Hindsley and his staff may be used in providing facilities for an instrumental program of any size and a community population in any stage of prosperity. The material is shared freely by Mr. Hindsley in the belief that his experiences connected with this construction opportunity (rare even at University level) will help others who may find themselves with a similar opportunity in their own communities.—*Ed.*

In University President David Dodds Henry's dedicatory address (March 7, 1958), he indicated that this $846,000 Band Building (as well as those of other departments on the campus) had been provided because of the success which the particular program had *already achieved* without it.

Figure 16: The $846,000 University of Illinois Band Building, dedicated in March 1958.

POPULATION EXPLOSION

As school bands gain more popularity each year, and school construction continues to break each previous record, many directors find that they have the heretofore rare opportunity of enjoying modern facilities. In many cases they actively participate in planning for them.

When making plans for the construction of band facilities, communication and cooperation between all participants in the project is essential to its ultimate success. A professional atmosphere of mutual respect in which no one either attempts to usurp the authority of another, or hesitates to offer suggestions out of his field, must be established and maintained.

The administrator secures the money, hires the others who will work on the job, sets limitations of space and cost, and coordinates all efforts; he determines *when* it will be done. *The band director* serves as the expert advisor on what is needed—now and in the future—

for the department. He must be ready with definite recommendations, based on experience and research; he determines *what* needs to be done. *The architect* plans facilities to meet the needs determined by the administration and the band director; he determines *how* it will be done. *The contractor* carries out the plan of the architect with all speed, ability, and economy; he *does* it.

PLAN—CRITICIZE—SOLVE

We were extremely fortunate to have the University of Illinois staff architects assigned to our project. Not only were they readily accessible for conferences, but they were also quite familiar with, and deeply interested in, the work of our musical organizations.

Every member of our staff was consulted as frequently as possible, but the man who was most closely associated with me in the formulation of plans, the actual development of the building process, and the selection and accumulation of equipment was Guy M. Duker, my administrative assistant, who is our buildings and equipment specialist in the department (*see* Fig. 17).

Figure 17: Guy M. Duker, Assistant to the Director of Bands at the University of Illinois since 1953, is an Associate Professor of Music. He is very active in the College Band Directors National Association.

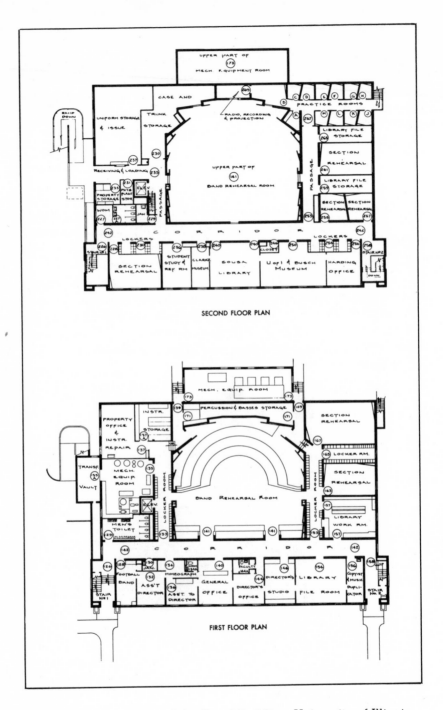

SECOND FLOOR PLAN

FIRST FLOOR PLAN

Figure 18: Floor Plans of the Band Building, University of Illinois.

172

First we prepared a list of the rooms desired, including the approximate sizes, explanation of the functions, and requirements of physical relationships and traffic patterns between rooms. Our contact with the architect then fell into a pattern:

1. They would submit a plan.
2. We would study it and make suggestions.
3. They would submit a new plan.
4. We would make new suggestions, etc.

The unique markings on the floor of our rehearsal area are a good example of the valuable suggestions which can come from the sort of close cooperation we enjoyed. From our mimeographed seating chart, the idea developed that the expansion dividers, necessary in terrazzo floor construction, be placed in such a position they they would outline a separate section for pairs of chairs and for music stands. The terrazzo was tinted one shade in the chair areas and another in the stand areas, adding both to the beauty and efficiency of our rehearsal room.

Figure 18 shows the floor plans of both the first and second floors. The dimensions and functions of the major areas are as follows:

FIRST FLOOR

Room	Size	Function
128	9' 8" × 21'4"	Football Band Office
132	13' 4" × 16'0"	Assistant Director's Office
136	15' 2" × 12'0"	Assistant to the Director's Office
137	26' 0" × 16'0"	Property Office and
	8' 0" × 7'0"	Instrument Repair
137A	11' 4" × 17'8"	Instrument Storage
140	16' 8" × 21'4"	General Administrative Office
141	64' 0" × 58'0"	Band Rehearsal Room
144	15' 8" × 13'8"	Director's Office
146	14' 4" × 21'4"	Director's Studio
154	24' 8" × 21'4"	Library File Room
156	8' 0" × 21'4"	Copying and Duplicating Room
157	20' 0" × 25'0"	Library Work Room
163	15' 4" × 25'0"	Section Rehearsal
167	33' 8" × 20'0"	Section Rehearsal
171	54' 0" × 6'0" (10'8")	Percussion and Bass Storage

SECOND FLOOR

Room	Size	Function
228	24′ 8″ × 17′0″	Section Rehearsal
	4′ 8″ × 4′4″	
233	9′ 5″ × 12′0″	Property Storage
236	13′10″ × 19′4″	Student Study and Reference Room
	9′ 2″ × 2′0″	
237	22′ 0″ × 37′4″	Uniform Storage and Issue
	11′ 0″ × 6′0″	
238	8′ 4″ × 19′4″	Herbert L. Clarke Library
239	642 sq. ft. (irreg.)	Case and Trunk Storage
240	21′ 4″ × 24′0″	John Philip Sousa Library
250	16′ 0″ × 31′4″	University of Ill. and Busch Museum
	14′ 0″ × 5′4″	
255	12′ 4″ × 13′0″ (11′0″)	Section Rehearsal
256	16′ 4″ × 16′0″	A. A. Harding Office
	4′ 8″ × 5′4″	
257	12′ 4″ × 13′0″ (11′0″)	Section Rehearsal
259	25′ 0″ × 8′4″	Library File Storage
261	25′ 0″ × 15′0″	Section Rehearsal
265	25′ 0″ × 8′0″	Library File Storage
267A	50 sq. ft. (irreg.)	Individual Practice Room
267B	100 sq. ft. (irreg.)	Football Band Chart Room
267C-M	7′ 4″ × 7′0″ (5′ 4″)	Individual Practice Rooms
269	16′ 0″ × 6′0″	Radio, Recording and Projection
Load	33′ 8″ × 8′6″ (6′10″)	Receiving and Loading Passage

CORRIDORS

Area number	Width
133	5′0″
139	4′8″
142	8′0″
153	5′0″
169	4′8″
235	5′0″
242	8′0″
253	7′8″ (5′4″)
267	6′2″ (4′8″)

LOCKER ROOMS

Room number	Size
165	8′ 4″ × 25′0″
230	20′10″ × 5′0″
254	20′ 0″ × 5′0″

THE FLOOR PLAN

The band rehearsal room is the heart of the entire plant. Students must have quick and easy physical access to the room through oversized doors. A large receiving and loading platform which opens to the street will assist in getting the equipment in and out.

The band's "home" should be close to the usual performance areas: auditorium stage, gym, football field. Auxiliary rooms must be located in such a way that a smooth, logical traffic pattern develops.

Sound can be isolated from the rest of the building by wise placement of corridors and storerooms to serve as buffers. Facilities for the storage, issue, and care of instruments, uniforms, music and other properties must also be provided. Both individual and section practice rooms are desirable.

In the Illinois building, bass and percussion instruments are stored in a long, closed corridor immediately to the rear of the rehearsal room (in an area which is often waste space behind band risers). Individual lockers in several corridors and locker rooms are provided for players of all instruments, where they are available throughout the day without disturbing rehearsals. Corridor wall space is available for pictures of past organizations and other "atmosphere" items. We have five rooms devoted to library associated functions, an instrument repair shop, four rest rooms, six section rehearsal rooms, and twelve individual practice rooms. There are also special rooms provided for the John Philip Sousa Library, the Herbert L. Clarke Library, the combined Carl Busch and University of Illinois collections of band instruments, and the A. A. Harding office and memorial room.

The Rehearsal Room

The University of Illinois Band rehearsal room (64' × 58') will accommodate up to 200 players on straight-backed chairs, plus an audience of almost 200, using both permanent type theatre seats, and portable folding chairs. Permanent six-inch risers are built in the semicircular formation a band normally uses. No one is seated higher than the conductor. Drapes, made in ten sections to careful acoustical specifications, hang from ceiling to floor back of the band, but they can be drawn completely into recesses when more sound reflection is desired. A control booth for radio, recording, and projection is visible at second floor level on the wall directly opposite the conductor. Five other openings, for television cameras, can be made available by removing sealed wooden doors. A large chalkboard is provided in the front of the room.

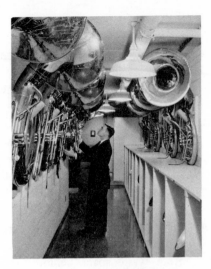

Figure 19-a: Bass Storage Area

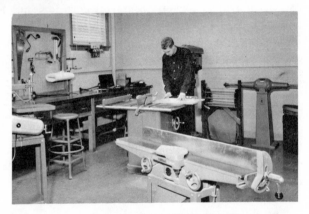

Figure 19-b: Instrument Repair Shop

Figure 19-c: Band Rehearsal Room

Every piece of equipment has its place and we do everything we can to keep it there, and thus to make the rehearsal room a place to do concentrated work with a minimum of confusion.

The Conductor's Podium

Since the conductor should have within reach all of the materials he needs (to eliminate wasted time and movement), and because of our knowledge that, to be used, equipment must be easily accessible, we have developed a podium not unlike the bridge of a ship, into which we have built the many electronic devices useful to a conductor. Figure 20 shows the late A. A. Harding, then *Director Emeritus* of the University of Illinois Bands, inspecting the facilities which his pioneer work in the field of bands made possible.

The Peterson Chromatic Tuner (every tone in six octaves, each with eight frequencies, or a total of 576 frequencies available), which

Figure 20: Band Director **Mark Hindsley** demonstrates the facilities of the podium to A. A. Harding, "the father of school bands."

is electrically powered, with a built-in speaker, is located to the conductor's left as he faces the band. An electric flashing-light metronome is below, not visible to the band. A one-half revolution of the stool brings him to a comfortable operating position for the tape recorder and disc turntable. Microphones, amplifier, and speaker controls are also included so that his directions, given in a normal speaking voice, may be heard throughout the room.

The Director's Office

The director—an administrator with no small task—should have an office of his own with proper office equipment. A desk and file placed in the rehearsal room can be used, but it is not nearly as pleasant, efficient, or as likely to inspire the kind of dignified leadership a progressive instructional program demands.

Practice Rooms

Students often have time available during the school day which can be used for individual practice if the facilities are available. Players of large instruments must have an opportunity to practice alone, without the necessity of carrying their instruments home. With both individual and group size rooms available, ensembles or sections may be scheduled for rehearsal simultaneously, thus increasing the efficiency of the department.

The Library

The fully equipped music library will include these items:

1. Steel filing cabinets

   a. 3″ × 5″ card size for three-way index cards (title, composer, classification).
   b. 5″ × 8″ card size for march size music, placed edgewise, trimmed to 5″ × 6¾″.
   c. letter size, for octavo size music, 7″ × 10½″.
   d. legal size, for folio (10″ × 13″) and quarto (9″ × 12″) size music, placed in separate drawers.

2. Music sorting racks, labeled, to hold a full set of either concert or march folios.

3. Concert folios should be labeled with the name of the school

and organization, the part, and the desk number. In the back pocket there should be a stiff manila folder for the student to use as a sign-out card for his entire folio (never loan parts separately), which can be left on the music stand or in the library. Music distributed when the concert folio is out is placed in this manila folder.

4. Tables and chairs for general work.
5. Paper cutters and scissors for trimming music.
6. Transparent tape for repairing music, heavy tape for repairing folios.
7. Rubber stamps to identify music and folios.
8. Music manuscript paper.
9. Pens, inks, paste.
10. Manila or jute envelopes.

Due to our large volume of work we are using an electric erasing machine, which operates on 110 volts, 60 cycle AC. Rubber revolves to make relatively effortless, complete erasures. We also have a Scotch Manual Edger which we use to mend old music and to join single sheets.

Both the increase in size, and the more widespread use of special arrangements for bands have made printing equipment a more common sight in band libraries. While we are careful to stay within the copyright law, there are ever increasing needs for part duplicating methods. We use the following equipment:

Multigraph Duplicator—Multilith Model 80. This machine will produce 70 top quality copies per minute. Paper sizes range from 3″ × 3½″ to 9¾″ × 14″. Copy to be printed is first prepared on a plate, which can be typed, or handwritten with a special pencil. Plates with pre-printed music staffs are available.

Reflex Printer—Bruning Copyflex Machine, Model 14. The Bruning process is a light-sensitive process by which positive copies are made from matter pre-written on a translucent paper.

Photocopy Duplicator—A. B. Dick, Model 112.

Music Typewriter—R. C. Allen, Model 814 C Musicwriter. This machine types all musical characters. It works well on multilith plates and Bruning transparencies, as well as on regular manuscript paper.

You must ask for help from the experts when planning a building or trying to decide on the best equipment for your own particular school needs. At the University we call on our recording engineer in the School of Music, electronic engineers from the physical plant department, and local dealers to advise us. Through investigation each band director will be able to find people in his own community with special skills and knowledge who will be glad to help.

Our architects procured the book, *Music Buildings, Rooms and Equipment,*[2] on our recommendation, and used it as a guide in many areas. Material later in this chapter on Acoustics, Lighting, Heating and Air Conditioning, are quoted or paraphrased from this source.

Help from Joel Tall, on tape recorders and microphones, is also referred to. The Instrumentalist Company has compiled a list of reference materials,[3] by numerous experts. Those which have been highly recommended (by still *another* expert) are the following:

BORG, EARL R., "Cabinets, Cases and Files for the Band and Orchestra Library," *The Instrumentalist*, January 1949, pp. 8–9.

BRANDENBURG, A. H., "Music Education Need Not Stop with Graduation," *Music Educators Journal*, June 1946, pp. 26–28.

CARTER, ELWIN, "School Building Planning for Music and Drama," *Music Educators Journal*, June–July 1959, pp. 37–41.

CHENOWETH, GENE, "Personality—Music and the Child," *Music Educators Journal*, September 1946, pp. 42–43.

KNUDSEN and HARRIS, *Acoustical Designing in Architecture* (New York: John Wiley & Sons, Inc., 1950).

NEWMAN, ROBERT, "Design for Hearing," *Progressive Architecture*, May 1959. Entire issue.

NEWMAN, R. B. and BOLT, R. H., "Architectural Acoustics," *Architectural Record*, Part I, April 1950, p. 165 ff; Part II, June 1950, p. 166 ff.; Part III, Sept. 1950, p. 148 ff.; Part IV, Nov. 1950, p. 158 ff.

SABINE, HALE J., *Less Noise, Better Hearing*. Celotex Corp., Chicago 1941.

---

[2] Published by Music Educators National Conference. A revision of Music Education Research Council Bulletin No. 17, this 1955 version was prepared by the 1952–54 Committee on Music Rooms and Equipment.

[3] The full list of approximately 130 titles is available from *The Instrumentalist*, 1418 Lake St., Evanston, Ill. These selections are those highly recommended by Lawrence Perkins, of Perkins and Will, Architects, Chicago.

TINKHAM, R. R. J., "Isolation of Sound in Buildings," *Architectural Record*, May 1946, pp. 114–117.

ACOUSTICS

Since music is an art of sound it is extremely difficult, if not impossible, to teach the subject effectively unless the properties of the room being used allow both the teacher and the students to hear the sounds accurately. There must be enough air space or other medium to absorb the great volume of sound produced by a band, without the excess reverberation which causes a confusing mixture of sounds.

Richard Bolt is a member of the firm of Bolt, Beranek and Newman, Cambridge, Massachusetts, which we employed as acoustic consultants. The following is condensed from his very thorough chapter on acoustics in *Music Buildings, Rooms and Equipment*.[4]

> There can be no full enjoyment or appraisal of music performance unless the sound can be heard with some measure of fidelity. Satisfactory acoustics is more than providing a musical performance space free from obvious acoustic faults; and it is more than isolating sound from persons in surrounding spaces where the sound is not desired. The acoustic properties of a room can enhance the quality of music for a listener, and can give the performer a sense of support which adds to the pleasure of performance.
>
> In order to achieve the best results which acoustical science is capable of providing today, we must integrate the acoustics with the other aspects of architectural design, engineering, and construction. If acoustical control is applied to a completed building as an afterthought, the results are frequently inferior and the cost is usually greater than necessary. On the other hand, if the technical requirements for good acoustics are incorporated into the planning and engineering of the building in a logical way, excellent results can be obtained, sometimes with little, if any, additional cost . . .

Architectural acoustics has two general purposes, Bolt continues:

1. "To provide a satisfactory *acoustic environment*" (". . . determined by (a) the intensity and character of all sounds existing in that space, and (b) the way in which sounds are prolonged and spread within that space").

---

[4] Music Educators National Conference, Washington, D. C., pp. 32–34.

2. "To provide good hearing conditions" requiring a "sufficiently low level of background noise, adequate separation of successive sounds (reverberation control), proper distribution of sound within the space, and sufficient loudness of sounds which are to be heard." The MENC publication is equally helpful on the subject of lighting.

LIGHTING

The quality and quantity of light in a comfortable classroom are dependent upon three factors:
1. Illumination level of the task
2. Reflectance pattern of the room
3. Brightness control of the light sources

. . . The American Standard Practice for School Lighting recommends 30-foot candles as a minimum to be maintained in *general classrooms;* 50-foot candles are recommended for *sewing, drafting* and *typing rooms.* These are feasible minimum standards under present conditions and not necessarily established ideal levels. Music room activities indicate levels *above* that of the ordinary classrooms and more in the order of the drafting and typing rooms.[5]

HEATING AND AIR CONDITIONING

". . . Proper ventilation, uniform temperatures and humidity play an important part in the health, learning and teaching abilities of the occupants of a building." The band director should alert the designer "to the following points" which are "peculiar to music education," MENC advises:

1. "Wind instruments require a great deal of inhalation and exhalation" by the many players in a band. Many of the "instruments require considerable physical exertion." [6]
2. Music classes are disturbed by the sounds so easily transmitted through the regular type of ventilating duct.
3. Musical instruments are affected (in varying degrees according to the instrument) by temperature changes. Uniform temperature is necessary for a consistent pitch level.

---

[5] *Ibid.,* p. 45.
[6] *Ibid.,* p. 51.

4. Relative humidity should be maintained at approximately 40–50%. Changes adversely affect pianos and other stringed instruments.

5. Quick mental responses are necessary for the production of music. The recommended dry bulb temperature is 68–72 degrees Fahrenheit.[7]

THE TAPE RECORDER

A good quality tape recorder has many uses beyond merely producing a souvenir of performances. Of course, we record all of our programs, both to make LP records for members of the band, and to use as reference material for my course in band literature. A copy of all satisfactory tapes (either rehearsal or performance) is sent to the University radio station which broadcasts a band program every week throughout the year.

To be really useful, tape recording equipment must be available at all times. We have units in the rehearsal room and my studio, which are ready to record merely by turning on the switch. We have purchased the tape recorders and other sound equipment listed below after consultation with various experts, as the best for our particular program. Each band director must survey his program and determine his own needs.

DESCRIPTION OF SOUND EQUIPMENT USED BY
UNIVERSITY OF ILLINOIS BANDS

Tape Recorders

Ampex Model 350-2R—a two-channel, rack-type, stereophonic recorder with speeds of 7½ and 15 ips.

Ampex Model 350-P—a two-channel, portable machine.

Amplifiers

Bell, Binaural 3 DT—used to amplify the sound of the tape recorder and turntable to the large speakers in the rehearsal room.

Bogen, Model 30 W—to amplify the conductor's comments and the sound of the tuner at the rehearsal hall podium.

Microphones

Altec system, non-directional.

Electrovoice 666—dynamic.

---

[7] *Ibid.*, p. 51.

Telefunken, Model U-47M—takes the place of five or six ordinary mikes, has a wide dynamic and frequency range. It can be either non-directional or cardioid field pattern.

Other

Mixer, Berlant—a four-channel unit, with transformers, allows up to four mikes to each side of the tape.

Speaker, Hartsfield Model D 30085 PN—has a theatre system with an extremely rigid straight-sided cone.

Tube tester—a portable machine which will test the validity and strength of any electronic tube.

Tuner—Scott AM-FM-Stereo, Model 333B.

Turntable, Rondine (Rek-O-Cut)—a four-speed player with a Gray tone arm and a Pickering Pickup cartridge.

In his book, *Techniques of Magnetic Recording,*[8] which is the most authoritative in the field, Joel Tall indicates that it is good business sense to buy a tape recorder on *performance* only. He advises the prospective buyer to look for the following features:

1. A quiet "erase" system. Record your whistling at a little more than full level, erase, then check.
2. A meter level indicator. Although more expensive, it is more accurate than the neon tube "magic eye" type.
3. Full track head. This type is best for highest quality.
4. Minimum "flutter" and "wow." Check this by recording the tone of a piano. The playback should have a natural, not "wobbly" or "tinny" sound.
5. A cool running machine. You should be able to keep your hand on the machine without discomfort after four to five hours of continuous operation.

MICROPHONES

Microphones perform the function of converting sound into electrical energy and are subject to all the laws governing the transmission of sound. There are four main types of microphone in general use:

---

[8] The Macmillan Company, New York 1950. The material on tape recorders and microphones has been condensed from this source and is used by permission of the publisher.

1. *The Velocity or Ribbon Microphone* operates as a result of the movement of a sensitive ribbon which is controlled by the velocity of the air hitting it. Since a blast of air can take the "crimp" out of the ribbon, it must be handled carefully and should not be used out of doors. Never blow into the microphone.

2. *The Dynamic or Moving Coil Microphone*, a rugged type suitable for all kinds of recording, converts sound to electrical energy through the use of a coil that moves with varying sound-pressures within a magnetic field.

3. *The Condenser Microphone* was used a great deal during the early days of radio and the "talkies"; it depends for its operation on the variation in voltage occurring in a condenser as a result of the movement of the sound-sensitive diaphragm. Complications inherent in amplifying the tiny pickup voltage and difficulties arising from its large size have been solved by design engineers and it is now coming back into popularity.

4. *The Crystal Microphone* operates when the Rochelle salt crystals from which most are made give off electric voltages as they bend and twist as a result of sound waves striking the small diaphragms which drive them. They should not be used in hot or humid climates.

Other Microphones

The Cardioid Microphone is a combination of the velocity and dynamic types, and is so named because the pickup pattern resembles a heart. Its negligible pickup to the rear reduces the danger of feedback when used with a public address system.

The Ceramic Cartridge Microphone, which operates much the same way as the crystal, is not subject to the effect of either heat or humidity.

High Impedance microphone cables must be short since hum, noise and loss of output result as the length increases. *Low Impedance* types, however, can use a cable up to approximately 100 feet in length without a noticeable loss of fidelity.

THE STROBOCONN

The stroboscopic device manufactured by C. G. Conn is an electronic method for rapid and accurate visual measurement or comparison of sound frequencies to within 1/100th part of a semi-tone. It is designed to be used almost entirely on an individual basis.

The Stroboconn has 12 scanning windows representing each note of the chromatic scale. Sound picked up by the microphone causes whirling stroboscopic disks in these windows to become illuminated by a neon tube whose rate of flashing corresponds exactly to the frequency of the tone sounded. On each of the whirling disks there are seven stroboscopic pattern bands, each representing a particular musical note as it occurs in one of seven octaves. Thus 84 (7x12) musical notes may be measured. By observation of the scanning unit, the operator discovers instantly whether a tone is in tune, sharp, or flat. No mathematical computations are necessary. If the black-spoked pattern in the window representing a tone stands still when the tuning unit is set on "0," the note is in tune to 1/100th part of a semi-tone, according to the American standard of A-440. If the pattern drifts to the operator's right, the tone is sharper than standard, but if it drifts to his left, it is flatter than standard.

Most students can play one tone in tune, but it is the relationship between different tones which is important to good intonation. By recording the playing of an individual (or even a small section), the performers listening to the playback will be able to watch the Stroboconn closely and *see* (as they learn to *hear*) where they have their intonation problems.

We keep our Stroboconns on "Pixmobiles" (a sort of electronic "tea-wagon"). Designed as a portable projection table, the pixmobile holds firm, even on inclining floors, because of its wheel brakes. A three-sided ledge around the shelves keeps the equipment from sliding off as we move it to any location.

The Strobotuner, also made by Conn, is a one-wheel model of the larger 12-wheel machine. You can still check all tones, but must move a dial to different positions to do so. The complete instrument (Stroboconn) should be purchased if you can possibly afford it, since the many uses made possible by being able to see all tones at once certainly make the added expense worthwhile.

There is no substitute for the ear, and neither machine is so intended, but both are valuable aids to study and training.

TUNING GUIDES

We find tuning guides to be so helpful in tuning the individual players and the entire band, that they are glued to the inside of our concert folios for reference by the student in tuning and testing his instrument. Each guide alerts the student to the specific intonation problems of his own instrument. For example, the one for cornet and trumpet explains, among other things, how to adjust the individual valve slides.[9]

THE DYNALEVEL

This instrument transforms the various dynamic levels of sound into light. The player can see each particular volume level he plays represented by a different color on a sort of miniature multi-colored barber pole. The individual can practice sustained tones at constant level, or *crescendo* and *decrescendo* at constant pitch (in conjunction with the Stroboconn). Since accents can be demonstrated visually, the student can develop a controlled, consistent increase of volume at the point of emphasis indicated by the accent mark. Parts can be balanced by asking each section to activate the same colored light on the column when they play separately.

THE ELECTRONIC METRONOME

There are many uses of the metronome which go beyond its usual role of time-beater. In a handbook by Frederick Franz called *Metronome Techniques*,[10] many very practical applications for the musician are suggested. Here are a few:

1. Measuring tempos by celebrated musicians, from broadcasts or recordings.
2. Teaching memory of tempos, just as tonal memory is taught.
3. Developing a smooth *ritardando* or *accelerando* by spreading the number of points of change equally over the intervening measures and marking the metronome settings in the score.
4. Acquiring an accurate sense of time division.
5. Learning complicated rhythms by assigning one metronome beat to the shortest note in the passage, figuring how many such beats should be given to every other note and rest, and gradually increasing the metronome setting.

---

[9] These excellent suggestions to players of each type of instrument are included in the book *Tuning the School Band and Orchestra*, and are published separately, in card form, by Ralph Pottle, Hammond, Louisiana.—*Ed.*
[10] Published by Frederick Franz, New Haven, Conn.

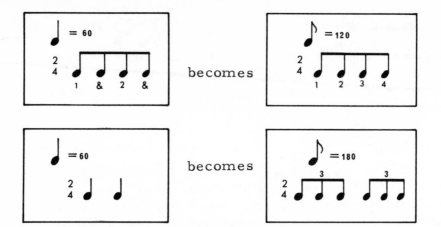

becomes

becomes

Figure 21: Metronome

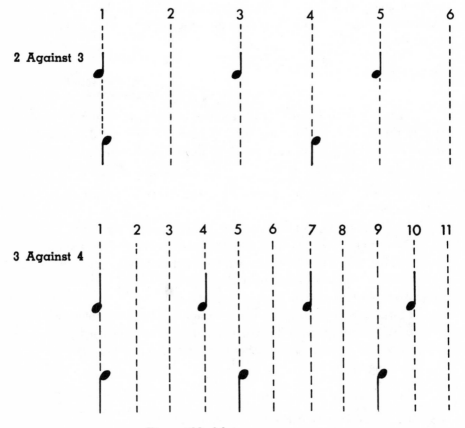

Figure 22: Metronome

6. Playing 2 against 3, or 3 against 4, by assigning one metronome beat to the lowest common denominator (6 and 12, respectively), then playing the notes on the indicated beats.

7. Controlling the *vibrato* by allowing only a set number of pulsations per metronome beat.

THE MOTION PICTURE PROJECTOR

Most schools provide one or more 16mm projectors for use throughout the system. The band director should take advantage of the many fine educational music films available either free or at a modest rental fee. Films of your own football halftime shows can aid in improving subsequent performances.

STORAGE CABINETS

In order to protect the investment of many thousands of dollars in instruments and other musical equipment, safe and adequate storage facilities must be provided. There are many fine commercial units available. Sometimes schools prefer to have cabinets built during the summer by the school maintenance crew. Cabinets should be provided for large school-owned instruments, small individual instruments, percussion equipment, uniforms, hats and plumes, library supplies, and instrument repair supplies.

OTHER EQUIPMENT

Our property office uses a Burgess Vibro-graver kit (engraver) to place permanent identification on mouthpieces and other metal equipment. Various decals and embossed adhesive strips are used on cases, folios, etc.

We use an Audio-Hailer Megaphone for easier communication out of doors. This model is self-contained, portable, weighs about 5½ pounds, and will amplify 1000 times.

OTHER AUDIO-VISUAL AIDS

Do not limit your use of audio-visual aids to a few sessions with the projector and the phonograph, but include in your planning a wide variety of equipment and techniques. Here are some of the many devices which can be employed:

chalkboard

bulletin board

duplicating devices

photographs

textbook illustrations

prints and etchings

cutouts

post cards

newspaper clippings

drawings and sketches

charts, graphs, tables

cartoons

pictorial statistics

posters

maps and globes

diagrams and schematics

lantern slides

filmstrips (also with sound)

opaque projections

35mm positive transparencies

micro-slide projections

tachistoscopes

motion pictures

phonograph records

electrical transcriptions

tape recordings

headphones

radio broadcasts (AM and FM)

television (open or closed circuit)

centralized sound system

field trips

museums

models

objects

specimens, collections, samples

relics

dioramas

floor representations

mock-ups

dramatizations

demonstrations

flash cards

albums

scrap books

Now I CAN RELAX?

Consult with experts in every field, but design the band's physical plant for the particular needs of *your own* school and community. Take your time, do a thorough job, and don't be afraid to experiment with unique ways of doing things.

Remember that the equipment you place in your room or building is just as important as the structure itself. Insist on top quality items that will last.

Don't expect a new building or the latest equipment to do your work for you, or to improve your band overnight. Even with all of the technological advances I have seen in my lifetime there has been no invention that has come even close to replacing the dedication, hard work, attention to detail, and personal leadership of an intelligent, well-trained, inspired human being.

Instrument Repair
And
Maintenance

by **Charles C. Rogers**

Elkhart, Indiana

Charles C. Rogers

has been Band Instrument
Service Manager for the
Conn Corporation since
1956. He writes an occa-
sional column for the *Conn-*
chord, and makes talks at clinics on various phases of instrument
repair.

Charlie Rogers was born and raised in Elkhart, Indiana, the
home of many musical instrument manufacturers. While still in high
school he took a part-time job after school and Saturdays with Conn,
in order to "legalize" his trumpet playing in their industrial band.
The group, which he describes as a "pretty fair country band," played
concerts in the park once a week throughout the summer and performed for a few employee gatherings during the winter months.
The band also supported the efforts of the Conn professional baseball team (made up of employees) which played on the circuit including Elkhart.

Following graduation from high school, Mr. Rogers went to
work full time for Conn. During his long service with the company
he has seen the shift away from the use of skilled craftsmen who
could carry out every step in the building of one instrument to the
use of modern assembly line techniques.

He has acquired a tremendous knowledge of instrument repair and maintenance as a result of his experiences in every department of the Conn manufacturing plant, working on every instrument
—both reed and brass—since 1927.

192

The cause of most troubles on band instruments we receive for repair is simply *poor housekeeping*—not keeping the instrument clean! A great deal of filth (we call it "debris") collects over a long period of time. It changes the acoustical properties of the instrument, leads to expensive repair work, and is very unhealthy for the player.

Many band directors send back to the factory instruments which they feel are basically defective, since they have "gone out of tune" or have "become stuffy." After we clean the sludge out of the woodwind tone holes and give the brass a good bath, they often play just like new.

We find brass mouthpieces which, through an accumulation of filth, have lost one-third of their inside diameter. Quite often the debris has eaten into the metal and caused deep pits. Some of it has been blown on into the valve section where it has mixed with the oil and formed a harmful abrasive. All of this trouble and expense can be avoided by simply flushing the instrument out with a good household detergent once a month.

If you want to convince your students of the danger to health of dirty mouthpieces, have the biology teacher come into band rehearsal (unannounced) and take some samples of debris from the mouthpieces, which he can allow to incubate at body temperature in a laboratory culture for 48–72 hours. Slides can then be prepared from the cultures and, by means of the microprojector, shown on the wall of your rehearsal room.

The shock of actually seeing the literally millions of harmful bacteria has a lasting effect.

With the many demands on the time and talent of the high school director, most men are able to do only a few emergency repairs—enough to get them through a concert or a show.[1] They must rely on a professional repairman, dealer's shop, or the factory.

The Professional Repairman

There is no organization which sets standards or authorizes some to wear a "button of acceptance." Like any other group, there are some "duds" in this field too. We get instruments for repair which have been nearly ruined by someone who did not know what he was doing.

A baritone saxophone was returned to us as "basically defective" by a director on the advice of a "qualified repairman." We concluded that he was not very "qualified," since even the most half-hearted attempt to get a leak light inside the sax would have revealed the girl's compact, lodged up in the small part of the body which was causing all the trouble!

Most repairmen will gain a reputation, either good or bad. If not, a director can usually sense whether they "know the language" or not. It is best to "audition" a repairman by letting him do something relatively simple for you, like replacing some pads. If he does *only* what you ask, and gives the instrument back still requiring minor adjustments and not in good playing condition, you should look for someone else.

The repairman who can actually play the instruments he is servicing has an obvious advantage over one who cannot, especially if he has been a teacher and is aware of the student's problems. He should remember that the flute, for example, which plays for a mature professional with full breath support and an "iron grip," may leak too badly for a student to produce even the first note.

The Dealer's Shop

Some stores are utilizing a sort of preventive maintenance pro-

---

[1] Several repair kits are available, among them the C. G. Conn "Emergency Repair Kit" designed for the bandmaster or student to make minor spot repairs. Erick Brand has a "Student Repair Kit" and a "Master Kit," which is advertised as a "portable emergency repair shop."

gram. They send a card 30 days following a sale, and at subsequent longer intervals, asking the customer to:

Please bring your instrument in;
We'd like to check it for you.

In this way they can keep their customers happy by preventing expensive repair bills, as they reduce the serious repair load on their store repair shop.

The Factory

We maintain a repair section to provide service to our customers and dealers. Although we will work on other brands, we do not promote the repair business, and would really prefer to confine our activities to the production of new instruments.

An instrument which is sent for reconditioning starts in our department where dents are bumped out, defective parts are replaced, and the other rough work is done. It is then sent through the new instrument assembly line where is is lacquered or plated, buffed, and assembled right along with our latest models.

We can schedule an instrument into the line with expectations for 30-day delivery so we must anticipate keeping it for at least a month, plus the time needed for the repair work.

"I NEED IT YESTERDAY"

Band directors can reduce the time their instruments will be out of service by following three rules:

1. *Send the instrument for repair as soon as it needs it.* This may seem obvious and elementary, but we receive instruments at the factory which have not been played for many months. Possibly repair has been delayed because of budget problems, but too often the director has just been too busy to get it shipped off.

2. *Send the instrument to the proper repair facility.* Decide whether it is a "band director," "professional repairman," "dealer's shop," or "factory" problem. Don't send a clarinet which just needs a few pads and springs back to the factory for a complete overhaul.

3. *Take advantage of repair slack seasons.* All repairmen are rushed throughout the summer, but during the period between January 1 and May 1 they have relatively little business. The sousaphone

which we take 60 days to overhaul during the summer can be returned in about 30 days during the slack season.

Any administrator or parent who invests money in band instruments expects normal depreciation through use, but not unnecessary repairs or premature replacement caused by misuse.

The band director must spend a portion of his instructional period teaching the students how to care for their instruments. Periodic inspections by the director or the section leaders should be held to make certain that small problems do not develop into major repair expenditures.

The following section contains a number of suggestions to the players of woodwind, brass, and percussion instruments, which high school students should be expected to carry out.

All Players

1. Those with instruments finished in lacquer should get a soft cloth and wipe off all fingerprints after each use. Since most lacquer finishes are not resistant to acid from perspiration, wiping clean will assure a longer lasting finish and result in a better looking band.

2. Carry only the instrument and those accessories which have space provided for them in the case (no socks, lunches, comic books, etc.). Serious damage may result from pressures in a crowded case.

3. Remove your instrument from the case with care, and don't throw it back in, hurriedly, on the way to your next class.

4. Instruments should be cleaned thoroughly before summer storage. Woodwinds should be oiled, and all keys lubricated, but brass should be cleansed of all lubricants and dried out.

5. Don't chew gum or consume soft drinks while playing; the sugar will be carried on into the instrument and cause woodwind pads and brass valves to stick. After eating, be sure to rinse the mouth well before playing a wind instrument.

6. Check the latch on your case. Great damage has been done in a bad spill when the lid flies open unexpectedly.

7. Box or tie down accessories in the case and avoid dents that result when these things bang around loosely.

8. Don't use the case as a seat. It was not built strongly enough for this.

9. Use rubber bands only in an emergency, and temporarily, because the sulphur in the rubber will tarnish and eventually eat into the metal.

10. A piece of camphor gum or a small bag of silica gel may be carried in the case to absorb moisture and retard corrosion.

11. A smooth pebble or other non-soluble object in the mouth will start the flow of saliva for a player who by general nature or nervousness is especially dry-mouthed. Be sure to remove before playing. Do not use chewing gum; the sugar water will cause trouble.

Woodwind Players

1. Each player should own a small screwdriver, mouthpiece brush, key oil and a bore oiling outfit (for wood instruments). By filing a notch into the point of a small metal crochet hook it can be used for pushing and pulling springs into proper position.

2. Dry the instrument out *thoroughly* with an accepted swab after *every* playing period, no matter how short.

3. Use a pipe cleaner or feather to keep tone holes completely free of dirt. Dust under keys can be removed with an old (dry) shaving brush, cotton tipped baby swab, pipe cleaner, or air pressure.

4. Dip a toothpick or fine wire in key oil and touch it to each moving part contact point once each month. Use oil sparingly; too much oil will collect dirt and lint. Work the key to distribute the oil and wipe off all excess. A thin film of oil on springs and screws will prevent rust.

5. Apply *cork grease* (the tallow base lasts longer than most other greases) to the corks on the tenons. It is expensive and sometimes impossible to replace a broken tenon which results from joints that are too stiff and dry to be assembled with ease.

6. Oil the bore of new wood instruments every two weeks for several months, later about three times a year. If you can get a woodwind instrument through the first six months without a crack it may never crack as long as it is oiled periodically.

Woodwind Players (cont.)

7. Wood instruments should not be subjected to excessive or abrupt changes of temperature. Do not attempt to play a cold instrument until it has gradually warmed to room temperature.

8. The very small upper joint of the oboe demands extra care, because it is more difficult to dry out, thus more liable to crack.

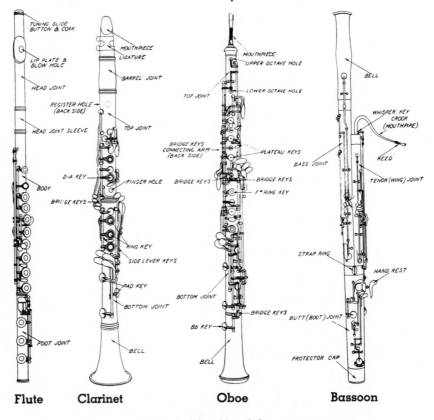

Flute   Clarinet   Oboe   Bassoon

Figure 23: Woodwind Instruments

9. When sending a cracked instrument for repair, be sure to mark the location clearly, since by the time it reaches the factory the crack may have closed up so tight it cannot be found.

10. Be careful in assembling and disassembling the instrument. Do not hold it any place where squeezing pressure will bend keys or rods. Be especially careful when fitting bridge keys together.

11. No woodwind instrument will play well unless the pads cover the tone hole sockets perfectly. Leaking tone hole sockets are the cause of squeaks and hard blowing tones. Detecting leaks and correcting them are important duties of the woodwind player.

12. One way to find a leak is to close all tone holes and the bell and fill the instrument with smoke. A wisp of smoke indicates a leak. This method leaves unsightly nicotine deposits on the pads, and should only be used if the leak cannot be found by the following methods.

13. Leaks can usually be located with a little gadget called a "feeler," made by cementing a narrow strip of cellophane to a match stick. Slip this feeler between the pad and the socket edge and close the pad with the key; then gently pull the feeler out. By repeating the process all around the edge of the socket, you will notice varying tension on the feeler. Where there is little or no tension on the feeler when it is pulled out, there is liable to be a leak.

14. Leak testing lights may be purchased. This is an electric bulb on the end of a cord which is lowered into the instrument. When the keys are closed, light showing through between the pad and the socket indicates a leak.

15. Try two methods for fixing the leak:

Recreasing: Dampen the pad and tie it down overnight.
Reseating: Melt the pad adhesive by heating the pad cup with a match or Bunsen burner. Press the pad down on its socket evenly and tie until the adhesive has re-solidified.

If neither of these methods works, take the instrument to an experienced repairman.

16. Pads, especially those nearest the mouthpiece, will last longer if kept dry with ordinary blotting paper.

17. Wash the mouthpiece out regularly with soap and lukewarm water. Special sanitary chemicals are not recommended because they might adversely affect the mouthpiece material.

18. Put the cap on the mouthpiece when not in use. This not only saves reeds from accidental snagging, but it protects the mouthpiece, which can be ruined by even a very small nick on the tip.

19. Loosen the ligature on the mouthpiece when putting it away. Constant pressure from a tight ligature is liable to warp the

Woodwind Players (cont.)

facing and in time may even cause a constriction in the tone chamber.

20. Wash the saxophone mouthpipe out (flexible brushes are available) and clean out the octave hole with a pipe cleaner or a feather.

21. The bassoon bocal should be cleaned often by running warm water through it. Three pipe cleaners joined by twisting ½" of the ends together will serve as a swab. The octave hole must be kept open. Blow through it or use a broom straw, but do not use anything which may damage or enlarge the hole.

22. Always use the saxophone and bassoon end plugs, because they protect the octave mechanism and insure a snug fit in the case.

23. Use the neckstrap with instruments requiring it, but do not depend on it so completely that you allow the instrument to hang freely from the strap without also holding it with the hands. Resting the bell of a saxophone, for instance, against a table, tends to cause the keys to bind.

24. Do not "tinker" with key mechanisms. One small action often causes a chain reaction which sends the whole thing out of adjustment.

Brass Players

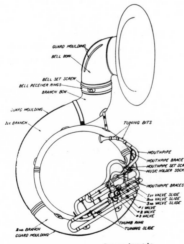

Figure 24: Sousaphone

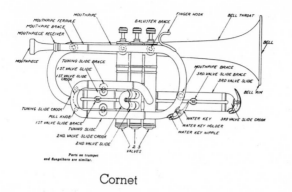

Cornet

1. Mouthpieces and mouthpipes demand special care. Carry the mouthpiece in a pouch or in the holder provided in the case. The French horn mouthpiece is especially small and narrow, the stem very thin, and both may be damaged easily.
2. The throat of the mouthpiece and the venturi of the mouthpipe are critical spots and must be kept clean. Avoid forcing a cleaning rod through these passages because it will enlarge them and damage the response of the instrument.

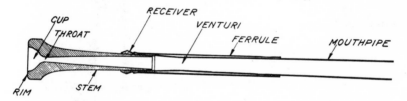

Figure 25: Trumpet Mouthpiece and Mouthpipe

3. Remove the mouthpiece after playing. In the attempt to loosen stuck mouthpieces, braces are torn loose, mouthpiece receivers are pulled away from the mouthpipe, and the mouthpipe itself is bent and broken. This is the greatest single cause of damage to cup mouthpiece instruments. If the mouthpiece becomes stuck, use the mouthpiece puller. If this fails, you'll save yourself the inevitable costly repairs by letting a repairman do the job in the first place.
4. Inside cleaning may be done with household detergent once a month. Do not use ammonia because it is a violent enemy of brass.

Brass Players (cont.)

5. Keep the valve slides greased. Each slide should pull smoothly without binding. Be sure to depress the corresponding valve key to release the air pressure. A sharp jerk with a handkerchief can often free a stuck slide (but a "dull jerk" with that same handkerchief may get stuck with a repair job that's not free!). Any corrosion can be cleaned off with gasoline or metal polish, but slides should never be buffed because then they might fit too loosely and drop or blow out.

6. Outside cleaning may be done with mild soap and water and a soft cloth or chamois. Abrasives and metal polishes should not be used; they will take the lacquer off, exposing the metal to air and thus tarnish.

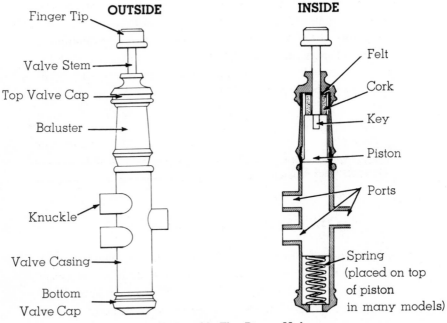

Figure 26: The Piston Valve

7. Keep the valves oiled. Wipe off the old oil with a soft cloth before applying new. Use more oil on the valves when playing outdoors in a dusty atmosphere, and clean the instrument after playing.

8. Push the valves *straight* down with the finger*tips*. Overlapping

the fingers will exert uneven pressure on the sides of the valve casings and cause uneven wearing, thus sticky valves, and eventual air leakage.

9. Clean the valves by removing the pistons and washing them and the inside of the casings. Pistons are hollow and will dent if not handled carefully. They should be wiped dry and laid on a clean cloth. The inside of the casing should be swabbed with clean cheesecloth. Do not allow lint to collect in the ports. Be careful not to scratch or gouge the inside of the casing.

10. Apply new oil after cleaning and replace pistons in the proper casing (each is numbered and it is essential that they match). Older valves will require a heavier oil to help seal the excess clearance which has worn between the piston and the casing. New clearance is about one-fourth of the diameter of a human hair.

11. If pistons are corroded in position, apply kerosene or penetrating oil. Let them sit overnight before attempting to remove. Do not try to poke them out with a stick.

12. Check springs to be sure the thrust is parallel to the valve casing. A "leaning spring" will exert uneven pressure and tend to wear the casing out of round. Open the coils on the side to which the spring leans to make it even again.

13. Any pressure on the valve slides will reduce the clearance of the pistons in the casings, causing that valve to drag; therefore pick up cornets and trumpets by the valve casings only, and keep the hand away from the second valve slide when playing. When necessary to lay the instrument down, do not allow any strain on the valve slides.

14. Do not further complicate the repairman's job by attempting to force frozen pistons out of dented casings.

15. By placing the thumb in the center of the tuning slide on any brass instrument, even pressure may be applied to prevent a cocked, stuck slide.

16. Do not give in to the nervous temptation to "fool around" with the moving parts (like finger tips, valve caps, slides, etc.) because it puts uneven strain on them.

17. Examine the water keys periodically. A thin coating of oil will help to prevent rust on the spring. If the cork is defective, replace it.

Brass Players (cont.)

18. Mutes, properly corked, will stay in the bell if pressed in firmly and rotated slightly. Recork mutes that require undue pressure, because forcing will tend to stretch the bell and eventually affect the playing qualities.
19. Use petroleum jelly or slide grease on detachable bell set screws and lyre holder screws.
20. Make it difficult for practical jokers to throw things into the bells of the larger instruments. Covers with school initials for the sousaphones solve the problem at public performances.

Trombone Slide Care

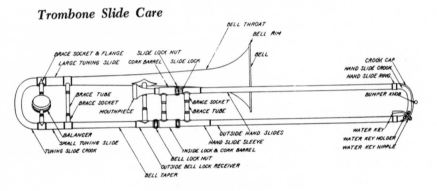

Figure 27: The Trombone

1. The average trombone slide tube wall thickness is approximately .009″. This is equal to about three human hairs. Lightweight slides are .006″ thick. When you consider that they are over four feet long, it is obvious that they require very careful handling.
2. If you force the lid of your case open when one end has a tendency to stick, you are liable to bend the slides.
3. Always take hold of the outside hand slide brace, even though the instrument has a slide lock. With this habit you will not need to worry about the lock.
4. Do not work slides when they are dry, because this causes scratches and will harm the surface of both inside and outside slides. Oil should be used for lubrication by most high school students; the cold cream treatment used by many professionals requires very regular attention.

5. To clean the slides use a strong cord about five feet long, weighted at the end, with a strip of cheesecloth six inches by six feet for the outside slide crook and the inside slide. A cleaning rod completely covered with cheesecloth may be used for the outside slide. Always hold the slide you are cleaning (not the opposite one) to prevent binding.

The French Horn

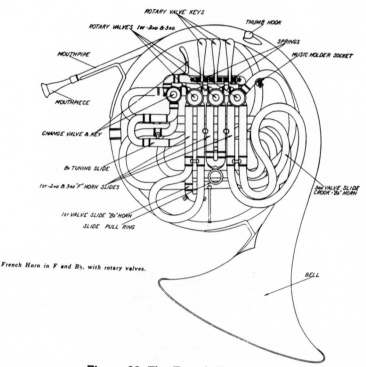

French Horn in F and B♭, with rotary valves.

Figure 28: The French Horn

1. French horn bells are made thin and soft in order to produce the characteristic tone, and consequently require the most careful handling.
2. Be sure the French horn is properly blocked and strapped in the case so that the bell does not take the impact of any dropping or jar. Keep foreign matter out of the case.
3. Oil should be applied every two or three months to the rotary valves—on the bearings only.

The French Horn (cont.)

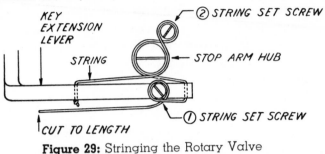

Figure 29: Stringing the Rotary Valve

4. Figure 29 shows how to string the rotary type of valve. Start at the knot in the string. Do not tighten the set screws (1) and (2) until completely strung and until ready to adjust the height of the valve keys. Leave an extra two inches when cutting the string, and this will allow you a good hold on it when it needs tightening later. A good grade of 27-lb. test braided fish line makes a suitable string.

Percussion Players

Figure 30: The Snare Drum

Hardware must be kept dry. A little machine oil will prevent rusting and keep the moving parts (bolts, screws, strainer, etc.) in good working order.

Covers should be used to protect the percussion equipment left set up in the band room from dust as well as from after-hours amateur percussionists.

Drum heads made from cowhide are affected by the humidity (plastic heads are not). Damp days will loosen the heads; dry days will tighten them. When you have increased the tension on a rainy day to get the desired tone, be sure to return the tension to its original position after you finish playing. If you do not and the next day is dry, the head will split as it contracts. Other than this humidity adjustment, leave the heads at playing tension all the time. Unnecessary loosening and tightening just weakens the heads.

Snare drum heads will stretch as they are used. When the top of the counterhoop is almost even with the edge of the shell they must be reset as follows:

1. Remove the snare head and moisten on both sides (but not near the edges or on the flesh hoop).
2. Place the head evenly on the shell and turn the tension collar screws only far enough to hold the counterhoops in place.
3. Set the drum on a flat surface, wet head down.
4. Let it dry slowly for at least 12 hours.
5. Do the same thing with the batter head. Since this is the side which gets dirty, you can take this opportunity to wash it with soap and water.

Bass drum heads may be adjusted the same way, one head at a time.

The Pedal Tympani   **Figure 31**

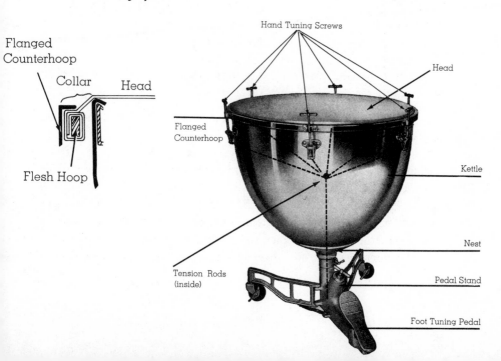

The tympani head must be kept pulled down evenly all the way around. This is not possible if one or more of the tension rods inside the kettle do not work easily. They should be greased at least every six months.

A one-half inch collar should be maintained in order to be sure of the lowest tones. Since atmospheric conditions vary from one hour to the next, almost constant head adjustment is necessary (plastic heads are not affected). When the tympani are not in use, do *not* release all tension from the heads, but leave them tuned to A (large) and D (small).

There is no sound more obnoxious to a conductor or contest judge than a loud squeak from the tympani during a pitch change. The pedal should be oiled regularly. If the head is making the noise, because of friction, the edge of the kettle should first be cleaned with emery cloth, then a dry lubricant (flaked graphite or talcum powder) applied to the top of the kettle, and rubbed into the edge of the head.

Old, hard, dry heads will not produce good tone or proper resonance and should be replaced. They are not helped by any kind of oil, grease, or so-called "head restorative." *To adjust the tympani tuning collar*, water should be applied to the head with a sponge or damp cloth at five-minute intervals until the skin is soft and shows some wrinkles. Two or three applications will usually do it. Do not allow water to run under the counterhoop.

If the collar is too small—increase tension with the hand screws and stretch the head.

If the collar is too big—release the tension and allow the heads to shrink.

If the collar is extremely large—turn the head completely over and re-set. Moisten one side only. Never remove the flesh hoop.

Cover the head with paper or a cloth. This will retard the drying process to a slow 24–48 hours.

Band Cymbals, always with straps and pads, should be struck with a full glancing blow (never straight in and out). This allows free vibration and reduces the possibility of breakage.

Metal cleaners and polishes should not be used and the cymbals should never be machine buffed, because these things will destroy the tone. Non-metallic kitchen scouring pads will do a good job.

As cymbals are used over a long period of time they have a

tendency to "build up" in tone. When playing a group of repeated notes, strokes of equal force will produce successively louder responses. Eventually this makes it almost impossible to sustain a *pianissimo* roll on a suspended cymbal. Some drummers attach a band-aid to the underside of the cymbal to compensate when this begins to happen.

STORAGE FACILITIES

Even before an instrument is put in use, adequate storage facilities should be arranged. Requirements are ample space, good ventilation, and proper humidity.

Extremely dry air (from general overheating in winter or from nearby radiators) results in cracks and loose reinforcing rings on woodwind instruments. It can also cause pads to become poorly seated or to fall out, lubricants to gum, and slides and valves to stick. Conversely, if the air is too damp, the wood may swell, mold and corrosion may develop, and glues may lose their adhesiveness.

Select a space for storage that has constant movement of air. Humidifiers, open vessels of water, or damp cloths can be used to maintain the relative humidity as close to 50 percent as possible. Temperatures of 65–75 degrees are ideal for most musical instruments. Do not leave any equipment exposed to direct sunlight.

THE CONN REPAIR SCHOOL

About 30 people were graduated every 16 weeks from this instructional program which operated until about 10 years after the end of World War II. As the "GI Bill" faded away, so did our students. We regretted its closing, but since it was a non-profit operation anyway, we could not continue it with only partially filled classes.

We feel it served a real need at the time. Many graduates are in business for themselves now or are working for other companies. The very fine *Band Instrument Repair Manual*,[2] by Erick D. Brand, was one of the texts used in the course.

There are some commercial schools offering repair instruction and many colleges are starting to include a class for their music educa-

---

[2] Originally copyrighted in 1939, this manual is still extremely valuable. It is available from the company founded by the late Erick Brand, which still bears his name, at 1117 W. Beardsley Ave., Elkhart, Indiana.

tion majors like the instrument repair course conducted by Frank W. Hill at Iowa State Teachers College.

THE SCHOOL REPAIR SHOP

A large school system with a qualified repairman on the staff, or enough work to justify hiring one, might include a repair shop in their building or remodeling plans. Erick Brand lists tools and supplies costing nearly $400 as necessary for general work in a one-man shop. In addition, the following other equipment is listed as necessary:

Furniture: Work bench and chair.

Machines: Buff, 1 H.P., with long arms. Lathe, 10″ with 30″ between
   centers.

Solution tanks: Lacquer remover: black iron tank (30″ × 12″ ×
   14″) on a three-burner laundry stove. Cyanide: one clean
   55-gallon oil drum, with the top cut out. Buffing dirt cleaner:
   black iron tank (30″ × 12″ × 14″).

TERMS

Many times we get requests for spare parts and because of a lack of standardized terms there are often unnecessary delays. For instance, we have received letters requesting a "valve cap." Since there is a great deal of difference between the top and bottom caps, we write back and ask which one they would like. Invariably the letter comes back with some statement like: "Oh . . . we don't want that, it's the one with the pearl on it that we need."

We call that the *finger tip*. The illustrations in this chapter indicate the names of parts of the various instruments. Inspection sheets for saxophone, clarinet, and flute are available from Erick Brand. They are designed for use in shops where the inspector is separated from the men doing the work, and many instruments must be inspected; however, they can be used to great advantage by the band director as a very detailed term reference chart. The man who has developed his ability to diagnose repair problems can use these sheets to remind himself of work he needs to do or have done, to communicate with his repairman, to keep a file of work requested, or to note repair work for instrument depreciation records.

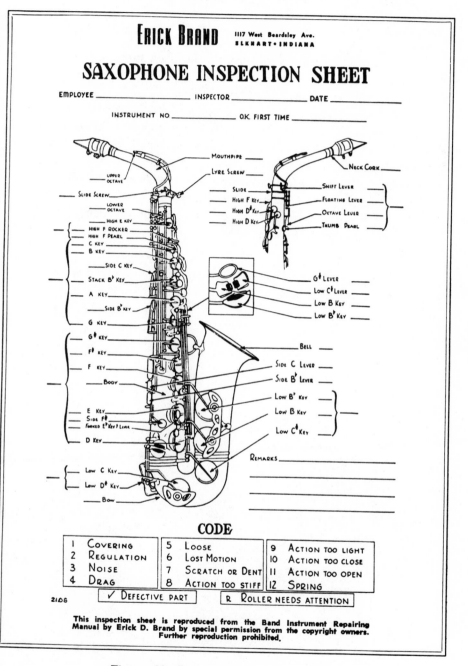

Figure 32: Saxophone Inspection Sheet

211

Each band director should make a thorough study of instrument repair and assume the proper degree of involvement according to his individual ability, interest, and available time.

The non-mechanic, if he just learns how difficult it is to fix a broken instrument, will be more diligent in his instructions on care and maintenance. A teacher with limited mechanical experience should learn to examine an instrument which is causing trouble and make an accurate diagnosis. Many men are excellent mechanics, but all do-it-yourself repairmen must *learn when to stop.*

Each band director will have to determine how difficult a repair job his knowledge and ability will allow him to try. The best rule seems to be:

If you don't know exactly what you are doing—just don't do it! Take it to your repairman.

CHAPTER X

The
Stage
Band

by **Stan Kenton**

Los Angeles, Calif.

Stan Kenton

organized a rehearsal band
in 1941 only to provide an
outlet for his own creative
arranging talents which
seemed to be of interest to
no one else at the time, but somehow an engagement at the Rendez-
vous Ballroom at Balboa Beach developed, and, except for brief
periods of re-evaluation, he has had a band ever since.

In every art form (and jazz must be included) there are those
who, because of their compelling exploratory spirit born of a sincere
belief in the future, so beat back the brush of unknown fields that
it becomes possible for others when they come along to recognize
the trail the forays have generally indicated but not pinpointed, and
to build a paved road for all—one complete with gas stations, bill-
boards, and people who will use it with pleasure, but never drive
far enough to even catch a glimpse of the group which has made
it all possible.

Seldom does one individual possess sufficient sense of direction
to expose, build, and perpetuate this path, but Stan Kenton is such
a man. He has always been interested in both a constant search for
new directions in jazz and in the training of young musicians who
will some day be the leaders of even more exciting movements in the
future.

To this end he has devoted many weeks each summer since
1959 (without pay) to the Stan Kenton clinics, sponsored by the
National Stage Band Camps. At these week-long sessions both students and teachers may study every facet of jazz under capable,
professional teachers.

214

"I've never seen such a vulgar display in my whole life," the high school music teacher scolded. An elderly woman who was quite a fine musician (she was typical of those who could not tolerate any kind of dance music) had just caught one of her students—*me*—playing jazz on the piano in the school cafeteria. Since there are now about 7,000 stage bands functioning as an integral part of music programs in high schools throughout the United States, there has obviously been a change of attitude on the part of music teachers.

Popular interest in this type of music first became apparent with the success of the many great dance bands of the 1930's. Significant changes occurred in the schools when the men began coming back from World II with a love for jazz and a realization that this music was being accepted throughout the world (if not completely in the United States) as a new art form, uniquely American.

In the early 1960's signs of another step in this gradual change became visible: the emergence of the colleges and universities as the leaders in performing jazz, in developmental experimentation, and in the training of teachers who in turn carried these advances to the high schools.

STAGE BAND OR DANCE BAND?

Not only is the attitude of music educators toward jazz changing tremendously, but even the name is being changed (to protect the innocent?). *Dance band* is becoming *Stage band*, since, with the acceptance of jazz as a unique American art form, the performing group is found more and more on stage, playing for careful listeners, rather than in the ballroom or nightclub providing functional music for dancers. The school groups play only an occasional dance, and that always under direct school supervision.

TODAY'S JAZZ MUSICIAN

The change in the musician himself has been especially significant. Years ago dance musicians were considered to be rather unreliable characters: floaters and drifters. Today the typical jazz musician is a college graduate who dresses conservatively, is extremely serious about his instrument, and totally dedicated to his art. Not only is he interested in the latest improvisations of his fellow jazzmen, but in the concert field as well. For instance, we have a tape unit on our bus which allows each man to listen through his own stereo earphones. The miles roll by very quickly as we enjoy our fine collection of Bartok, Richard Strauss, Sibelius, Stravinsky, and other serious composers.

I find the men in my band are not so interested in going out and abusing themselves physically, because they can't afford to. I don't have any rules about this—the music itself is far more demanding in this respect than any leader could possibly be. With the increased technical and artistic demands of contemporary jazz a man needs all of his faculties to present a performance consistent with his own high standards.

Some Schools Are Hesitant

So, although the high school stage band has its roots in jazz and dance music, with all the associations of the past, it is fast escaping from this stigma. Many students are not even aware that it ever existed. Still, some schools will not allow stage bands. Sometimes we find the reason to be a music instructor who does not understand this music and is terrified to imagine himself in front of a group of students who know more about the subject than he does.[1] On the other hand there are some directors who have had professional jazz experience, or who attend clinics or camps in an honest effort to learn, but who cannot convince their administrations of the value of the group.

---

[1] *Developmental Techniques for the School Dance Band Musician*, by Rev. George Wiskirchen, Berklee Press Publications, 1961, contains an excellent bibliography of instructional texts.

Figure 33: Stan Kenton at an Interview

LET'S GET STARTED

You know your students will be pleased when you announce the formation of a stage band, because they have been reminding you every day; the middle-aged civic club members will welcome your programs of some of "their" swing-era music; if the group involves many students, but is not so expensive to transport to public relations appearances as the concert band, your superintendent may smile; and it will allow you to teach a sort of "current events" music history course, as you continue to teach good playing habits.

INSTRUMENTATION AND PUBLISHED MUSIC

In the "stock arrangement" method of writing there is a great deal of doubling of a basic trio of trumpet and two saxophones, thus almost any combination from this minimum on up will sound fairly full. However, with larger groups this factor produces a concentration in the middle register which results in a monotonous muddy sound. The following table shows the minimum instrumentation and how to add other instruments.

Section	Minimum	Maximum (add in order)
Rhythm	piano dance drums	bass violin guitar
Reeds	1st sax–alto 2nd sax–tenor	3rd sax–alto 4th sax–tenor 5th sax–baritone
Brass	1st trumpet	1st trombone 2nd trumpet 2nd trombone 3rd trumpet 3rd trombone

In the "special arrangement" style, the arrangement is conceived for the full stage band and must be played by the complete instrumentation for which it is written. There are an ever increasing number of very fine arrangements in this style and they are *much* preferred over the stock arrangements.

Each year Matt Betton, with the assistance of the staff of the National Stage Band Camps, prepares a list of the stage band music published that year.[2] Each selection is graded as to difficulty, and rated as to musical quality. I find the lists to be thorough, carefully graded, and extremely impartial.

In the following list of stage band music and other recommended materials, only those rated A, B, or C (as a result of reading and listening sessions held at the Stan Kenton Clinics) are included. Complete lists include VII (professional level), and D, E, F ratings.

Grading	Rating
I, II (Elementary–Easy)	A–Excellent
III, IV (Intermediate–Medium)	B–Very Good
V, VI (Advanced–Difficult)	C–Good

[2] Annual lists are available from Matt Betton, Box 1010, Manhattan, Kansas.

Grade	Selection	Arranger	Publisher	Rating
II+.	Trebie Ahead	Bob Seibert	KSM	C plus
	Cool to the Touch	Lloyd Conley	Kendor	C
	Browsin'	Bob Seibert	KSM	C minus
II.	Blues Chorale	John LaPorta	Colin	C plus
	Pavloram	Bud Estes	Kendor	C
	Trumpet Rock	Russell Ward	Presser	C
III+.	Off the Wall	Bob Seibert	KSM	B
	No Spring This Year	Dick Fenno	Westlake	B minus
	You're My Thrill	Larry Wilcox	Fox	C plus
	Cincinnati Tatamatati	Norman Beatty	Kendor	C
	Brush Off, The	Art Dedrick	Kendor	C minus
	Exactly Like You	Dave Grusin	Shapiro	C minus
III.	Low Tide	Bob Seibert	KSM	B minus
	Easy Terms	Bob Seibert	KSM	C plus
	Rhee! Oh Rhee! (Vibes solo)	Norvo-Fry	Morris	C plus
	Diggin' Roots	Larry Wilcox	Fox	C
	Indiana	Dave Grusin	Shapiro	C
	Mode for Spring	Don French	Berklee	C
	On Stage Blues	John LaPorta	Kendor	C
	Side by Side	Dave Grusin	Shapiro	C
	Twistin' the Blues	Larry Wilcox	Fox	C
	Teach Me Tonight	Glenn Osser	Leeds	C
	You'll Be There	Dick Fenno	Westlake	C
	Gumshoe	Sammy Nestico	Kendor	C minus
	Wild Onion, The	Dick Fenno	Fenno	C minus
IV+.	Back to the Beat	Glenn Osser	Leeds	B
	Color Blind	John LaPorta	Kendor	B minus
	Virginia Creeper	Bob Seibert	KSM	B minus
	Mopsy	Ralph Mutchler	Berklee	C plus
	Automatic Transwingin'	Bob Seibert	KSM	C
	Anema E Core	Glenn Osser	Leeds	C
	Country Cousin	Don Sebesky	Colin	C
	Dave's Tune	Wally Barnett	Deagan	C
	The End of a Love Affair	Glenn Osser	Leeds	C
	Four Other Brothers	John LaPorta	Berklee	C
	Mais Oui	Glenn Osser	Leeds	C
	I Remember Basie	Dick Fenno	Fenno	C minus
	Lover Man	Glenn Osser	Leeds	C minus
	Miss Boss	Mercer Ellington	Colin	C minus

Grade	Selection	Arranger	Publisher	Rating
IV.	Bluer Than Blue	Ernie Wilkins	Colin	B
	Li'l Darlin'	Neal Hefti	Neal Hefti	B
	Young Man With the Blues	Glenn Osser	Leeds	B
	Golden Apple, The	William Russo	Colin	B minus
	Groovin' Easy	Sammy Nestico	Kendor	C plus
	Boston Bound	John LaPorta	Berklee	C
	Introducing the Band	John LaPorta	Berklee	C
	Lover Come Back to Me	Art Dedrick	Kendor	C
	Skin and Bones	Art Dedrick	Kendor	C
	Sleepy Serenade	Glenn Osser	Leeds	C
	You Don't Know What Love Is	Glenn Osser	Leeds	C
	Captain's Riff, The	Davis-Polhamus	Highland	C minus
IV—.	Play It Cool	Dick Lieb	Fox	C
V+.	Clef Dwellers, The	Tim Dennis	KSM	B
	Swinger, The	Don Sebesky	Colin	B
	Swingin' Room Only	Bob Seibert	KSM	C
V.	You Turned the Tables on Me	Ray Wright	Fox	B plus
	Jet Out of Town	Glenn Osser	Leeds	B
	Heaps of Creeps	Bob Seibert	KSM	B minus
	Let Me Love You	Glenn Osser	Leeds	B minus
	Medium Rare	Bob Seibert	KSM	B minus
	Swing, Swang, Swung	Bill St. Laurent	Berklee	B minus
	Exit Swinging	Bob Seibert	KSM	C plus
	Like Being In Love	Fred Karlin	Fox	C plus
	Sing, It's Good for You	Glenn Osser	Leeds	C plus
	Chapter & Verse	John LaPorta	Kendor	C
	No Strings Attached	M. E. Hall	KSM	C
	South of the Border	Dave Grusin	Shapiro	C minus
V—.	Beach Hop, The	Harry Betts	Pell Mell	C
	Cross Currents	Don Hannah	Kendor	C
	Two to One	Mercer Ellington	Colin	C minus
VI+.	Copley's Folly	Johnny Richards	Berklee	B
VI.	Pickwick	William Russo	Colin	B plus
	Groovin' High	Glenn Osser	Leeds	B
	Dizzy Atmosphere	Glenn Osser	Leeds	B
VI—.	Hat Full of Blues	Don Sebesky	Colin	B

Other Recommended
Materials

Organizing the School Stage Band   Don McCathern, Southern Music
The Professional Arranger–Composer   Russell Garcia, Criterion
A Manual for the Modern Drummer   DeMichael-Dawson, Berklee
First Steps to Improvisation   Phil Rizzo, Modern Music School
Spread Chord Voicings   Cleveland, Ohio
How to Play a Good Jazz Chorus   Dick Fenno Publications
Six Jazz Originals for any 2 horns   1261 S. Hickory
How to Improve your Jazz Chorus   Santa Ana, California
A Modern Method for String Bass   Berklee Press, Boston, Mass.
Theory Method and Workbook   National Stage Band Camps, Inc.
                                               Box 221, South Bend, Indiana

Recordings

Leeds–Get-Together   Leeds Music Corporation
    For trumpets, saxophones, trom-
    bones–each with 11 tunes and a
    score.

King Super 20 Saxophone Showcase   H. N. White Co.
    For five saxs, drums, string bass.
    Four tunes.

For Drummers Only   Music Minus One
    Fifty page book and 12″ LP.

Trading Solos (Drums)   Sam Ulano
    For training a drummer in art of
    ad lib solos. 12″ LP.

Jazz in the Classroom Series   Berklee Press
    Educational LP's and scores—
    for analysis, study, and perform-
    ance of jazz.

PICKING THE MEMBERS

Most directors find that the music encountered in the stage band repertoire serves as a challenge to their better players, who may be in danger of becoming bored with the repetition necessary in a concert band rehearsal to teach the younger players or the slower students.

While each director will know his own students best and have his own methods for choosing ensemble members, a few words about how the sidemen for my band are hired may be helpful:

1. I avoid formal auditions, because I become so emotionally involved that it is impossible to make a fair judgment of the man's
playing. I'm far more frightened than he is.

2. Whenever I run across an outstanding player I talk to him about
his future plans, and make it a point to remember his name. Whenever we have an opening we usually know where there is a man
who is capable of filling the chair, and anxious to join the band.

3. I expect a man to be able to read and execute in the jazz idiom,
almost immediately at sight, any piece of music which is put before him.

4. I don't believe in having fourth or fifth trumpet specialists. Unless the man is ambitious and desirous of some day playing first
trumpet, and even eventually going out on his own, we do not
want him.

5. When one man is doing an acceptable job I never bring in another and set up a competition for the chair, since I find that this
is the greatest way to have insecurity run rampant in a band.
Musicians are not machines. Their psychological condition has a
great deal to do with the way they play. The chief responsibility
of music teachers is to help students to find a reason for their
existence here on earth—to help them to come out of themselves
and to develop their natural gifts. The great music teacher is
probably 75 percent psychologist and 25 percent musician, in
that he spends much time in a mental conditioning process with
the student, trying to remove the fear and insecurity which in-
hibits so many good players.

Figure 34: Stage Band Seating Plan

TRUMPETS

2	1	3	4

TROMBONES

2	1	3	4

SAXOPHONES

2	3	1	4	5
tenor	alto	alto	tenor	baritone

Physical arrangements
and equipment

Figure 34 shows a seating plan for the stage band. In this set-up, the "lead men" (first saxophone, trumpet, and trombone) are directly in line from front to rear, and the traditional jazz soloists (the second trumpet, saxophone, and trombone) are closest to the rhythm section.

A stand and light should be purchased for each individual part. Fibre carrying cases will prevent loss and excessive wear of the music. Many brass mutes are available, and may be purchased as needed, but the *cup* and the *straight* are considered to be the minimum requirement (*see* Fig. 35, next page).

A jazz concept

The stage band player is subject to all of the usual musical demands of both the large and the small ensemble. Few of the arrangements written today especially for the high school stage band are too technically demanding, and today's players are certainly sufficiently well developed to handle them. Interpretation brings the real problems, and to maintain an effective group, each member must develop a jazz concept.

This is probably the most difficult thing to teach, since it involves the rhythmic subdivision of beats, the dimension of sound, attacks, releases, and so many other fundamentals. Although listening to records may help a student to establish a background, we find at the National Stage Band Camps that you can't beat having the leader right up in front of the band singing or playing the passages as he rehearses the group. The stage band director lacking this ability can attend clinics, seek help from friends, or listen to recorded and live jazz groups in order to learn. Each summer at our camps we have many directors who choose to sit in the groups along with their students and rehearse under a top-notch jazzman.

Rehearsal techniques

Dr. M. E. Hall, who was among the first to teach college courses in jazz, both at North Texas State College and at Michigan State University, feels that it is absolutely necessary for the successful high school band director to investigate this music thoroughly. He has written: [3]

---

[3] *The Instrumentalist*, May 1962, p. 65.

Figure 35: Brass Mutes *

STONE-LINED DERBY | STONE-LINED STRAIGHT MUTE | VEL-VE-TONE MUTE | WA-WAH MUTE | NON-TRANSPOSING FRENCH-HORN MUTE

CUP-MUTE | CLEAR-TONE MUTE | MIC-A-MUTE | BUZZ-WOW | GLEN MILLER (TUXEDO PLUNGER)

* Reproduced by courtesy of Humes & Berg, Chicago, Ill.

In terms of community relations and support I believe that the director who does not understand stage band techniques is in a worse situation than the director lacking concert band knowledge, because the average citizen can recognize popular music played poorly whereas in concert music his standards for judging are less secure.

Having developed a jazz concept of the style he wants, the director must then convey this to his students. Dr. Hall, who has done a great deal of work on some of the technical problems involved in training an effective stage band,[4] feels that the leader can play records, or take the students to hear outstanding dance bands and combos in person, but ultimately he will have to give them some method of marking their music as a reminder of what style will be used.

Figure 36: M. E. Hall earned his doctorate at New York University after a full career as a "road musician."

Experience has shown that two marks will take care of a great many situations. They are the $\wedge$ and the ———

---

[4] The material immediately following was adapted from *The Teacher's Guide to the High School Stage Band*, by M. E. Hall, copyright 1961 by H. and A. Selmer, Inc., Elkhart, Indiana. Reprinted by permission.

Figure 37: Attacks, Releases, Combinations

Attacks

♩ —"tah"—the normal, legitimate attack.

♩̄ —"dah"—the breath push; continuous air flow with periodic tongue interpolations.

Releases

♩ —tapered—the normal, legitimate release.

♩̂ —"bop"—stopped abruptly with the tongue, maintaining volume level and intensity until the very end (sometimes "taht").

Combinations

♩̄ ♩̂ —"dah-daht"—the attack of the second note serves as the release of the first.

♩̂ ♩̄ —"daht-dah"—reversed, with a space in between.

NOTE VALUE CHANGES

As in any other particular style of music, the notes are not always played exactly as they are written. Figure 38 shows the most common changes.

SPECIAL SECTION PROBLEMS

The successful director must have just as definite a conception of a stage band sound and style as he does that of an acceptable marching

Written	If Marked	Should Be Played

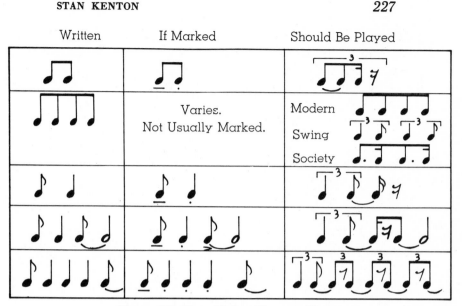

Figure 38: Note Value Change Chart

or concert band. His judgment must be equally secure when he is setting the tempo for Debussy's *La Mer* or "kicking off the beat" for *How Deep Is the Ocean?*

In discussing some of the specific section problems in his *Teacher's Guide to the High School Stage Band,* Dr. Hall notes that rhythmic subdivision of beats is the real essence of jazz. Melodies are written and performed in such manner that their rhythmic aspects oppose the basic underlying pulsation. The function of the rhythm section is to play these strong beats of the measure as the reeds and brass emphasize the weak beats. This creates a cross rhythm effect, which can be amplified by pitting one section against the other, both of which oppose the basic beat set up by the rhythm section. When this is done with taste, including frequent variation to avoid monotony, it creates a basic and important difference between poly-rhythmic jazz and the uni-rhythmic music of the 19th Century European Romantic period from which so much of our legitimate repertoire comes.

The Rhythm Section

Published parts for this section are to be considered merely as a guide, or suggestion. The rhythm section, as it provides the basic pulse of a steady, even tempo in an appropriate two or four beat style, must complement and enter into subtle inter-relations with the wind instruments. Since it is only by taking certain liberties with the written part that a jazz feeling may be achieved, the necessity for each student to acquire a real jazz concept is even more pronounced.

Wind Instrument Sections

It is up to the "lead man" to set the vibrato, phrasing, balance, and basic tone quality of the section. The competent section member ("sideman") must adapt to the style desired. Considering saxophone sound, for example, Carmen Lombardo says one thing and Lee Konitz another.

The matter of balance is affected not only by how loud each member is playing, but by the pitch of the tones played and the brand of mouthpiece and instrument he is using. Section rehearsals are essential to work out all of these important details.

Vocals

The emotions in most popular songs are best expressed through the intimate quality of the low register of the female voice, and the most successful performers are those who convey both emotion and an impression of personal intimacy with the listener.

The choice of key is a crucial factor in achieving a jazz quality. We find the lowest comfortable note for the girl and never write below that. With the boy we look for the highest comfortable note. The usual one-octave range of pop tunes will take care of the other extreme. Generally speaking, the following ranges are best:

GIRL

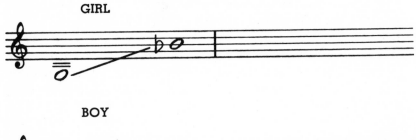

BOY

Figure 39: Voice Ranges

The boy's note will sound an octave lower than written, of course. Standard keys are usually best for boys, and a fourth or fifth lower than standard is best for girls.

Most stage band arrangements are conceived and written as instrumental numbers, but some can be used as vocal accompaniments. Since it is undesirable musically to allow anyone to play the melody along with a vocal soloist, all main melody lines should be edited out of the instrumental parts. The form of the arrangement should be analyzed and adjusted so that the vocalist begins and ends the piece, and the band is featured for no more than 16 measures in the middle. One common pattern is that in which the vocalist sings the first chorus after an instrumental introduction, and the band plays the first 16 measures of the second chorus. The singer then comes in at the bridge (seventeenth measure) and finishes the song.

STANDARDIZED STAGE BAND ARTICULATIONS

Matt Betton and the staff of the National Stage Band Camps,[5] have prepared a chart of the markings generally accepted as standard. (*see* Fig. 40, next page).

JAZZ IMPROVISATION

Jazz, in its basic improvisational form has been beyond the capability of most high school musicians, thus the emphasis has been on playing prepared arrangements. While this not as rewarding musically as self-created jazz, it has complied with the desire of the average student to play popular music.

Bach improvised two-part inventions at the keyboard during the church services for which he played the organ. While it would be musically satisfying for each of us to do this (pity the poor parishioner), most of us are content to play, after many hours of practice, those same notes which his genius was able to create extemporaneously.

Those who excel in improvisation—and there are many high school players who are doing extremely well—are those who have that one God-given talent which we call "taste."

Improvisation, if it can be taught, can assist in the development

---

[5] Ken Morris, President, Box 221, South Bend, Indiana.

Figure 40: Standardized Stage Band Articulations

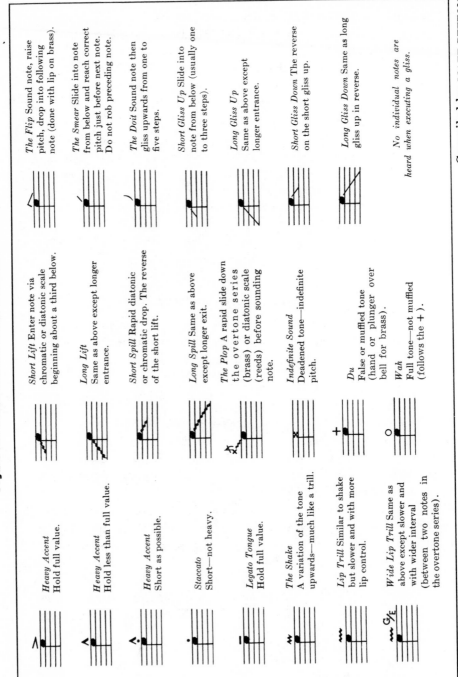

Heavy Accent Hold full value.

Heavy Accent Hold less than full value.

Heavy Accent Short as possible.

Staccato Short—not heavy.

Legato Tongue Hold full value.

The Shake A variation of the tone upwards—much like a trill.

Lip Trill Similar to shake but slower and with more lip control.

Wide Lip Trill Same as above except slower and with wider interval (between two notes in the overtone series).

Short Lift Enter note via chromatic or diatonic scale beginning about a third below.

Long Lift Same as above except longer entrance.

Short Spill Rapid diatonic or chromatic drop. The reverse of the short lift.

Long Spill Same as above except longer exit.

The Plop A rapid slide down the overtone series (brass) or diatonic scale (reeds) before sounding note.

Indefinite Sound Deadened tone—indefinite pitch.

Du False or muffled tone (hand or plunger over bell for brass).

Wah Full tone—not muffled (follows the +).

The Flip Sound note, raise pitch, drop into following note (done with lip on brass).

The Smear Slide into note from below and reach correct pitch just before next note. Do not rob preceding note.

The Doit Sound note then gliss upwards from one to five steps.

Short Gliss Up Slide into note from below (usually one to three steps).

Long Gliss Up Same as above except longer entrance.

Short Gliss Down The reverse on the short gliss up.

Long Gliss Down Same as long gliss up in reverse.

No individual notes are heard when executing a gliss.

Compiled by **MATT BETTON**

of creativity which educators call for in our school systems. John La-Porta, who teaches at the Berklee School of Music in Boston, has a course in jazz improvisation.

Figure 41: John La Porta has earned two degrees at the Manhattan College of Music and was a member of the American Youth Symphony Orchestra directed by Leopold Stokowski. He was the arranger and coach who assisted Marshall Brown in the development of the famous Farmingdale High School jazz group.

LEARNING JAZZ

John LaPorta feels that everybody learns jazz in one way or another, although much of it is certainly "unconscious learning," *i.e.*, through environmental influences. Some of the Negro musicians, for example, have been exposed to jazz influences from their earliest years: the gospel singing style at their churches, the records and folk music at home, and the entire racial tradition and close association with the

beginnings of jazz. In this way some musicians have been able to cir-
cumvent most of the basic jazz training which is necessary for the
young fellow in Elephant's Breath, Iowa, who never heard a jazz record. It is difficult to determine the ratio of talent to experience without
being able to measure the exact amount of "unconscious learning."

TEACHING JAZZ

Mr. LaPorta separates his conscious teaching of jazz into two
phases: performing techniques, and instrumental ear training. *Legato,
staccato,* slides, fall-offs, etc. are all performing techniques, and concern the *way* things are said. The object of this phase of his teaching
is to give the student sufficient technique to be able to communicate
clearly any musical idea he may have.

Instrumental ear training leads to melodic composition in the
jazz idiom, and concerns *what* things are said.

In his course at the Berklee School of Music, Mr. LaPorta first
plays rhythms on his instrument and the students answer with exactly the
same rhythms. Then he plays simple melodies, using only notes in the
major scale, in all keys. Once again the student must play back exactly
the same melody. Continuing to concentrate on melody, he makes it
progressively more difficult by widening the intervals in the tunes.
Students are encouraged to play along with records to learn the
repertoire, and to transpose these standard tunes to different keys.
This step continues to develop the ear and memory and also teaches
interpretation.

The next step is "rhythmic displacement," in which students improvise changes in note values, but do not change pitches. This is
basically the style Louis Armstrong employs so well, since although
he adds an occasional note and many special effects, including a distinctive *vibrato,* the melody notes are seldom altered significantly.

The student should know all of his major scales before he begins
this training, and he should be studying chords as he progresses. Using
the chord progression and melody of any tune as a base, he eventually
will be able to improvise original melodies which are theoretically
correct and in the jazz idiom.

LaPorta recreates in the classroom the working combo situation
where one man suggests a melody and the others pick it up, caress it,
harmonize it, pass it around, develop it, and discard it for another
which has been suggested in the process.

At Least Correct

Mr. LaPorta explains that one of the reasons the classically oriented musician experiences difficulty with jazz improvisation is that he has already spent many years developing the control necessary to play accurately what is on the printed page—at least 99 out of a 100 times. Now, as a jazz improvisor, he is expected to produce, extemporaneously, fresh melodies in such a way that his own individual mark is unmistakably apparent. Once the opportunity has been afforded the legitimate student to play jazz he seems to learn quickly. Solo quality may range all the way from "correct . . . and sterile" to "correct . . . and inspired," depending on the natural ability of the student. Very few people are creative jazz artists. At least the rest can learn to play *correctly*, even if they lack the God-given quality of true artistic genius.

A Look at the Future

Although the theoretical aspects of jazz (overtone series, melody, harmony, form, etc.) are really no different from those of the European influenced musical periods, the approach to the performance of the music is vastly different. As crude as the present form will some day appear to have been, and as long a time as it will take to develop, I feel that we have had the privilege of witnessing the beginnings of a truly American musical era.

Since the professional is so bogged down with the commercial demands placed upon him, I feel that the leadership in developing this American music will come from the colleges and universities. Every day more schools are adding jazz courses and many are building first rate jazz departments. Students from North Texas State College, for example, have come directly into my band with no other professional experience. I expect most schools to have recording contracts in the future so that the end-products of their experimentation can be heard by the "people."

DON'T FORGET THE PEOPLE

We have seen composers and players become contemptuous of "the people," label them "musical illiterates," and turn their creative genius so completely in upon itself that they are no longer able to communicate and their art reverberates, unencumbered by human flesh, in a hollow ivory tower forever.

I have found that the challenge of trying to develop a salable product somehow keeps you honest. In arranging for my band through the years I have occasionally written arrangements strictly "for the people," in order to attract attention to the band during a period of poor record sales, or to give me the time and money to work on other assignments that I thought were really important. Looking back years later, I have realized that these times when I felt I was "selling out" have resulted in some of the most important recordings the band has ever made, and the things I thought were "really important" were really quite *un*important and have (appropriately) been forgotten. Often in searching for something that will be attractive to "the people," you discover things that make a great deal of sense.

Great art seems to have thrived when the creators had their "backs to the wall." Those in charge of the university programs will have to be very careful that the no-pressure, cloistered atmosphere which they will enjoy does not allow the art to become so over-refined, narrow, and uncommunicative that it dies the death of self-indulgence.

Just as music once emanated from the churches of Europe, I feel that the music of the future will come from the American colleges and universities. When jazz has completed the move to its new home, all of the old stigma of the corner saloon and the houses of ill repute will become a part of those earthy roots which are common to the history of every living, growing form . . . be it botanical, organizational, or aesthetic.

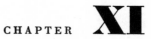

Summer
Music
Camps

by **Joseph E. Maddy**

Interlochen, Michigan

235

Joseph E. Maddy

was born at Wellington, Kansas in 1891, and became the first Supervisor of Instrumental Music in America (Rochester, N.Y., 1918). In 1922, working with T. P. Giddings, he developed the "Universal Teacher"—the basis for all instrumental class method books. With this book one teacher could instruct large classes, and thus the way was opened for tremendous growth in public school instrumental music programs.

In 1927 the National Convention of School Superintendents resolved to urge all American schools to give music and art equal recognition with "the other fundamental subjects" in education. This important decision came as a direct result of a concert by the All-American High School Symphony Orchestra, organized and trained by Joseph E. Maddy. Regional and all-state groups have been formed everywhere based on the pattern set by Mr. Maddy with this group.

As a result of the begging of orchestra students, who wanted to keep the group together all summer, the National Music Camp at Interlochen was established. In 1957 The Interlochen Press, and in 1962 The Interlochen Arts Academy (a year-round boarding school offering both artistic and academic training) became two more of Mr. Maddy's vital ideas which have grown to reality.

In the foreword to *Joe Maddy of Interlochen*, published by Henry Regnery Company, Chicago, in 1963, Van Cliburn wrote: "Nowhere in the world is there a place—or a man—turning out more musical missionaries than Dr. Joe Maddy's summer music camp at Interlochen, Michigan."

236

When I was about 12 years old I played piccolo and clarinet in a boy's band from my home town of Wellington, Kansas. We went out of town on a week's camping trip and were supposed to have band practice every day and give a concert in the little town of South Haven, Kansas, which was about 15 miles from home. I remember that we gave the concert, but we didn't do much practicing.

Contrasted with that experience is the fact that today hundreds of high school bands attend a camp for at least a week, often many miles from home, where they spend hours every day in very serious practice, and give numerous concerts. During the eight weeks at Interlochen, for instance, we average between 350 and 400 programs by our 1,700 campers.

TYPES OF CAMPS

The Comprehensive Camp, like the National Music Camp, offers a variety of experiences in all of the arts.

The Special Camp concentrates on one area, like baton twirling, precision marching, or stage band.

The Professional Camp features a staff which will take over your band and work up specific shows or routines.

The College Camp allows your band to stay in college dormitories on the campus and to use the facilities of the school.

The Cooperative Camp is operated by several bands and directors, who get together to share the work, expenses, and profits.

The Local Camp is organized and run by the director with the help of his band boosters club.

How to choose a camp

You should be certain when you choose a camp that your students will receive training which is more specialized than that available to them every day at home.

The conductor is the most important single factor to be considered. He must be the sort of man who can inspire your students to accomplish as much as possible within the camping period. "Learn more in less time" is the motto at Interlochen.

Figure 42: Joseph E. Maddy conducts one of the many Interlochen performing groups.

The organization must be such that no time is wasted. A good librarian and set-up crew must see to it that everything is ready and that rehearsals start on time.

The faculty must be varied enough to give sufficient attention to the specialized training of the youngsters. At the National Music Camp we usually have one instructor for every 15 students.

The staff must contain all the people necessary to maintain a home away from home: medical, maintenance, food service, etc., depending on the size of the camp. Counselors must possess real leadership qualities.

The physical facilities, while they do not have to be "plush," must

meet adequate health standards in the living areas, and musical standards in the rehearsal areas.

The recreational program is a very important part of every music
camp. Good medium temperature swimming must be available.

The purpose of the camp must be consistent with your own
educational philosophy and purpose.

The carefully supervised life should include excellent food and
regular hours.

The balance of instrumentation is very important and a good
camp will consider this carefully when accepting students.

The other students should serve as a challenge for yours. Ability,
as well as instrumentation, must be balanced. We use audition tapes
for this purpose.

The music library must be large enough that the students who
return each year can play different programs.

The fees should be realistic, not necessarily cheap. It takes a
great deal of money to operate a camp properly.

The schedule should be full, well-planned, and balanced. The
following are schedules for both the comprehensive and the local type
camp:

HIGH SCHOOL DIVISION DAILY CLASS SCHEDULE

National Music Camp
Interlochen, Michigan

All classes meet daily, Tuesday through Saturday.

Bands, orchestras, choir and certain other major classes
also meet Monday mornings.

8:20–10:50 A.M.	Orchestra (major)
	Dance (major)
	Drama Production (major)
9:00– 9:50 A.M.	Survey of Music Literature
	Beginning Music Composition
	Beginning Organ Class
	Ensembles (brass and woodwind)
	Vocal Sight Reading
	Voice and Diction
10:00–12:50 P.M.	Basic Ceramics and Sculpture (major)
	Advanced Ceramics and Sculpture (major)

10:00–10:50 A.M.   Beginning String Instrument Class
Beginning Wind Instrument Class
Ensembles (brass and woodwind)
Music Theory
Sculpture
Organ Class (advanced)
Costuming
Oral Interpretation
Stagecraft

11:00–11:50 A.M.   Choir (major)
Conducting
Beginning Harp Class
String Instrument Workshop
Piano Tuning
Music Laboratory (beginning)
Acting Technique
Art
Ceramics

12:00–12:50 P.M.   Girls Glee Club
Music Theory
Advanced Music Theory
Creative Counterpoint
Beginning Piano Class
Music Laboratory (advanced)

12:30– 1:20 P.M.   Beginning Ballet Technique
Advanced Ballet Technique
Advanced Modern Dance Technique
Piano Repertoire (Thurs. only)
Piano Literature (T.W.F.S.)

1:20– 3:20 P.M.   Band (major)
Drama Production (major)
Fundamentals of Radio and Television (major)
Basic Art (major)
Advanced Art (major)

1:30– 2:20 P.M.   Beginning Wind Instrument Class
Beginning String Instrument Class
Beginning Percussion Class
Music Theory
Beginning Music Composition
Survey of Music Literature
Piano Ensembles
Voice and Diction
String Instrument Workshop
Beginning Modern Dance Technique

2:30– 3:20 P.M.	Ensembles (brass and woodwind)
	Advanced Music Composition
	Orchestration
	Ceramics

3:30– 4:20 P.M.	String Orchestra (3 periods weekly)
	String Ensembles (2 periods weekly)
	Operetta Workshop
	Ensembles (Wind or Percussion)
	Music Laboratory (beginning)
	Make-up and Theatre History
	Stagecraft
	Oral Interpretation
	Art
	Costuming

| 4:30– 5:20 P.M. | Piano Ensembles (girls) |
| 4:30– 6:00 P.M. | Swimming, Sports and Recreation |

| Evenings | Concerts, sight reading, recitals, plays, operetta, dance performance, parties. |

Five periods daily in arts activities are considered a normal load for a high school camper because of the many special activities and recreational advantages that are open to them. Students enrolling for private lessons should reserve at least one hour daily of practice time for each weekly lesson to permit adequate preparation.

DAILY SCHEDULE [1] (Local-Type Camp)

W.Y.A.H.S. Band Camp
Camp Mizpeh

Monday, August 21

8:00–11:00	Enroute to Camp Mizpeh
11:30–12:00	Orientation meeting and unloading
12:00–12:45	Lunch
12:45– 1:30	Move into assigned cabins
1:30– 3:00	Music rehearsal, dining hall
3:00– 5:00	Swimming
5:00– 6:00	Dinner
6:30– 8:30	Marching drill (no instruments)
8:30–11:00	Square dance (Al Hughes, caller)

---

[1] From *Band Training Camps*, copyright 1962, by Alan Wyand (1100 W. Market St., York, Pa.).

Tuesday thru Friday, August 22 to 25

6:45	Rise and shine
7:45	Breakfast: big day ahead, so eat plenty
8:30– 9:45	Music rehearsal: dining hall
10:00–11:30	Marching drill: football field
12:00–12:45	Lunch
12:45– 1:15	Free time
1:15– 3:00	Marching drill
3:00– 5:00	Swimming, softball, etc.
5:00– 6:00	Dinner
6:30– 8:30	Rehearsal (to be announced)
8:30–11:00	Tuesday: Planned recreation, scavenger hunt, and cabin skits (Mr. Umbarger and committee)
	Wednesday: Bowling party (transportation to alleys by bus)
	Thursday: Planned entertainment (wait and see!), bonfire, and marshmallow roast
	Friday: Dance (music by our own W.Y.A.H.S. dance band)

Saturday, August 26

6:45	Up and at 'em
7:45	Breakfast
8:30– 9:45	Rehearsal (to be announced)
10:00–11:30	Rehearsal (to be announced)
12:00–12:45	Final meal at camp
1:15– 2:30	Rehearsal (to be announced)
2:30– 3:30	Pack and load busses
3:30– 7:00	Enroute back to York

NOTE: Tentative schedule is included with information sheets and sent to all parents and students two weeks prior to camp.

So you want to start a camp?

There should be a considerable amount of money available. We had $15,000 to start the National Music Camp, and at the end of the first year we were $40,000 in the red! The end of the second year found us $65,000 behind and this was back in the 1920's!

The thing that often leads to the failure of a camp—and I do not like to see them fail—is when several directors get together, decide to donate their services, and operate the camp on "volunteer help." They will help—as long as they do the conducting—and when they are finished, they leave! People really have to be paid in order to be dependable. Volunteer helpers do not do very well in anything.

While a college campus may not have the same atmosphere as a beautiful spot on a lake, it is a good way to get started. A valuable experience for the students can be created through the relatively inexpensive use of already established facilities. The important thing is a good conductor who is backed up by a good organization and a good faculty.

Figure 43: Clarinet Section students practice on their instruments.

PURPOSE

Learning to play better should be the chief goal of a band at camp. In a camp atmosphere with a full schedule of musical activities free of the many interruptions of normal home and school interests, a great deal can be accomplished.

Every Interlochen activity is mildly but persistently competitive—just as every activity is in mature life in America. We have five performing organizations rehearsing at the same hour. While more expensive to operate, it is certainly more efficient, since whenever the first chair player of a lower organization can outplay the last chair player of the next higher group, the students can be exchanged. This represents the active philosophy of the National Music Camp: "Promotion through achievement rather than age."

Those who win superior ratings at Interlochen are assured of success in their life ambitions in the arts, while those who fail to excel seek other vocations, but continue as supporters of cultural activities in their communities. While it may at first seem harsh to say that one of our prime purposes at Interlochen is to get students *out* of music, let me explain.

In 1962 our students played a concert on the White House lawn. On that occasion I met the President's administrative assistant, Henry Hall Wilson, who reminded me that he had been a "pretty poor second oboe player at camp," and that he had "decided to go into something else." A former staff member is the President's electronic advisor, while still a third person (who was just an ordinary cornet player at camp) was the legislative assistant to Vice President Nixon. We did those men a service by allowing them to see that they did *not* have the talent to follow music as a profession.

But even though the chief purpose of a large comprehensive type camp may be to serve as a proving ground for youthful talent, most band camps throughout the country do (and should) simply try to improve the quality of the band by helping each individual student to make progress on his own instrument, in an atmosphere of healthful outdoor living and recreation.

RECREATION

Many musicians are so intent on their playing that they neglect recreation, both at home and at camp. We find that we must *require* students to get some exercise. An hour and a half is set aside each day for swimming, sports, and recreation, and we do not allow any music during that time.

While we do not absolutely require it, we feel that everyone should be able to swim, and our athletic staff makes it interesting for them to learn. We stress the individual and small group sports, such as volleyball, badminton, and tennis, rather than the large team spectator sports.

ALL-STATE SUMMER CAMP

In 1942 the Michigan All-State Band began coming to summer camp at Interlochen. The best players are selected from about 600 cities and towns. Financing is handled locally through PTA's, local clubs, and various fund raising techniques. Whereas most other all-state bands meet only for a few days, each summer these Michigan students spend two full weeks in vigorous rehearsal and performance of a comprehensive repertoire, under the baton of well known successful conductors, and under the guidance of the National Music Camp faculty.

As a result of the motivation of this all-state system the standards have increased tremendously throughout the state of Michigan. In 1962 we took a very select group of 103 players to Washington for the White House lawn concert. The members were carefully chosen by tryout. *Six times* as many Michigan students were chosen for the trip as were students from a neighboring state with an equally outstanding school music program (and Michigan camp enrollment was just slightly higher).

I can heartily recommend this system to every state in the Union, because I have seen the results. The camp can be held almost anywhere (a college campus is fine). The important thing is the incentive for achievement which such a plan offers each individual instrumental student in the state.

THE FUTURE

American music teachers have developed the finest instrumentation—one which has been adopted throughout the world—probably because we have been able to develop fine players of *all* instruments by teaching *music* first, and the mechanics of the instrument second. Our best oboe players at Interlochen for years have come from little towns in Texas, communities which are far away from any professional oboe instructor. This is in direct contrast to the European system, which seems to be developing soloists who cannot read music at sight, have little knowledge of literature, and lack personal repertoire.

In our free society, where such fine teaching is so generally available, everyone should have the opportunity to study music if he desires. However, American education has shortchanged the potential musician, artist, actor, and dancer. This is true today more than ever because many schools are dropping their arts courses to make room for more science. Surely the intention is not to make everybody scientists so we can develop more weapons to kill off more of those who share life on this planet with us. But preparation for war has always led to

war. While we certainly must keep our top scientists at work developing weapons for our defense, at the same time we ought to be working
just as hard developing the arts—which are the sinews of peace.

During a period of time at a summer camp, away from home, in
an artistic atmosphere, close to Nature, with an opportunity to work
and relax, to think and dream, your students may discover (and you
may rediscover, before a tough football season sets in) all of the
wonderful things which music can accomplish *now* in your community, and ultimately what a significant contribution the arts can
make to the fate of the world.

We feel the importance of the arts so strongly that we have
dedicated the Kresge Assembly Hall at Interlochen to "*The Promotion
of World Friendship Through the Universal Language of the Arts.*"

Baton Twirling

by **Don Sartell**

Janesville, Wisconsin

Don Sartell

is in constant demand throughout the United States for twirling camps, clinics, and contests, although he calls twirling and the training of majorettes "strictly a non-professional hobby."

He is primarily a publisher. He founded *The Drum Major Magazine*, the oldest, largest, and most widely circulated twirling magazine in the world, in 1945, when he was 17. Several other magazines are also under his direction, including *Young and Beautiful*, the official magazine of the charm and beauty field.

Mr. Sartell was born in 1928, in Janesville, Wisconsin, the son of a career army bandmaster. Both facts worked to introduce him to twirling. When his father was stationed in the deep South, this young Yankee sixth grader soon discovered he was not too popular in town. Spending a lot of time on the post, he saw a twirling performance by Don Williams, a former national champion and the originator of the fire baton. Lessons followed. Six months later young Don Sartell had won the Wisconsin State Championship and was started on a phenomenal performance career which was to include innumerable medals and trophies, and an appearance before President Roosevelt; an organizational career which includes "Miss Majorette" contests in nearly every state, twirling camps in every area of the country; and an extremely successful private teaching career through which he has helped literally thousands of girls, but has never charged a student for a lesson.

248

There are nearly one million baton twirlers in the United States. This activity—sometimes classified a "sport," but more accurately called an "art" by those who really know—ranks second only to the Girl Scouts in the number participating throughout the country. The third week of July has been designated "National Baton Twirling Week" and state governors sign proclamations recognizing the values of the "art."

USES ARE VARIED

Law enforcement officers have long called twirling a "great deterrent to juvenile delinquency," and recently children in deaf, crippled, and blind schools have profited from its therapeutic value.

Girls who do not exercise or practice in a sport tend to gain weight, become thick-thighed, and lose firmness of body as they grow older. Not only does the twirler develop a strong, healthy body with the ability to move quickly, coordinate between baton and body, and use either hand with comfort and skill, but she sharpens her reactions and improves her mental agility as well.

Above all, the girl who twirls has the opportunity to gain self-confidence. Every little girl finds something wrong with herself; she is in her own little dream world. Twirling provides the "safety-valve": the outlet for her inner desire to do something, to achieve, to accomplish.

STANDARDS ARE IMPORTANT

The girl who is intelligent, possesses qualities of leadership, and who will practice diligently will be both an excellent student and a top-level majorette. I very seldom find a really outstanding twirler who is not on the honor roll. However, if a band director allows 30 girls to march in front of his band and has no requirements other than wearing a short skirt and doing some dancing, he has problems. He must set and maintain high physical, moral, and academic standards. The girls should be taught to always remember that:

Talent is God-given—be humble.
Fame is man-given—be grateful.
Conceit is self-given—be careful.

REWARDS ARE SATISFYING

Many colleges and universities offer financial aid for excellent twirlers who will blend with and add to their band programs. High school band directors should advise the girl seeking such help to:

1. Make a list of the colleges she would like to attend.
2. Write letters to both the admissions office *and the band director* of each school asking for information about the majorette program, explaining her intentions.
3. Arrange for an audition and personal interview with the college band director. Very few directors will accept a twirler on a letter of recommendation alone, and they resent pressure of any sort.

Although a few become professional twirlers or go on to movies and TV, most of the girls settle down in a community, raise families, and enjoy the benefits of a quick mind in a healthy body, plus the poise and personality developed through the self-confidence that twirling helped to provide.

Most girls will teach a few students. Fees vary from 50 cents for class to $2.50 for private lessons. As they make "pin money," there are occasional opportunities to travel, and they experience the satisfaction of helping other young girls find that important "safety valve."

Twirling is a tremendous steppingstone. For the vast majority of the nearly one million who participate, it picks them up in adolescence and drops them off as they are graduated from high school; it gives them something to fill their lives during that very crucial stage of their physical and emotional development.

WHAT ABOUT THE BOYS?

Up until 1935 there were relatively few twirlers and they were all boys. My inspiration, Major C. W. Boothe, a baton twirler, juggler, gun spinner, Swiss flag swinger, and the first twirling instructor in Chicago, started holding a contest at the Chicagoland Music Festival. At that time more girls began to twirl and within five years outnumbered the boys 10 to one. Now they are ahead by well over a thousand to one.

Because the overwhelming number of twirling students were girls, within just a few years they had grown up and were dominating the teaching field as well. The masculine style of the early 1940's began to disappear as some of the younger male twirlers picked up the mannerisms of their female teachers, resulting in performances that were not always a credit to twirling.

Band directors can do a great deal to correct this embarrassing situation. The boy drum major, for instance, should have a very firm military posture and beat. He should be just as masculine as the majorettes are feminine, but sometimes instructors allow their boys to execute a frilly little beat, and ask them to kick their legs in some ridiculous fashion.

A uniform which fits exactly will help convey the desirable image of masculinity, but as I travel around the country I see stock size, or hand-me-down affairs with pants too long, in-seams too low, and shoulders drooping. While the majorettes are called "fit-misses" by the spectators, it is no wonder that the drum major is sometimes known as a "misfit."

There are a few dozen very fine professional, obviously masculine twirlers and there will probably always be some very good ones at all levels. I personally do not encourage boys to go into the twirling field, because, due to the extreme shortage of male teachers, they are almost always forced to study with girls. Besides, there are so many other wonderful physical activities for boys, as opposed to a very limited number for girls.

THE DESSERT

Not many years ago band directors generally were uninformed about majorettes. As a result they were so ashamed of the poorly trained girls who went on the field, that some became discouraged and eliminated twirling from their programs.

I consider the marching band the "main course" in any show and the majorettes the "dessert." Of course, there are times when the dessert can be used to carry the meal for a while.

Let's consider the director in a small community with a new program.

Since it takes less time to train proficient majorettes than it does to build a top band, the director might want to use a fairly large majorette corps in the early years, playing down the inability of the band. As the band develops, the twirling group should take its place as the "dessert." The proper balance in an ideal program is one drum major, three featured twirlers, and one majorette at the head of each marching file of the band.

Sometimes the dessert can get the meal out of an uncomfortable position. I remember when I was doing a lot of performing, I came into a town in Wisconsin which had a good band, but not nearly as good a group as their rival's band which they were meeting that night. The band director was worried. I offered to help his majorettes work up a special routine, but he felt it was too late (and when I saw the majorettes I agreed). He asked me to perform, and I consented after three seconds of urging (twirlers were real egotists in those days).

After the 150 members of the visiting band had presented a beautiful show, we turned out the lights, and I did my act which involved one, two, three, four, and five fire batons; we stole the show! The people never were able to decide which school had the better band!

SETTING UP THE ORGANIZATION

I believe in the delegation of duty in an organization. The band director who does not set up a chain of command, feeling that everything demands his personal attention is: (1) kidding himself; (2) passing up a wonderful opportunity to teach students; and (3) needlessly restricting his activities. He should have more freedom to observe, check, and improve the operations of his groups.

The following groups can be set up, each feeding the next one in a graduated scale of selectivity:

The Community or Recreational Corps may be formed by a non-school group, such as a dance studio, or the city recreation department. In towns which still frown upon twirling, the director might (off the record) arrange for a local girl with twirling experience to start a group. Once established, the people will generally see the advantages and support a school program.

The Elementary or Intermediate Training Corps may be guided by the girl's physical education teacher, since twirling can be put to good use in a physical fitness program, or instruction may be handled by the high school majorettes as an extracurricular activity. You must not forget the "masses" when dealing with the public education of children.

The High School Twirling Corps can serve as a separate performing unit and as a feeder for the band majorettes. The director should tell the entire group, "Girls, if you work hard, I'll let you march in the annual Homecoming Parade" . . . and he should live up to that promise. By attaching his junior high school drum section to the group, he can provide experience for his young percussionists as he adds another attraction to his show package.

The Select Precision Unit of the Twirling Corps has become so popular that a National Twirling Corps Contest is being held. At least 12 members are required for competition; 16 is an ideal size for ease of maneuvering, balance, etc.; however, it is best to leave the number flexible, depending on the number available and the size of the full corps.

As with any ensemble, doing everything *together* is the important thing. The unison group can advance only to the level of its weakest member. Absolute precision on a few basic twirls is a beautiful effect and should not be destroyed by trying to do routines that are too difficult.

BAND MAJORETTE, RECREATION, OR CONTEST TWIRLER?

Although tremendous individual differences will be noted, there are basically only three categories of twirlers:

1. *Recreation Twirlers.* I call these "baton carriers." This group usually consists of those twirlers connected with playgrounds, dance schools, etc.
2. *School Level—the Majorette Group.* These include those majorettes and twirlers who are primarily concerned with school band performances and other activities.

3. *The Contest Twirler Group.* This takes in about 30,000 people across the country who are dedicated artists. They work several hours a day for 8–10 years to perfect top contest level routines.

The largest number fall into the middle group who work quite hard, but never make it to the top category. If the band rehearses on school time, and the students receive credit, the majorettes should also have these privileges, if the band director has set up a systematic program of instruction and advancement for them. They must not be simply turned loose to practice the wrist spin and the figure 8 throughout their entire high school career. A good precision routine with sufficient variety will take anywhere from six weeks to three months to learn.

Those in the *majorette* category should play a musical instrument and remain a part of the band program throughout the year; but the technical demands on the *contest twirler* are equal to those in any art, and they should spend the concert season working to perfect this skill.

CHOOSING THE BAND
MAJORETTES

Many times a contest is held, all participants graded, and the top girls are "in." This places the band director in the frustrating position of having to accept a poor twirler who had a good day as he watches a fine twirler who had an off day return to the feeder corps.

I prefer to use a series of private auditions in contest form. This allows the director to get to know the girl, to understand her problems at home, to share her dreams and ambitions, and to show the genuine interest *in her* which breeds that friendship and mutual concern on which sound teaching is based.

The head majorette should be chosen with a great deal of care since the situation resulting from a bad choice is not so much a reflection on the girl chosen, but on the ability of the band director to make a proper selection.

THE UNIFORM

In general the trend is toward those outfits which allow the freedom of movement so vital to an effective performance, but at the same time display excellent taste.

Judy Lynn Anderson

Photo by *Aida*, Milwaukee.

Sherry Lou Daly

Figure 44: Twirling costumes have changed greatly. The bulky 1907 model * has given way to the ideal school band style worn by **Judy Lynn Anderson** of Hays, Kansas (center), and the ideal costume for contest twirling worn by former national champion **Sherry Lou Daly** of Milwaukee, Wisconsin.

* From the DeMoulin Brothers' 1907 catalog; reproduced by permission.

A few schools have failed to accept the modern American concept that "pretty legs are here to stay," and they still require bulky knee length skirts. On the other hand I see uniforms which seem to have been inspired by a traveling "girlie show." An investigation of the feelings of the girls and their parents should be made, and the accepted standards of the community determined. The school administration can then make clear to the band director what is considered "proper attire."

Although the band boosters club should assist in the selection and purchase of the uniforms, the final choice must rest with the band director, since it is *his* concept which determines the balance of every element in the "package deal" he places before the public (which holds *him* solely responsible).

WEATHER AND MEDICAL PROBLEMS

Over the years improvements in training techniques seem to have produced majorettes who have amazing resistance to extremes of both heat and cold. Band directors in ultra-cold areas can help by allowing flesh colored leotards (indistinguishable at 10 feet), insisting on warm undergarments and extra sweaters, and by limiting the period of exposure.

Heat prostration (a serious thing in parades) is quite often of psychosomatic origin, due to anxieties and frustrations connected with a "prima donna" feeling. Those who are chronic sufferers should be eliminated from the band program on hot days. The director who knows his band is going to be in a long parade in Florida during August, for instance, can combine showmanship with concern for the students by providing not only salt tablets, but yellow parasols . . . or some such unusual solution.

There should be a medical advisor on every trip and at every band performance. Although a doctor would be ideal, a person who can administer first aid and who knows when to call in a physician can be of tremendous help.

The normal healthy high school girl will experience no adverse effects from physical activity during the menstrual period; the only difference seems to be that her perspiration at this time has a tendency to "de-chrome" the baton.

The "U" system of
teaching

In 1949, while returning from a twirling clinic, a friend and I were involved in an automobile accident. After about a year's recuperation, I still found it difficult to concentrate on performing, and I began to think about sharing some of the material which I had so zealously guarded for years.

I made forays into several teaching areas, and finally settled on super-advanced contest twirling—the thing I felt I knew best. Every once in a while I would run into a "diamond-in-the-rough": a girl with ability beyond local training. In 1951, one of these girls, Hilda Gay Mayberry, defeated the national champion in open competition. This first big victory for one of my students gave me a great deal of hope and confidence, and from that time on I have concentrated in this area.[1]

While working with each girl I gradually developed the "U" system of teaching, which involves very intricate timing and is based on a consideration of the problems and capabilities of each individual student.

Figure 45: Hilda Gay Mayberry as National Baton Twirling Champion . . . and 10 years later, as **Mrs. Cortland K. Cox,** wife and mother.

---

[1] Mr. Sartell's "concentration in this area" has resulted in his students winning over 15 national championships.—*Ed.*

Many teachers waste a great deal of time looking for the "gimmick" which will make their students stand out. I believe in doing the ordinary extraordinarily well, and in developing techniques which will bring out the individuality of each student so well that anyone else can copy the trick, but no one can equal the presentation of it.

Gary Cooper once said to me: "Set your goals high. It isn't necessary that you always reach them, but it is important that your best qualities will be brought out while you're trying to."

BEST AGE TO START

Twirling at an early age can be as detrimental as it is advantageous at a later time. Although *elementary* twirling is certainly to be desired, the bones of the human body are not ready for *advanced* baton training until a girl is at least nine years old. I know girls whose crooked fingers and twisted bodies are evidence of advanced finger work and contorted positions before that time.

The director should advise parents to be wary of the occasional unscrupulous dance studio operator who sees the financial advantage of starting large groups of twirlers at age three.

PRACTICE

Three 20-minute periods per day will get the best results. This one hour is the maximum for most high school students, and many girls achieve satisfactory results with less.

CAMPS

The best way to learn twirling is by direct contact with an outstanding teacher, and there are many fine summer camps which provide an opportunity for the interested girl to do this. Since a camp can be only as good as the teaching staff, the band director must investigate the instructional phase of the program in order to separate the "play" camps from the "twirling" camps. A list of camps as well as a state-by-state list of registered teachers is available from the National Baton Twirling Association.[2]

---

[2] NBTA was organized by Mr. Sartell as the "National Board of Technical Advisors," but most people assumed it meant "National Baton Twirling Association," so it was changed to that. Help on *all* twirling problems is available by writing to NBTA, Box 266, Janesville, Wisconsin.—*Ed.*

BOOKS

Learning from books is very difficult in the twirling field due to the problems of the missing third dimension. The "sequence approach" which we are using with pictures, in which the camera shoots like a machine gun, is a step in the right direction, but there is still no completely satisfactory way of illustrating twirling routines or techniques in a book or on film.

SELECTING THE BATON

The average girl is twirling a baton which is hindering her advancement. Out of roughly 700 students at a university twirling camp we found only about 10 girls who had batons which fitted them properly.

The length of the baton should be the same as the distance from the armpit to the tip of the longest finger.

The thickness is determined by the inside size of the middle finger joint. The fingers should close comfortably around the shaft of the baton.

The balance point should be about one-fourth to one-half inch off center, towards the ball.

FUNDAMENTALS AND RUDIMENTS

Posture, poise, and strutting should be taught immediately, and all early instruction should include a great deal of active participation by the pupils. Students are bored very quickly by long explanations without accompanying action. Exercises to develop a healthy body with strong arms and wrists should be included in the instruction.

Each teacher has his own set of rudiments. Most include the wrist spin, figure 8, two-hand spin, etc. The National Baton Twirling Association is developing a standard list of rudiments in three categories: basic, advanced, and super-advanced.

TERMS

There are a great number of terms in both general and local use. Much confusion can be eliminated by using descriptive phrases, rather than nicknames. Instead of asking a student to do the "jet series," for instance, I prefer to say, "Do the back-catch, turn-left, catch-under-left-leg series." After all, we are only dealing with left and right arms and legs, and fingers which can be numbered (1,2,3,4 and thumb).

The majorette must hold her head up and chin in, assuming a tall and majestic appearance. The abdominal muscles are pulled *up and in* rather than *just in*. One knee must remain straight while the other is bent.

As long as a girl maintains a basically healthy, natural looking posture, slight variations in movement are pleasing, but when these additional motions cause her to look awkward and unnatural they are certainly not in good taste and should be eliminated.

A smoothly graceful strut with a compelling, yet restrained, rhythmic drive requires careful training and a great deal of practice.

As a very *short* sequence in a show, after the majorettes have *first* established themselves as a dignified unit, a little hip-swinging might show versatility and serve as a good change of pace, but the girl who is constantly gyrating or who pumps her arms and legs up and down is completely out of place. Strutting is merely exaggerated marching, but exaggerated strutting is often distasteful.

COMPOSING THE ROUTINE

Whereas the contest twirler is trying to squeeze as many tricks as possible into the allotted two and one-half minute period in order to impress a professional judge, the band majorettes are performing for an audience of laymen who will like them only if they can understand and appreciate the things the girls are doing. Obviously the routines must be conceived from contrasting viewpoints.

The band majorette routine should be basically simple, have frequent repetition of impressive movements, contain many pleasing visual effects, and be integrated with the music. Twirls should be executed for a set number of measures and changes made at phrase endings whenever possible.

The contest twirler executes within the rhythmic framework of the music but progresses from one twirl to the next with no attempt to integrate with the musical form. Her primary objective is to trick the judge into thinking that he is seeing tricks more difficult than she is actually performing.

Those tricks which are similar, or which follow each other smoothly, should be arranged in order of difficulty and organized into various series. It is much easier to combine 15 or 20 series than it is to take 150 tricks and build an acceptable contest routine. Careful consideration must be given to transitions between series, and the really artistic baton routine composer will use many of the techniques of the music composer.[3]

CONTESTS

The late Fred W. Miller, who was assistant director of the first twirling contests at the Chicagoland Music Festival used to say, "Where there are top-notch twirling contests, you find twirling improving at a fast rate."

He also noted that without these, the girls become content to learn simple dance numbers employing only a few basic twirling rudiments.

In all my years of association with twirling I have never seen a crooked contest, but I have seen thousands of incompetently run events. In most of these cases the people were trying very hard to conduct a good contest but their experience was so limited that they simply didn't know what to do. Judges of the majorette events in regional and state band festivals are too often men who are extremely capable musicians, but not at all qualified as twirling judges. Any girl who takes an hour out of her day, and spends money traveling to contests and clinics to learn, deserves an equitable chance. It is extremely unfair to subject her to non-professional judging.

I was once invited to a southern state to judge the twirling events in a band festival. The state association president explained that trumpet and clarinet and bassoon players had been doing the baton judging and everyone was used to high ratings. Since they asked me to judge by the national standards, most girls (who were used to AA ratings) ended up with C's and D's. There were no A's! I have not been asked to return. The twist is that while I was there they also asked *me* to judge the bassoons!

---

[3] Editor's note: Although many twirlers will not know the terms, the principles of sequences, imitation, augmentation and diminution will be employed, to name only a few.

Gradually people are becoming aware of these situations and they are being corrected. The National Twirling Judges Association selects and trains judges for all events which they sanction. There are rigid requirements for certification as a "Class A" judge. Band directors with considerable twirling knowledge and experience who can prove their ability in elementary examinations may apply for the "Class C" rating for judging school-level events.

The festival manager with too few entries in his majorette events to justify hiring a special twirling judge might consider scheduling a baton clinic the same day. He can then hire one person who is both a top clinician and an outstanding judge. A small fee to offset expenses could be charged. A list of competent judges is available from NBTA.

Score sheets are available in two well known forms (*see* Fig. 46). In the early 1930's a group of band directors developed a rudimental score sheet. Since that time other band directors have made revisions. The latest version is the 1961 NIMAC form.

In 1935 Major Boothe introduced the sheet which has since evolved into the 1959 NBTA form.

Both have their merits and their problems. Actually the only thing a first-rate judge needs to do the job is a plain white sheet of paper. Those who feel that by developing a perfect adjudication form they can do away with human error do not realize that the score sheet can only be a way for the judge to record his thoughts, to communicate with the entrant, and to show justification for his conclusions.

Complaints at contests generally stem from:

1. A lack of competent judging.
2. Poor organization by the contest manager: starting late, poor music, no time for refreshments, rest-room facilities lacking, etc.
3. The frustration of parents who cannot find a local instructor capable of taking their daughter beyond her present level of achievement.
4. The failure of contestants, their parents, and teachers, to admit that it was the hard work they did *not* do which beat them, not some complaint they have invented or magnified in order to save face.

Band directors who find themselves in charge of twirling contests must be sure that the students understand exactly what is required; if they lose they must know that they got a "fair shake."

Figure 46: Twirling—Solo or Ensemble

Twirling—Solo or Ensemble

Order or time of appearance ______ Event No. ______ Class ______ Date ______ 19__

RATING

Use no plus or minus signs in final rating

Name ______

School ______

City ______ State ______ District ______

Adjudicator will grade principal items, A, B, C, D, or E, or numerals, in the respective squares. Comments must deal with fundamental principles and be constructive. Minor details may be marked on music furnished to adjudicator.

SINGLE HAND FUNDAMENTALS—Check List ______ ☐

LEFT		RIGHT
☐	Vertical wrist twirl	☐
☐	Horizontal wrist twirl	☐
☐	Vertical Figure 8	☐
☐	Horizontal Figure 8	☐
☐	Finger twirl	☐
☐	Time toss-with catch	☐
	Forward whip	☐
☐	Reverse whip	☐

ADDITIONAL FUNDAMENTALS—Check List ______ ☐

- ☐ Forward cartwheel
- ☐ Reverse cartwheel
- ☐ Two-hand twirl—right to left, left to right
- ☐ Pass around back—right to left
- ☐ Pass around back—left to right
- ☐ Low aerial
- ☐ High aerial
- ☐ Salute

ROUTINE—TECHNICAL MASTERY (ambidexterity, continuity, retention of baton, revolution, smoothness, speed) ______ ☐

ROUTINE—SHOWMANSHIP (originality, rhythm, stage personality, variety) ______ ☐

GENERAL COMMENTS (confidence, facial expression, posture)
(Ensembles only: Uniform style and ability) ______ ☐

*May be continued on other side.

Signature of Adjudicator ______

Figure 46-a

"The National Standard"

OFFICIAL NBTA SCORE SHEET

All Purpose Solo Sheet

(For One Baton, Flag, Duets, Two & Three Batons, Strutting And Divisional Contests)

GIRL ☐ BOY ☐

AGE GROUP ______

EVENT ______

NO. ______ LANE ______

FOR DIVISIONAL ☐ OR STRUTTING ☐ CONTESTS ONLY

NBTA PLACE

Name of Contestant ______ Age (Day of Contest) ______

Address ______

City ______ Zone ______ State ______

Code: Scale of Proficiency — ✓ (Checked) = Very Good; Encircled = Unsatisfactory or needs more

Below Average: Unsatisfactory			Average: Fair	Av.	Good	Above Average: V.G.	Exc.	Sup.
0 to 11	12	13	14	15	16	17	18	19

POOR 5	FAIR 4	GOOD 3	VERY GOOD 2	SUPERIOR 1

←STRUTTING CAPTIONS / DIVISIONAL CAPTIONS→

Strutting caption (5 4 3 2 1)	Divisional caption	Points	Comments	Score
APPEARANCE	Variety (40)	20	AMBIDEXTERITY, LEFT HAND RIGHT HAND, FINGER TWIRLS, LEG WORK, ROLLS SLIDES, HORIZONTALS, FULL HAND MOVES, AERIALS, TOSSES THROWS, NOVELTY TWIRLS	
POSTURE	Difficulty	20	SPECTACULAR TRICKS, DIFFICULTY OF TRICKS, DIFFICULTY CREATED THROUGH FOLLOW THROUGH, TIMING & CONTINUITY	
GRACEFULNESS & SHOWMANSHIP	Speed Control (GENERAL PRECISION)	20	GENERAL HANDLING, RELEASES, RECOVERIES, CONSISTENCY, RAPIDITY, BATON PATTERN: VERTICALS, HORIZONTALS	
TIMING	Smoothness Graceful-ness (40)	20	CO-ORDINATION, BODY MOVEMENTS, USE OF: ARMS LEGS, UNIFORMITY, FREE HAND, FOOTWORK, HAND CHANGES, RELEASES, CATCHES, BALANCE	
VAR. & DIFF. OF STEPS	Showman-ship Presentation	20	FACIAL EXPRESSIONS, SPIRIT, PERSONALITY PROJECTION, POSTURE, ATTITUDE, EYE CONTACT, APPEARANCE, SPARKLE, BRILLIANCE	

SCALE / DIV.: 1-5 Sup. 1; 6-10 V.G. 2; 11-15 Good 3; 16-20 Fair 4; Less Poor 5 — DIV. RATING

Penalties

DROPS: .5 1.0 1.5 2.0 2.5 3.0 3.5 4.0 4.5 5.0

BREAKS SLIPS / OFF PATTERN UNINTENTIONALLY / STAYING OUT OF POSITION: .1 .2 .3 .4 .5 .6 .7 .8 .9 1.0

TIME — NO PENALTY 2:20 TO 2:30 (NOVICE 1:30 TO 2:00)

☐ UNDERTIME (.1 Per Sec. Under 2:20) ☐ OVERTIME (PENALTY .5)

PENALTIES

SCORE ______ LESS PENALTIES ______ TOTAL SCORE ______

Clerk's Initials ______ Judge's Signature ______

ENTRY	EXIT
☐ SUPER	☐ SUPER
☐ GOOD	☐ GOOD
☐ POOR	☐ POOR
☐ OUT OF STEP	☐ OUT OF STEP

JUDGES PERSONAL COMMENTS—UNOFFICIAL VIEWS

SCALE	
Superior	95 - 100
Excellent	90 - 95
Very Good	85 - 90
Good	80 - 85
Average	75 - 80
Fair	70 - 75
Unsatisfactory	Below 70

Figure 46-b

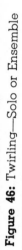

The prime function of the drum major is to represent the band director: a sort of company commander–first sergeant relationship. The band director should say, "Jim, I want the band here at 6 o'clock; I'd like the majorettes to have this equipment; I want these duties delegated." The drum major should then take charge and carry out the desires of the director.

By using the same practiced eye with which he chooses the junior high school student who has just the right ear, intelligence, lip formation, fingers, and personality to some day play first oboe in his concert band, the band director should groom a student for the position of drum major. The actual techniques involved are not difficult to learn. Physical appearance and leadership qualities are the really important considerations.

For the flashy show band, a girl may be more in character as drum major, but for a military type band a boy is undoubtedly superior. The use of *twin* (two boys or two girls), or *paired* (boy and girl) drum majors can be a beautiful thing when employed artistically, but is not recommended just for sheer novelty, since a great deal of careful planning must be done to insure a smooth operation.

The U.S. Army drum major manual is still proper for a strictly military band, but gracefulness of body and arm movements cannot be gained through this system. Actually I do not believe in any stereotyped system, but would prefer to see each band develop its own unique style.

I recall seeing a Texas cowboy band with a drum major who marched at the side of the group, had no baton, but carried a pistol in a holster. Periodically he would come out front, do three or four spins with the pistol and fire a shot—the signal for the next maneuver. Simple, and maybe silly as it sounds, this is the sort of thing which is very effective in developing a unique *band personality* which people talk about—and remember.

SHOWMANSHIP

There are many groups and special effects generally associated with baton twirling which can be of tremendous help to the band director in attracting a lot of attention and building spirit.

Possibly because of my own love for the circus, I believe in the three-ring type of performance. The band, majorettes, pompon girls, color guard, flag swingers and twirlers all should participate in a fast moving show with tasteful change of pace, so that the audience can look upon the whole thing as one unified production, rather than a series of single performances by the individual groups.

The Horace Mann High School Band of Gary, Indiana uses a great number of these auxiliary features. When they come down the street it is a show all in itself (*see* Fig. 47).

Figure 47: The Horace Mann High School (Gary, Indiana) group, winners of more than 50 first place trophies and two international championships; it is directed by Mr. and Mrs. Kenneth Resur, and is broken down as follows: 90-piece band; 15 baton twirlers, plus leader; 10 flag swingers, plus leader; 10 gun spinners, plus leader; 10 cape swingers, plus leader; 15 pompons, plus leader; 30 guidons, with pole and pompons; 9-member color guard; drum major and mascot.

The color guard will add to the appeal of any group. The Madison, Wisconsin Scouts twirl full size flags with sharp points on the poles. At one place in their performance they march directly towards one another and the points just miss by inches. It's tremendous! I've never seen anything in any phase of showmanship surpass this for winning the audience, because here is our American flag presented in the most beautifully perfected routine I have ever seen in my life.

To eliminate the giggling and talking sometimes seen during the playing of the National Anthem, the majorettes should serve as the leaders in proper flag etiquette by executing a very majestic salute and remaining at attention.

Mascots, when allowed an occasional performance are a pleasant addition to the over-all picture, but their overemphasis will detract from the program since the audience is inclined to focus on the cute little girl doing the wrist spin and to ignore the big girl who has worked extremely hard to perfect a difficult routine.

When I was very young my dad commanded an Army band in Louisiana. On one special occasion three bands came together and did a clever precision number in which the percussion was gathered in the center of the field. At the end of the show, just as one of the drums swung around toward the audience, I jumped out of it (they had taped the head in after me) and did a three-fire baton act.

The show was carried by the precision drum routine, but that extra, spectacular punch ("the dessert") was added by the surprise of seeing a little boy pop out of a drum, and further surprise everyone by actually doing something!

Pompon girls were once a part of the cheerleader group, and later associated with the majorettes. Now the pompon corps is often highly competitive with its former parent organizations. More beauty of body and motion are required than for cheerleading, but not as much as for twirling. Their routine, even while the band and the majorettes are performing, adds a great deal of color and provides the necessary change of pace. The best use is at a basketball game or between the stands and the sidelines at a football game.

Fire Baton Twirling, although it must be approached with caution and intelligence, is not dangerous for anyone beyond the beginner stage. Inside performances are much more exciting than those outdoors because of the assurance of complete darkness, and the shadows which can be created by keeping the body between the baton and the wall.

I prefer to have the band play some very rhythmic tune like "Sabre Dance," and without notice, suddenly stop. The twirler then gradually increases the speed of the baton and fills the room with that characteristic "oooiiisssssshhhhhhhh . . .", which is so exciting when all else is silent. Then the band comes back in and the routine is completed with music. You can keep audiences applauding for many minutes with this sort of performance.

Swiss Flag Swinging was brought to the United States by Major Boothe, but because of the slow performance speed and the great skill required, it has never achieved widespread popularity.

Flag Twirling, however, is very fast, very tricky, very cute—and very easy to do. Almost any trick possible with a regular baton may be performed by twirling at the end of the shaft (about 12 inches beyond the flag) with the flag serving as the counterbalance.

Hoops, although they require great precision, are easy to learn to twirl. They were originally made by screwing a baton onto a bicycle wheel. Now they are made from drum hoops. By tacking a 1½-inch braid to the hoop some very beautiful effects may be achieved.

Lighted Batons, because of battery corrosion problems and the competition of the fire baton, have lost most of the great popularity they enjoyed when first introduced in the early 1950's.

Juggling involves manipulation from the end of the shaft, whereas the baton is *twirled* from near the mid-point on the shaft. It would take me a month to teach a girl to *twirl* three batons, but she could learn to *juggle* them in about two weeks.

All of these auxiliary features should be used as the "dessert," and sometimes even the "dessert to the dessert." The key phrase to remember in planning their use is "change of pace."

WHERE NOW?

Twirling has grown from an occasional professional performance of mild interest only to vaudeville audiences, into an activity directly involving a very large portion of every school's student population, and indirectly affecting nearly every person in the country. The successful band director must have a sufficient knowledge of baton twirling and the associated fields to set up an effective organization—always for use as "the dessert to the main course" of a fine band.

But always remember, you must never follow up champagne and pheasant under glass with a plastic bowl of sour ice cream!

CHAPTER

Precision Drill

by **A. R. Casavant**

Chattanooga, Tenn.

A. R. Casavant

started the present style of
precision drill in 1953 and
has been in demand for
clinics and workshops
throughout the United
States ever since. As Director of the Chattanooga High School Band
from 1949–59, he produced a precision unit which was never defeated
in competition, and was given the unbelievable score of 100% in a
recognized interstate event . . . two years in succession.

He holds degrees in science from Tennessee Military Institute
and the University of Chattanooga, and a Master's degree in music
from the Vandercook College of Music where he has served on the
summer faculty since 1949. Further studies have been pursued at
the University of Tennessee, Boston University, and Chicago Musical
College.

Originally interested in becoming a physician, Mr. Casavant has
been engaged in almost constant study and research in the areas of
anatomy, kinesiology, physiology, psychology, and the eurhythmics
of conducting, marching, and percussion. His leg rest for field drums,
and carriers for bass drum, tuba, and bell lyra, made from stainless
steel and designed to follow the contour of the anatomy are tangible
results of this interest.

A long list of publications (see p. 284) and his many clinic and
workshop appearances provide band directors with a wealth of authoritative information and instruction from this hard working expert.

270

The superior precision drill performance is the result of the show creator's artistic sense of balance of all factors, plus the polish obtained through careful preparation by the group.

One outstanding precision drill routine per season is probably the limit for most situations and directors, but since precision drill is simply *the controlled movement of individuals and groups*, these techniques can be used for the flashy entrance, the smooth transition between formations, and the memorable exit in any type of show.

Through the years there has been a difference of opinion as to the educational value of marching bands—much of it in print. I do not intend to add to that already bulging literature, since there are two facts which render any serious consideration of the issue meaningless:

1. The people like to see it. Marching contests draw extremely large crowds far in excess of the friends, relatives and rooters you would normally expect.
2. The students like to do it. Teen-agers are in a "physical activity stage" of their lives. High school students can be talked into wanting to sit down and play music all the time, but their normal inclination is towards vigorous physical activity.

SPATIAL MOVEMENT

"Precision drill" in the 1930's and 1940's usually meant that a band would march downfield, turn, proceed so many steps in the opposite direction, and turn again. The relationship between individuals always remained the same. Some bands today remain in block formation and do facing movements, kicks, jumps, and chants. People are executing motion uniformly, but the formations are stationary.

The increased popularity of football and the accompanying half-time show on TV has put a lot of pressure on bands. Something must be happening—visually—at all times. You must change your formation or you lose your audience.

The drill I have been doing is concerned primarily with "spatial movement." Not only do individuals move with precision, but the entire formation is constantly changing. This is accomplished by changing from line (company front) to block band, moving from block to a staggered block formation, or altering the direction of a line (*see* Fig. 48).

A definite advantage for the director who uses precision drill shows is the carryover of training from one show to the next. He can add maneuvers to a basic skeleton of precision entrance, exit, and transitions throughout the entire season—each week a little more difficult, more exciting, with greater uniformity.

THE MARTIAL CONCEPT

Precision drill is really the martial form of the dance. It is a combination of physical education and music, sometimes called *eurhythmics*. Note the differences between the terms *military* and *martial*. Whereas our military concept, as influenced by the U.S. armed forces, has been changing from cavalry to mechanized to push-button, our martial concept has always been the same, *i.e.*, dignity, elegance, pomp, pride, and self-confidence just short of arrogance. With the introduction of fatigue clothing, shorts, and the like, we seem to be losing this martial appearance in our military uniforms.

The uniforms of the Napoleonic era probably best express what I mean by a "martial appearance." This uniform contributed directly to the morale, esprit de corps, and confidence of the men who were asked to stand in straight lines of skirmish, watch their friends fall at either flank, and continue to fire away at the enemy. Effective precision drill must convey this *martial* feeling.

VARIOUS TYPES OF SHOWS

Most precision drill shows are of the *mechanical* type, in which each movement fits with the next very neatly, like the moving parts of a fine engine. The *composite* show[1] approaches a genuine work of

---

[1] An early effort in this aesthetic direction is Mr. Casavant's "New World" show, published by Southern Music Company, 1100 Broadway, San Antonio 6, Texas.—*Ed.*

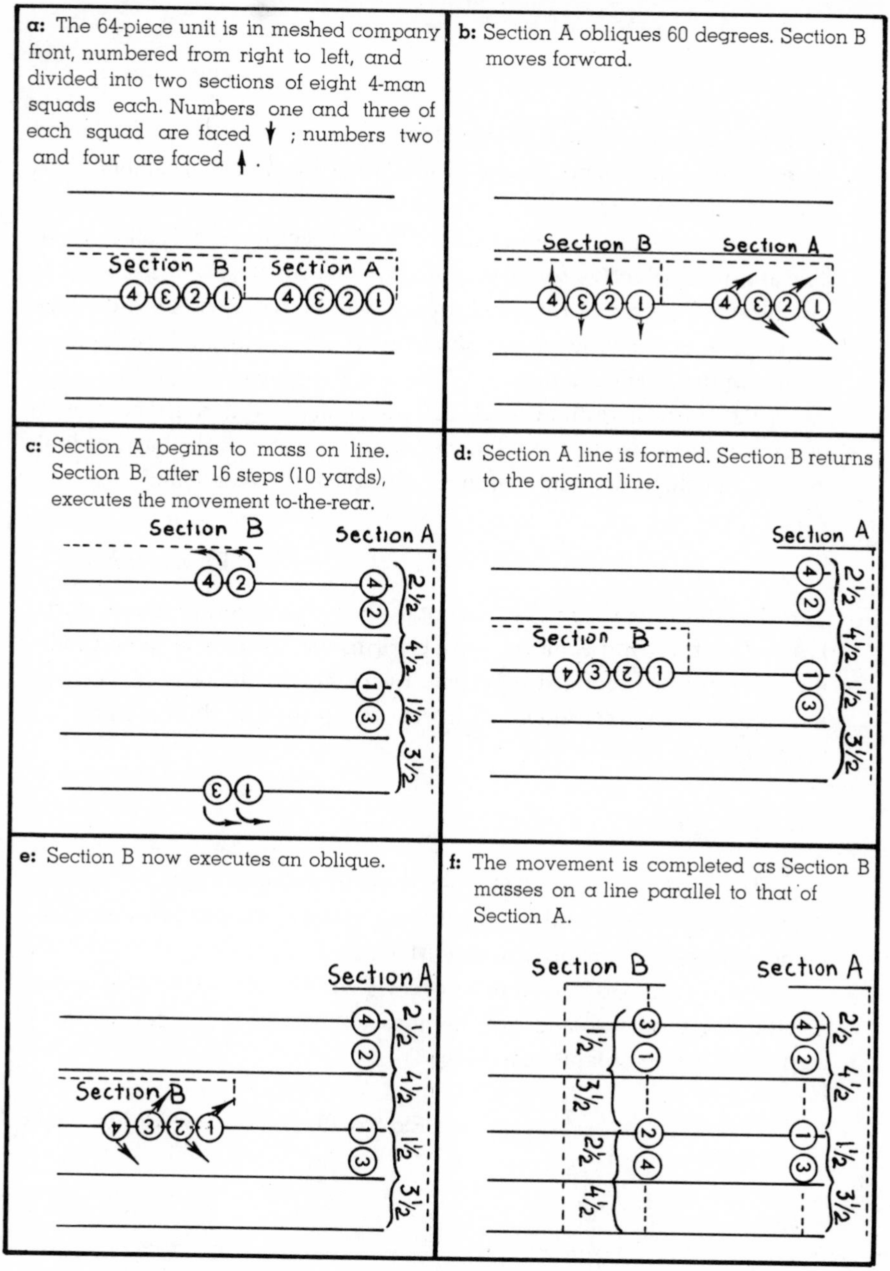
a: The 64-piece unit is in meshed company front, numbered from right to left, and divided into two sections of eight 4-man squads each. Numbers one and three of each squad are faced ↓ ; numbers two and four are faced ↑ .
Section B
Section A
b: Section A obliques 60 degrees. Section B moves forward.
Section B
Section A
c: Section A begins to mass on line. Section B, after 16 steps (10 yards), executes the movement to-the-rear.
Section B
Section A
2½
4½
1½
3½
d: Section A line is formed. Section B returns to the original line.
Section A
Section B
2½
4½
1½
3½
e: Section B now executes an oblique.
Section A
Section B
2½
4½
1½
3½
f: The movement is completed as Section B masses on a line parallel to that of Section A.
Section B
Section A
1½
3½
2½
4½
2½
4½
1½
3½

Figure 48: Altering the Direction of a Line *

DRILL KEY:

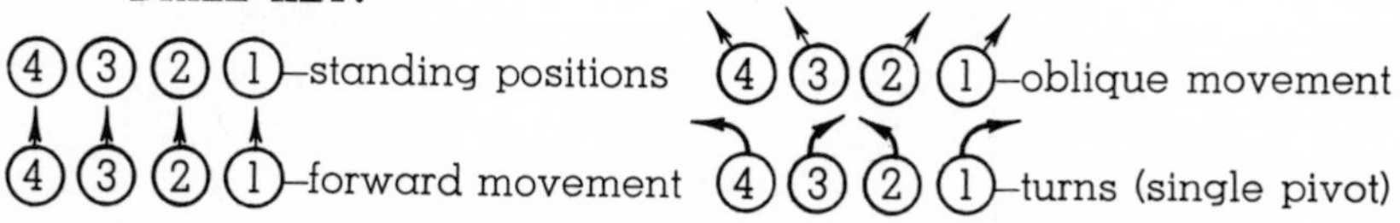
—standing positions
—oblique movement
—forward movement
—turns (single pivot)

* From *Precision Drill Line Movement*, by A. R. Casavant, copyrighted by Southern Music Co., San Antonio, Texas.

art in that the music and the martial form of the dance are so integrated in both conception and execution that they become inseparable. This type of show is rare.

The many geometric patterns which precision drill makes available are quite effective for large stadium performances, but if you have low bleachers, some of the other aspects will be more useful. Individual work, such as "by-the-ripple" movements in which students execute actions in order (like dominoes falling in a line) is very appealing when viewed from near-ground level. Fast movements and contrary motion of sections may also be used. Downfield motion allows the band to look its best, but the cross-field march will produce the best sound.

FUNDAMENTALS

I prefer to teach the fundamentals thoroughly before school starts. Even after the band achieves top performance level these same fundamentals must be practiced regularly. Every hour you spend in this way will save you an hour and a half in rehearsing specific shows. Three are basic:

1. The Steps

The highknee step—22½"—8 steps to every 5 yards ("8 to 5"). The motion is flashy and good for brisk tempos. Proper lift action becomes impossible at approximately M.M. 148.

The stride—30"—6 steps to every 5 yards ("6 to 5"). This step is suitable for moderate and slow tempos (M.M. 120), and for the long step necessary in oblique marching.

Figure 49: High Knee, Stride Steps

I consider my basic step "8 to 5," and my auxiliary step "6 to 5." There are not two systems, but rather one system which includes both steps. Unless you make use of both you are needlessly limiting yourself.

2. *The Single Pivot Turn*

In this movement the right foot is always the pivot foot regardless of the direction turned, thus a cross-over with the left foot is required for a right turn. This allows the creation of a *musical* drill since it is possible for everyone to change directions either to the right or to the left on the same beat, rather than on succeeding beats, as in the military turn. Start the turn *on* the beat and use one-half count to execute at tempos below M.M. 140.

3. *The Step-Two*

This is the movement of individuals in a given direction at two-step intervals. Variations of "step-one," "step-four," etc. are possible. All drill is based on rhythm, and obviously students must be taught to move rhythmically. All major movements must begin and end at major divisions in the music and each marcher must feel the rhythmic pulse of "step-two . . . step-two . . . step-two . . ." so that he steps off on the pulse following his neighbor's move. You must never tell students to "count to 43 and step off."

TRAINING TECHNIQUES

The director should accustom himself to a regular rehearsal routine. I use the following:

1. Secure the attention of all.
2. Explain thoroughly.
3. Demonstrate in detail.
4. Illustrate, with students.
5. Practice diligently.
6. Check details.

Listen, Look, Think

Remember that the unit must *listen* to hear, *look* to see, and the director must *think* in order to say something worthy of the students' attention.

Figure 50: Step-Two

The Individual

The performance of the individual marcher is the critical factor in the evaluation of a precision drill show. Perfection in the mechanics of drill, a personal conception of martial bearing, and a sense of individual responsibility are essential. Three rules are basic:

1. *Keep the head up.* This is the mark of the well-trained precision unit as well as an indication of character in the individual.
2. *Stand between two people.* "Dress right!" becomes "Dress Both!" The individual senses the interdependence of members of a drill unit, since each person is the middle one of three.
3. *Do not anticipate.* The drillmaster must eliminate all premature motions by alerting the student to their presence. The use of music with the drill will aid in this project.

Esprit de Corps

Discipline and morale are inseparable. Self-discipline is essential to the perfect performing group and is attained only through constant repetition of details until there is a correct conditioned reflex. Esprit de corps is present when enthusiasm, devotion, and jealous regard for the honor of the unit become factors common to all members. This is an objective of precision drill training which ranks well ahead of any other single factor.

Effort yields results

There is no accurate method of predicting how long it will take to build a competent precision drill unit. How long does it take a cornet student to learn to play "The Carnival of Venice"? Some do it in five years, some in 20, most never do it. I have seen precision drill installed effectively as a system in just one year, but usually it takes a "hand-me-down" process from student to student to establish an effective program. Since the younger players learn a great deal by listening and watching, the older, more experienced students must be excellent examples of correctness. In addition to serving as models, I expect these leaders to pass on those things which I have taught them. I believe in the cadet system: direct instruction of the inexperienced by a veteran cadre.

Neither is there any accurate method of predicting how long it will take to perfect a given show. The rule that "every minute on the field requires an hour of rehearsal" has not proven reliable for me. With a good band I can often work up a good five-minute show in 50 minutes, although with another band, or another show with the same band, it might take me two hours to get one minute. A great deal depends on how well the band has been trained in the fundamentals and on how much time the director wastes.

Many directors consume five minutes of valuable rehearsal time lecturing a student who has been three minutes late, when a simple "see-me-after-class," or a standing rule to that effect, would have been sufficient. Band directors probably waste more time than students.

RELATIONS WITH STUDENTS

Students enjoy the hard work which is necessary to achieve the top physical condition precision drill demands. The director must also honestly enjoy the hard work which his position as drillmaster demands or his dissatisfaction will influence the enthusiasm of his students. Just marching with a highknee step throughout a complete show requires a tremendous amount of stamina, but when you blow an instrument at the same time it is very much like swimming under water during the entire half-time break.

Whenever a student says he does not feel well he always has my permission to drop out of drill, without question. I find that very few do. It is probably because every student involved in precision drill has equal responsibility and realizes that *his* mistake will blur the over-all performance. This situation requires strict group and self-discipline, but also teaches teamwork.

Teen-agers love the feeling they get from personal achievement (don't we all?). In a pageantry type of presentation each individual is certainly a vital part of the total picture, but the roles are not *active* ones. Students compare the passive outlining of a heart while playing "Let Me Call You Sweetheart," to the active execution of precision maneuvers and prefer the immediate sense of accomplishment which the *active* performance gives them. For this reason they are quite unenthusiastic over other types of shows after they have learned precision drill.

DRIVE AND CHANGE PACE

You have to know how hard to drive students. I find it best to push them as far as they will go, and then change pace. One boy I had been driving quite hard at a summer camp made another mistake, and I turned on him and glared. I saw that he was about to burst into tears, so I continued to glare, but at the same time I winked at him. Well, this great big young fellow broke into a wide grin and he was my buddy for the rest of camp.

Since the students realize that one uncooperative person can seriously mar their otherwise effective performance, they are always on your side on those few occasions when you have to deal harshly with the "smart aleck."

THE DRILLMASTER

He must "know his stuff." This includes knowing his show so well that he does not have to waste time and destroy student confidence in him by constantly referring to his charts to "see what comes next." A good band director will have a better band in a better situation, but he will always have a good band, no matter where he is. The successful drillmaster must: (1) know the capabilities of the individuals and understand their problems; (2) accept responsibility and have pride in his work; (3) work hard as an example and get things done; and (4) be fair; admit mistakes without any show.

Figure 51: A. R. Casavant takes a short break during one of the many clinic sessions he conducts throughout the United States.

THE DRUM MAJOR

In the 1930's most bands did "command drills" in which the drum major gave the signal to move. The point at which he gave it might vary from eight to ten steps every time the show was rehearsed or performed. Today most bands do "set drill." Each movement is done exactly the same way, at the same time, at the same place in the music, and at the same place on the field. The drum major now gives "cue," not "command" signals.

With the use of the company front band the drum major must hold the group together through precise musical direction. Pumping the baton up and down has impressed audiences for many years, but has done little to help the band to stay together. Although the function of the drum major has been changed drastically, we have done little to develop the techniques which are needed in his role as field conductor. Instead most bands have retained the military drum major manual and attempted to "modernize" it by having him run, jump, dress up like a peacock, and do any number of fancy maneuvers—all usually carried to the point of absurdity.

Each drum major should develop his own style, or "personality," just as each band should be different and unique.

THE THEORY OF DRILL

Although understanding the theory of precision drill may require considerable time and effort, the successful director is the one who, in addition to being able to rehearse and present the published shows he buys, can apply the principles of precision drill to every facet of his marching band activities. As in any field, the person who acquires a thorough knowledge of the basic theory will be better able to understand each specific application of that theory.[2]

Point and Period

The basic terms to be understood in the theory of drill are point in time, and period of time. Consider the space flight advertisement of the future:

---

[2] Additional material may be found in A. R. Casavant's *Precision Drill*, published by Southern Music Company, San Antonio, Texas, from which the following material has been adapted.—*Ed.*

MOONFLIGHT SPECIAL
Launching Tomorrow
Lift off 7 A.M.
One week guided tour—get your tickets here!

The *point* in time is "7 A.M. Tomorrow." The *period* of time is one week. In precision marching *points* occur when a marcher (1) starts moving; (2) changes direction or speed; (3) stops moving.

A *period* is the distance, or time lapse, between two points. To insure precision in the marching step, all marchers must hit the *points* at exactly the same time, and the intervening *periods* must be of identical length.

Points in the marching step:
1. Start—toe of shoe breaks contact with the ground.
2. Peak—foot changes direction at the highest elevation.
3. Stop—toe of shoe resumes contact with the ground.

Periods in the marching step:
A. From point 1 to point 2.
B. From point 2 to point 3.
C. From point 1 to point 3.

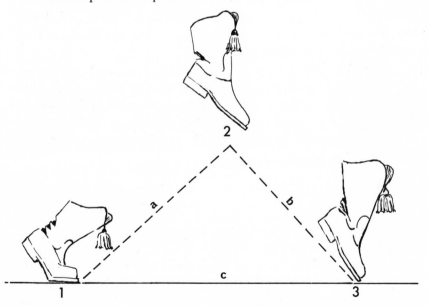

Figure 52: The Marching Step

Beat and Count

The principles of point and period may be applied in understanding the difference between the terms *beat* and *count*. A *beat* is a point in time which represents a regular pulsation. Like the markings on a yardstick, beats point out a particular location. "After-beats" are notes occurring other than on the beats. A *count* is the period of time between two successive beats. Therefore a whole note is not "over" until the first beat of the following measure, since it receives four *counts*, not four *beats*.

> Beats: 1——2——3——4——1
>
> Counts: ——1——2——3——4

THE THEORY OF FOURS

The majority of march music is written in units of four, therefore the use of this figure is natural. There are many applications beyond those mentioned in the following two paragraphs.

Four marchers form a squad; four squads form a platoon; four platoons form a 64-piece band, which is exceptionally flexible for drill purposes and can be instrumented to sound large enough to fill any stadium. In schools with a marching band enrollment far exceeding this number, the best qualified members ("horses," I call them) can be formed into an elite drill company.

Most marching is done on football fields. The yard lines had best be considered in the planning of a show because the audience will compare the band's moving lines with the fixed stripes on the field. Using the theory of fours, the best size of step in one-eighth of five yards, or 22½ inches; this allows phrase endings in the music to coincide with yard line positions.

THE THEORY OF INTERCHANGEABLE PARTS

Each sharply defined, regular, and consistent movement is made up of only a few component parts, which are common to many movements. These parts must be executed in exactly the same manner regardless of the movement in which they may be found or the physical differences of the individuals performing them. Just as the same spark plug will serve as an important part of the operation of a lawnmower or an expensive car, a sharp "instruments up!" motion may be used preparatory to playing, accompanying a parade rest, or while making a single pivot turn.

THE THEORY OF FUNDAMENTAL EXTENSION

While the various movements have a definite purpose they also present a picture which is pleasing to the eye. Those motions without any real function are called "flash." "Precision flash" [3] is additional color added to the fundamentals of drill and may be accomplished through:

1. Various exaggerations in execution, such as flourishes, kicks, jumps, lifts, and dips.
2. Change of pace, such as shifts from line to block, or altering the step from highknee to stride.
3. Diversion, such as using slides, feints, and compound turns. Precision flash may be extended by using *LaDeDa* and *Razzle Dazzle*, which is the addition of motions without any useful function. For example, the normal precision drill right flank takes one-half count, but the *LaDeDa* right flank may be extended to eight counts by adding various hand, foot, and body motions.

WHAT ABOUT THE FUTURE?

Just as every band director does not have the talent, training, or experience to compose and arrange all of the music his band plays, neither is every one able to conceive, plan, and write a complete precision marching show. If each director were to arrange all of his own music, we would be hearing some strange sounding bands. No one expects this, yet we are seeing some stranger looking bands for precisely the same reason: generally each man is composing his own marching show. The solution to his musical problem is relatively easy since he can choose what he needs from a wealth of fine literature available from many publishers. Unfortunately there is no easy solution for his show problems, as yet.

---

[3] See *Precision Flash* by A. R. Casavant, Southern Music Company, San Antonio, Texas.—*Ed.*

Better publishing techniques need to be worked out for shows, since most are very difficult to understand from the printed page alone. Films have been made and distributed.[4] These offer some help, but no solution, since there are still many questions dealing with the third dimension which must be left unanswered.

In my clinic and camp sessions I find that directors are seeking help with specific shows, but they do not seem too interested in the theory of drill. I think that each director should realize that working with the composer of the shows he is using is a great help in understanding those things which cannot be written with sufficient clarity in the score, but unless he also learns the theory of drill, this help will only be temporary. It is somewhat like the student who may memorize long division answers without first learning the principles involved, and before becoming thoroughly familiar with the multiplication tables.

As shows become easier to transfer from the printed page to the field, I think we will see the development of a standard repertoire of 20 or 30 precision marching shows.[5]

With the increase in the number of qualified show composers which more widespread knowledge of the theory of drill [6] will bring, there will be many new and exciting developments in the years ahead.

---

[4] Most of the Chattanooga High School shows produced by Mr. Casavant are available on film.—*Ed.*

[5] Two of Mr. Casavant's shows—the "1955" and the "New World," have already been performed by bands in many parts of the country.—*Ed.*

[6] *A. R. Casavant Publications:* Fast Break; Precision Drill; Precision Drill Line Movements; Block Formation Drill; Precision Flash; Street Parade Drill; Six to Five; Staggered Block Drill Movements; Manual of Drill; Field Entrances; and Phalanx Drill Movements.

Football
Half-Time
Shows

by **Frederick C. Ebbs**

State University of Iowa

Frederick C. Ebbs

Professor of Music, is Director of University Bands at
the State University of Iowa,
in Iowa City. He is well
known in every part of the
country as a guest conductor, show clinician, and as a contest judge.

Born in 1916, at Amherst, Ohio, he received his B.S.M. degree
at Baldwin-Wallace College, Berea, Ohio, in 1937, and the M.M. at
the University of Michigan in 1940. He also studied privately with
the most influential clarinet teacher of recent times, Daniel Bonade,
from 1934–39, and during the summer of 1950.

Mr. Ebbs became Music Supervisor of the Rittman, Ohio public
school in 1937, and by 1940 had developed the prize-winning Class C
Band that is still legend in Ohio music circles. He introduced the
first football marching band in the Hobart, Indiana city schools, and
led both the Junior and Senior High School Bands to Division I ratings in district and state contests every year from 1941 to 1948. He
returned to Baldwin-Wallace as Director of Bands in 1948, remaining
there until he accepted a similar position at Iowa in 1954.

Mr. Ebbs not only directs the Symphony Band in performances
of a repertoire selected from the finest compositions in band literature, but he has also developed the Hawkeye Marching Band into
an extremely entertaining half-time marching, dancing, singing and
playing show band.

Bandleader Horace Heidt called the group "a mighty impressive
combination of Fred Astaire and Harry James—and that's an unbeat-
able combination." Meredith Willson has said: "The Iowa Band is
the finest university band I have ever seen."

286

Organization is the most important factor in the development of a successful marching show band. The director must evolve an effective system—a method—to be followed by himself and his students for everything that is done from his first germ of an idea for the show through the actual performance and the evaluation which should follow.

Since the band which makes a presentation during the half-time break of a football game is there to *entertain* the crowd, the director ought to have either a natural sense or an acquired knowledge of those tangible and intangible elements of show business which result in a performance that captures the imagination of the audience—that "appeals."

CULTURAL VALUES

Those of us who have a musical education, and a background filled with many years of association with fine music, recognize the fact that the marching show band, while it may have some *educational* value, has little or no *cultural* value—for us. But for some (perhaps even a majority) of the people who sit in the football stadium, the music heard at the half could be, culturally, as far advanced as any they will ever be able to appreciate. While one can attempt to raise the cultural level through the use of various types of music (always performed well), don't ever forget that the audience wants a show band there to *entertain*, not to *elevate*.

SECURE ADEQUATE PERSONNEL

Obviously no band can function properly without a sufficient number of qualified members, and the correct balance of instrumentation. What is "correct," of course, will be determined by the sound and style the director seeks. The approach may be completely different according to individual tastes. The average member of the crowd will usually like most of the different concepts equally well, as long as the performance is good, although the connoisseur and the loyal alumnus will always have a preference for one over the other.

A student staff should be organized to assist with certain elements in the show production process. At the State University of Iowa, we have six graduate students who serve without any form of payment other than the opportunity to gain experience on the staff headed by the director and the assistant diector. There are also three librarians, a four-member equipment crew, two drum majors, 12 rank leaders, four music arrangers, and an announcer. A high school band can be organized in the same way, with the possible exception of the graduate staff and the music arrangers, although high school students can copy parts, and a few have learned to make some very acceptable marching band arrangements.

ARRANGE PROPER FACILITIES

In addition to the usual indoor facilities of the concert band, an outdoor, regulation size football field, properly lined, with a surface that is smooth enough to be safe for marching, should be prepared for rehearsals. A tower (or some means for the director to observe from above ground level) and a public address system (or at least a portable amplifier) are essential. The area should be readily accessible so that valuable rehearsal time is not wasted in traveling to and from the site.

THE SHOW CONCEPT

In creating entertaining half-time shows you are bounded at one end of the scale by *what cannot be done*, and at the other end by *what everyone does*. By overlapping into "what cannot be done," and using only the best (the "sure-fire") of "what everyone does," you find *your own* area in the middle, made up of the things: *that have not been done . . . that can be done . . . that everyone does not do*.[1]

---

[1] A few of the things achieved by the State University of Iowa Band (under the leadership of Director Ebbs and Assistant Director Tom Davis) are: simultaneous two-speed marching, entry in a design, adjustment of concert formation during playing to feature various sections (staging, not animation), and a special musical arrangement calling for the band to turn several times (as a whole and by sections) to follow directors on opposite sides of the field.—*Ed.*

UNITY, VARIETY, AND
CLIMAX

The three essential elements in the construction of a show are unity, variety, and climax.

While it is certainly possible to achieve unity without doing a *theme* type of show, we prefer the use of the central idea because all of the varied types of marching, formations, and music can be more easily tied together in this way. We strive for a "unified variety," with climaxes spread throughout the show, building to a peak at the end.

In one of our shows the central theme of "Harper's Bazaar"—the Iowa Memorial Union (student activity building), and its director, Dr. Earl Harper—allowed a wide variety of action and music, all tied together by the central theme as explained in the script. The spirit of a downfield march (in formation) provided the initial climax; a strong musical climax came with a concert rendition of Moussorgsky's "Pictures at an Exhibition"; the peak was achieved through the very rhythmic actions and music of the "Down By The Riverside" drill, emphasized by the exciting effect of all bandsmen blowing directly at the home audience.

ELEMENTS OF SHOW
BUSINESS

"Gee that show was great . . . I wish you would do it again sometime."

Although many directors hear this from appreciative members of their audiences, few of them ever repeat a show, because they know that audiences will often enjoy one number as a *reminder* of a past show, but there is usually not sufficient depth to this type of production to bear complete repetition.

The practice of doing things in sequences of three has been employed by nearly every artist, writer, and composer throughout history. In the common ending you would not want to take the repeat

Figure 54: Ending

HALF-TIME SHOW

THEME: *Harper's Bazaar*

ANNOUNCER: *Bob Snyder*

DOWNFIELD MARCH

"Ladies and gentlemen—presenting—in its first half-time performance of 1962—the Hawkeye Marching Band with Drum Majors Jerry Kesler and Bill Parisi. (FANFARE) Today the band pays tribute to one of the most remarkable institutions on the campus, the Iowa Memorial Union, and to its great director, Dr. Earl Harper, who retires at the end of the current school year. We hope you'll agree that this show could only have one title—'Harper's Bazaar'!

"Funiculi, Funicula"

"Best Things in Life Are Free"

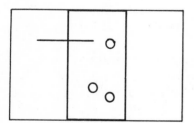

BILLIARD TABLE

"In mentioning the Union, the first thing that comes to most minds is its outstanding recreational facilities: the Gold Feather Room for snacks, the River Room for dancing, and the game rooms for table tennis, bowling, and billiards. Let's keep an eye on 'Frankie and Johnny' as they cue up for this difficult three-cushion shot.

"Frankie and Johnny"

"School Days"

290

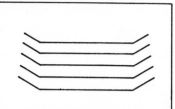

CONCERT FORMATION

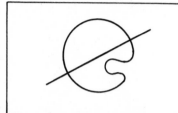

ARTIST'S PALETTE

"One of the Union's finest contributions is in the field of culture. The wonderful art exhibits and the outstanding concerts of great music are a continual delight to all who enjoy the finer things in life. Combining both of these areas the Hawkeye Philharmonic presents a special concert arrangement of Moussorgsky's 'Pictures at an Exhibition.'

"Pictures at an Exhibition"

"Promenade"

"The Hut of Baba Yaga"

"Great Gate of Kiev"

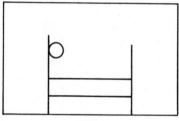

BED

"After several years of legal entanglements you are privileged to watch the construction of an entirely new section which will be known as the guest house unit. For graduate students seeking new areas of research, here is an interesting title for a dissertation—'Does the Bubble Gum Lose Its Flavor on the Bedpost Overnight?'

"Best Things"

"Does the Bubble Gum Lose Its Flavor on the Bedpost Overnight?"

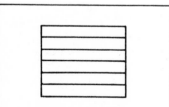

DRILL ROUTINE

"Recreation, culture, entertainment—the Hawkeye Band concludes its salute to the Union with a sparkling drill routine. The South may sing about its 'Swanee River,' and Hoosiers point with pride to their 'Banks of the Wabash,' but SUIowans will never forget the Iowa Memorial Union—'Down by the Riverside.' "

"Down by the Riverside"

291

one more time, but just playing the figure two times is not enough.

Since there are an almost unlimited number of even more subtle elements which become fused by experience into a "show business sense," any comprehensive listing would be impossible. By an examination of the "Harper's Bazaar" script a few can be illustrated, however.

The unexpected cleverness of the title (saved until the very end of the PA announcement), and the downfield march in the fanfare formation rather than the block band which audiences generally expect.

The ridiculous contrast of the "Great Gate of Kiev" followed by "Does the Bubble Gum Lose Its Flavor on the Bedpost Overnight?"

Saving and strengthening the punch of the final peak by using only limited, restrained action (only *parts* of the formations move) throughout the show to foreshadow, but not compete with the rhythm and extreme movements of all bandsmen in the concluding drill routine.

The familiarity of the theme, enhanced by the introduction of *human interest* through reference to a man loved by the students and the alumni (who make up the bulk of the audience).

The "inside" appeal to the specialized audience with a reference to ridiculous dissertations in "Does the Bubble Gum," etc.

The contrast in transition movement—squads and ranks in orderly movement with "scatter" saved for the final bubble breaking sequence.

WATCH, ANALYZE, AND LEARN

In watching band shows either in the stadium or on TV, do not merely attempt to pick up new techniques, but spend some time observing and analyzing the reactions of the crowd as well. If you rent or borrow show films try to get those which have sound recorded at the stadium. Those which have dubbed-in, studio-recorded sound never present a true report of the audience response. Through sensitive observation you may discover that what you like personally may be vastly different from what "goes over best" with the audience.

THE FOUR TYPES OF SHOWS

The Marching Show features a full precision drill routine, with coordinated music—the military concept.

A. Word

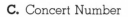

B. Precision Drill

C. Concert Number

D. Moving Figure

Figure 55: The Variety Show

The Pageant Show may include the Boy Scouts, Girl Scouts, Fire Department, everything—the three-ring circus concept.

The Formation Show has letters, words, and outline representations of various things—the picture concept.

The Variety Show is a combination of the others. We use this type, emphasizing formations, but including some precision drill as one part of nearly every show—the change-of-pace concept.

SPECIAL TRAINING FOR SHOW BANDSMEN

In addition to all of the usual considerations in the training of a marching bandsman, the half-time show band makes special demands. We expect each bandsman to possess the attitude and intense desire which will allow him to polish the basic individual movements to the point of flawless execution, and to completely control his own physical characteristics and personality so that the entire membership of the band can execute a maneuver as if they were of one body, mind, and spirit. When this is done with absolute precision the effect is spectacular.

However, the show bandsman should be taught a skill even beyond the attainment of absolute precision: he should learn to exaggerate his actions, to execute with a flair, in short—to be a showman!

GETTING IDEAS FOR A SHOW

The theme of a show may come from any one or a combination of many sources: a song title, birthday, anniversary, newspaper item, local celebration . . . anything! Sometimes one sequence of a published show will suggest an original idea to you. One must constantly gather raw materials with the eyes and ears, and then allow the imagination to work overtime. Many times we have an idea in the back of our minds for several years before it is developed to the point of performance.

The rough plans for your full season of shows should be made during the summer. Potential *audience appeal* is the important consideration in choosing the best among many ideas. Shows which are merely different and cute may not necessarily be appealing. While a show could be too sophisticated for general acceptance, seldom do you hear objections that one was "too corny."

Fresh ideas for annual special occasions (like Homecoming)

seem to run out very quickly. Rather than trying to do an annual show on the same theme it is often better to do a regular show and announce: *"With a hearty welcome extended to all alumni and visitors, the band presents a show featuring . . ."*

We use a rather simple, but extremely helpful, chart to plan the continuity of a show (*see* Fig. 56).

HAWKEYE MARCHING BAND			
State University of Iowa			
SHOW_____ DATE_____ GAME_____			
FORMATION	MUSIC	ACTION-ANNOUNCEMENTS (PROPS)	TIME

Figure 56: Continuity Planning Chart

TYPES OF MUSIC

Marches are used for straight military style marching.

Show, dance and pop tunes are used for dance, or drill routines which employ kicks, flips, etc.

Formation music is played while in a particular outline. It may be arranged to coordinate with an internal or external movement of the figure (like rolling eyes, or a marching soldier).

Entry, exit and transitional music should be short, snappy, direct, and designed to get the band on into the next formation, or off, with all deliberate speed.

Preparing the Music

Because of the special requirements of marching show band music, it is difficult to use stock arrangements unless they are completely adapted to fit your show and your band. Special arrangements are best. Many band directors are capable of writing music that will fit their bands and their production ideas a lot better than a published arrangement or show can be designed to do. Remember that special arrangements also require special permission from the publisher.

Arrangements must fit the ability of the band. Parts must be clear, accurate, and easy to read. The rehearsal numbers or letters and the points at which movement occurs should be marked clearly. Remember that the music will be performed outdoors by musicians who are moving at a brisk pace over a large field, often pointing their instruments in different directions. A basic simplicity, exploiting the full band sound, should be sought.

CHARTING THE FORMATIONS

Miniature men and a scale model of the field will aid in planning formations and animations. Several types are available and may be purchased, or you can make your own, using screws to represent the band members.

Charts which can be given to each individual bandsman can be prepared by using either spirit duplicator, mimeo, or multilith masters. The "Patterns of Motion Band Guide," [2] an overlay containing 160 evenly spaced holes, is designed for use with mimeograph stencils and liquid duplicating masters. It will fit over the field outline of each and provide fast, precise marking. With this guide you can diagram any size block band formation up to and including 160 (10 × 16) pieces at a 2½ yard (4 steps apart) spacing, or any other formation that you may choose. To chart a company front or any line at 1¼ yard (2 steps apart) spacing, scribe every other man, move the guide to the open space between men and scribe the remaining positions.

The charts and corresponding photos (from the "Harper's Bazaar" show) indicate very clearly how careful planning, using the grid, will insure the proper distribution of bandsmen on the field (*see* Fig. 57).

Putting a Drill Routine
on Paper

Although it is very difficult to transfer to paper the simultaneous actions of a complicated precision drill routine, each bandsman must know what he is expected to do. We give a sheet similar to the "Riverside" Drill shown in Figure 58 to each member of the band.

The letters and numbers in the first column on the left refer to rehearsal letters and measure numbers in the music. For instance,

---

[2] Available from H. C. Berger Company, 433 N. Grand Street, Lansing, Michigan.

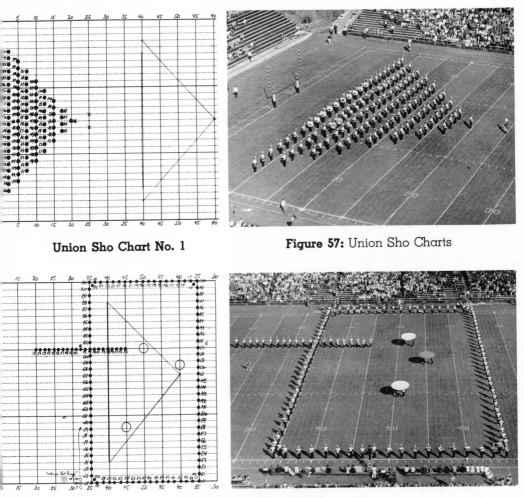

Union Sho Chart No. 1

Figure 57: Union Sho Charts

Union Sho Chart No. 2

Union Sho Chart No. 3

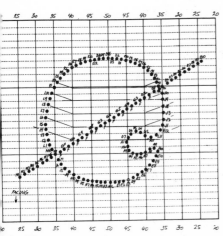

A 8–2 means rehearsal letter "A," the eighth measure, second beat. The band is divided into eight groups for this particular drill. These groups, in the original starting position, are shown on the field chart (*see* Fig. 58).

Abbreviations used in the drill are as follows:

TTR—to the rear.
MT—mark time.
RF—right flank.
LF—left flank.
FM—forward march.
L—left foot.
R—right foot.
K—kick.
XL 'bout—cross left foot over right and turn.
N,S,E,W—the four directions (see compass on field chart).
FM 12—forward march for 12 steps.
TTR on 12—to the rear, executed on the 12th step.
Rare-back—a flashy movement exaggerating the up-down instrument
    movement. The instrument is pointed up at a 45 degree angle as

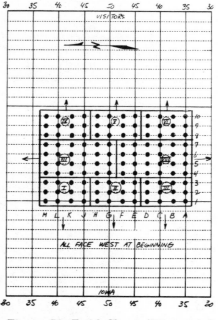

Figure 58: Field Chart: "Riverside"

the body leans back and the right or left leg comes up (with the toe pointed).

Flip—slang for pivot to the right, left, or rear. Executed *on* the beat.

Drill Routine

"DOWN BY THE RIVERSIDE"

INTRO: Block Band: A-Rank on South 35. Band divided into 8 Groups:
Grp. I: 1,2,3 of J K L M; Grp. II: 1,2,3 of E F G H; Grp. III: 1,2,3 of A B C D;
Grp. IV: 8,9,10 of J K L M; Grp. V: 8,9,10 of E F G H; Grp. VI: 8,9,10 of A B C D;
Grp. VII: 4,5,6,7 of G H J K L M; Grp. VIII: 4,5,6,7 of A B C D E F.

(NOTE: All TTR's in this routine are executed with a RARE–BACK!!)

1–1: All Stand Fast—no MT.
4–1: All MT 8 steps.
8–2: Grps. IV,V,VI—TTR; Grps. I,II,III–no flip; Grp. VII–RF; Grp. VIII–LF.

A
1–1: Grps. I,III,IV,VI: FM 12, TTR on 12, FM 4.
Grps. II,V: FM 16.
Grps. VII,VIII: FM 12, MT 4.

8–2: Grps. I,IV–Flip S; Grps. III,VI–Flip N; Grps. II,V,VII,VIII–TTR.

B
1–1: Grps. I,III,IV,VI–FM 4, TTR on 4, FM 8, TTR on 8, FM 4.
Grps. II,V–MT 8, FM 8.
Grps. VII,VIII–FM 8, TTR on 8, FM 4, plus: 1   2   3   4
MT MT XL 'bout

8–2: Grps. I,III–Flip E; Grps. IV,VI–Flip W.

C
1–1:

Grps. I,III,IV,VI:	1 2	3 4	5 6	7 8	9 10	11 12	13	14	15 16
FM:	L K	R K	L K	R K	L K	R K	L	K	R K

Grps. II,V,VII,VIII:	1 2	3 4	5 6	7 8	9 10	11 12	13	14	15 16
MT:	L R	L R	L R	L R	L R	L R	L	R	L R
		LF		LF		LF			LF

D
1–1:

Grps. I,III,IV,VI:	1 2	3 4	5 6	7 8	9 10	11 12	13	14	15 16
MT:	L R	L R	L R	L R	L R	L R	L	—	— Flip
		LF		LF		LF	FREEZE		

Grps. II,V,VII,VIII:	1 2	3 4	5 6	7 8	9 10	11 12	13	14	15 16
FM:	L K	R K	L K	R K	L R	L R	L	—	— Flip
					FM		FREEZE		

8–2: Flip: NORTH   EAST   SOUTH   WEST
         M–Rank   10's of BCDEFGHJKL   A–Rank   1's of BCDEFGHJKL
         2–9 of L   9's of CDEFGHJK   2–9 of B   2's of CDEFGHJK
         3–8 of K   8's of DEFGHJ   3–8 of C   3's of DEFGHJ
         4–7 of J   7's of EFGH   4–7 of D   4's of EFHG
         5–6 of H   6's of FG   5–6 of E   5's of FG

E

1–1: A & M–Ranks, 1's & 10's of BCDEFGHJKL: FM 16, TTR on 16, FM 16.
      2–9 of B & L–Ranks, 2's & 9's of CDEFGHJK: MT 4, FM 12, TTR on 12, FM 12, MT 4.
      3–8 of C & K–Ranks, 3's & 8's of DEFGHJ: MT 8, FM 8, TTR on 8, FM 8, MT 8.
      4–7 of D & J–Ranks, 4's & 7's of EFGH: MT 12, FM 4, TTR on 4, FM 4, MT 12.
      5–6 of EFGH: MT 16, TTR on 16, MT 16.

16–2: All Flip West.

F

1–1: All: 1 2   3 4   5 6   7 8   9 10   11 12
      MT: L R   L R   L R   L R   L R   L R
              LF   LF   LF   LF

X   (IN FOUR)

1–1: Files 1, 3, 5, 7, 9: MT 4, TTR on 4th.
      Files 2, 4, 6, 8, 10: Right Oblique and move in between odd-numbered files—done in
                  FOUR EQUAL STEPS, TTR on 4th.

2–1: Files 1, 2, 9, 10: FM 4
      Files 3, 4, 7, 8: FM 2, MT 2
      Files 5 & 6: MT 4

2–4: Files 1, 2, 3, 4, 5, 6: TTR

G

1–1: All: 1 2   3 4   5 6   7 8   9 10   11 12   13 14   15 16
      FM: L K   R K   L K   R K   L K   R K   L R   L R

5–1: Files 1 & 2: Down on right knee; all others MT.
5–3: Files 3 & 4: Down on right knee; all others MT.
6–1: Files 5 & 6: Down on right knee; all others MT.
6–3: Files 7 & 8: Down on right knee; all others MT.
7–1: Files 9 & 10: Down on right knee.

All Play to End, add "and Down" after cut-off.

TRANSITIONS

Each individual part of the show must be tied together with a transitional movement which is rapid and smooth. Allow the rank and squad leaders to choose the best way for their group to move out of one formation and into the next, and watch the result of all these decisions so that you can make any suggestions for improvement that seem necessary. In the Billiard Table formation chart (*see* Fig. 57), the triangular formation which immediately preceded it is superimposed, to assist the squad leaders in plotting their courses.

THE SCRIPT

The actual script is prepared next, although of course the general form of it has been known since the selection of the original idea or theme. Announcements should be brief, with uncomplicated sentences that can be clearly understood by the ear without any help from the eye.

THE REHEARSAL SCHEDULE

We use the following rehearsal schedule for each week's game:

MONDAY: Pass out and run through the music, on the field. "Walk through" the formations. Allow rank and squad leaders to make their transition choices.

TUESDAY: Review the music. Combine the music and the formations. Attempt to go straight through the complete show.

WEDNESDAY, THURSDAY AND FRIDAY: Polish the show. Theoretically the only parts that need a great deal of practice are the drill routines and the transitions. About half of the period on Wednesday or Thursday is used to learn the Pre-Game show.

SATURDAY MORNING: Final Rehearsal—the day of the game.

Rehearsal Tips

If your field and rehearsal room are immediately adjacent to each other (and they should be), play through the music first and then go directly to the field to learn the formations. If your field is a great distance away, play through the music on the field as the roll is being taken by one of your student assistants (use the vacant space method).

If the wind players' lips seem to be tiring out during a long rehearsal, we usually ask only one group to play at a time, while the others rest. One time through it might be the lower brass and reeds who play, another time the soprano and alto instruments, still a third time it could be the drums who play alone. Not only does this save lips, but it also helps to balance out the band.

PERFORMANCE MUST BE GOOD

The band's performance level must keep pace with the ever-increasing popular music critical ability the general public is acquiring as a result of the constant flow of music from radio and TV, plus the background music which is heard everywhere from the barber shop to the chiropodist's office. Although it may be mediocre music in many cases, *the performance of it is usually good.* The laymen, perhaps unconsciously, will always compare the over-all impression he gets from listening to a nonprofessional, live, school band with the sound put in his head by this pre-recorded, top quality, completely professional, product. Unless the man in the football crowd has some musical background he may not be able to analyze what causes the difference, but he will recognize that it exists.

STUDENT CONDUCT AT GAMES

The band members should stay together all the time they are in the stadium. With a university crowd of 60,000 it is impossible to allow members to leave the band section, but regardless of the size of the crowd, it is not good discipline for band members to move around individually. They belong in the band section ready to play.

When the band is dismissed, students should get the uniform off as quickly as possible, not only to save wear and tear, but to avoid the inevitable loosened tie, the coat slung over the arm, the relaxed (sloppy) appearance, which is understandable after a performance, but nonetheless very unbecoming to the prestige of the band.

COMPETITOR RELATIONS

Although there is an undeniable element of competition between bands during the half-time show period, the director should place the emphasis on improving his band's own previous level of attainment, rather than on beating the other band. The conductor who considers only the devious ways he can devise to defeat the other director, may, in the long run, not only "lose" the halftime, but also the friendship and respect of his colleagues and his own students as well.

You may have adequate, well-trained personnel, outstanding rehearsal facilities, a well-planned show, exciting special arrangements, beautifully clear charts, a clever script, and your students may be able to do the fundamental drills in their sleep. In short, everything may be "right," but the really important question is, "What was the reaction of the audience . . . did the show appeal to the crowd . . . were they entertained?"

The best way to find out is by viewing a sound movie of your performance. State University of Iowa films are taken by our own audio-visual department, at a cost of about $100 per show. I can have black and white films without sound the day after the game (Sunday), and complete with sound, on Tuesday. I preview them and make notes on the technical things as well as analyzing the crowd reactions. When the students see them on Wednesday I bring these things to their attention. There is always a loud groan if someone made a mistake and the offender certainly is "needled" by the other bandsmen. We find these sessions to be very educational. Remember also that without films, or unless students are temporarily sidelined through illness, many students complete a full career as a band member without ever having seen a performance given by their own band.

Synchronized Sound Films

Taking pictures alone is no problem, because there are many good, and inexpensive, movie cameras available, but to get synchronized sound is more difficult.

In some communities there are professional photographers, and even music dealers, who will shoot sound films for a fee. These audio-visual records of the half-time performance can be so important as an aid to the improvement of the band that the expense should be included in the budget.

Sound motion picture equipment serves as the impartial evaluator and electronic motivator in the marching show band, just as the tape recorder does in the concert band. It just happens that tape recorders are usually within every department's budget and sound motion picture equipment may not be. It is to be hoped (possibly even anticipated) that research, technical advancement, mass production, and competition will cause sound movies to be more readily available to all.